The Economics of Insurgency in the Mekong Delta of Vietnam is the most complete work to date dealing with the economy of the Mekong Delta. The results of this study demonstrate significant shortcomings in past U.S. policies. They have already produced striking changes in U.S. economic policy in South Vietnam, particularly in the essential areas of economic assistance and land reform.

Much of the material for this book was obtained through interviews with farmers, landlords, moneylenders, and laborers in the Delta. The author discusses historical and general economic conditions in the area, agricultural productivity, capital and labor, land tenure, fertilizer use, and a subsistence innovation involving the use of an intermediate technology. The analysis focuses not only upon the theoretical issues of development economics, such as disguised unemployment, innovation, and investment decisions, but also upon their larger social and political implications.

Several chapters are devoted to a detailed examination of the Viet Cong and South Vietnamese government economies at war. Particularly significant is the role that economic issues and policies played in the successful efforts by the Viet Cong from 1960 to 1964 to gain the support of the peasant. Land reform, rent reduction, and even a minimum rural-wage policy were employed. The author provides the first documentary evidence that the Viet Cong were a major force for constructive economic and social change in the Delta.

On the other hand, by 1967 massive U.S. economic assistance had gone some distance toward putting the Vietnamese government in a more favorable position with regard to the economic benefits associated with the South Vietnamese government's continued management of the economy. No doubt, however, long-standing economic and social grievances are still a potent force for the Viet Cong, and there is as yet no complete assurance that the revolutionary social and economic changes wrought by the Viet Cong would not be reversed if the Vietnamese government gained complete control in the countryside.

Robert L. Sansom is a member of the National Security Council staff and a captain in the U.S. Air Force. He is a former Rhodes scholar, Fulbright scholar (in Argentina), and White House fellow.

Sansom graduated first in his class from the U.S. Air Force Academy in 1964 with a B.S. degree. He holds an M.A. degree in economics from Georgetown University (1965) and B.Phil. and D.Phil.

degrees from Oxford (1969). From October 1965 through September 1968 he studied economics at Oxford and during this time spent eleven months in Vietnam doing the research on which this book is based.

The
Economics
of Insurgency

Robert L. Sansom
THE
ECONOMICS
OF INSURGENCY
in the
Mekong Delta
of Vietnam

The M.I.T. Press
CAMBRIDGE, MASSACHUSETTS, AND LONDON, ENGLAND

Copyright © 1970 by
The Massachusetts Institute of Technology

Designed by Dwight E. Agner. Set in Linotype Electra
and printed by The Heffernan Press Inc. Bound in the
United States of America by The Colonial Press Inc.

SBN 262 19064 8 (hardcover)

Library of Congress catalog card number: 70–90753

Contents

Preface   xiii

Abbreviations and Units   xvii

1 Introduction   1
   Scope and Method   1
   The Area of Study   5
   The Sample   13
   Outline   17

2 Land and Income: A Historical Inquiry   18
   Introduction   18
   The Settlement of Cochinchina   19
   Tenancy as a Means of Development   23
   Tenancy as a Means of Exploitation   25
   The Export Model   34
   Wages: Another Indicator   39
   Harvesting Techniques   42
   Conclusions   45
   Appendix to Chapter 2: Historical Footnotes   46

3 Recent Conditions of Land Tenure   53
   From 1945 to 1960   53
   Viet Cong Reforms   58
   The Vietnamese Government's Response   66
   Landholdings and Land Use   72

4 The Production Opportunities of the 1960s   75
   Primary Agricultural Activities   76

Contents

Secondary Agriculture   88
Transportation   94
Marketing   99
Summary   103

5   Capital   104
Usury or a Reasonable Return?   104
Interest Rates and Indebtedness   105
Credit Institutions   109
The *Hui*   114

6   Labor   123
Labor Supply, Labor Policies, and Wages   123
Disguised Unemployment   135
Conclusions   148

7   Irrigation   151
Introduction   151
A Framework for the Analysis   153
Irrigation Developments in LBD and TCN   154
Conclusions   160

8   The Motor Pump: A Subsistence Innovation   164
Introduction   164
The Innovation   165
Diffusion of the Innovation   169
Conclusions   176

9   Fertilizer: A Subsistence Investment   180
Introduction   180
The Yield Response   183
The Determinants of Fertilizer Use: Profitability versus
    the Subsistence Need   188
Multiple Regression Analysis   194
Conclusions   197

10   Income and Investment   198
Income   198
Investment   201

Contents

11   *Notes on Economic Aid and Viet Cong Tax*
      and Trade Policies   211
      Introduction   211
      The Role of Aid in the Village Economy   212
      The Macroeconomic Role of Aid   215
      Viet Cong Taxes   216
      Viet Cong Trade Policies   222

12   *The Economics of Insurgency*   228
      United States Policy and Land Reform   228
      The Balance of Interests: Viet Cong versus
      GVN Economics   236
      Old Realities and New Myths   241

      Appendix A: Interviews   246
      Agricultural Production Questionnaire   246
      Question Outline for Land Tenure Field Research   255

      Appendix B: Historical Data and Statistical Notes   258
      Historical Data (Table B.1)   258
      Statistical Notes to Table B.1 and Text   264

      Bibliography   268

      Index   275

Tables

2.1   Rice Prices and Exports   34
2.2   Rice Export Model   36
2.3   Wages   41
2.4   Rice Production Techniques   44

3.1   Upper Delta Land Prices   62
3.2   Distribution of Landholdings by Size   72
3.3   Land Utilization and Average Product   73

4.1   Transportation Costs, 1966/67   96
4.2   Rice Marketing   100
4.3   Disposition of 1966/67 Rice Crop   100

5.1   Annual Real Interest Rates   106
5.2   Monthly Interest Rates   107
5.3   Indebtedness   108
5.4   Use of Loans   108
5.5   Types of Credit by Number and Amount   111
5.6   Government Loans in LBD   112
5.7   *Hui* Data   116
5.8   Average *Hui* Interest Rate   121

6.1   Family Earnings, by Occupation   134
6.2   Labor Requirements   140

9.1   Fertilizer-Paddy Price Ratios and Nutrient
      Fertilizer Use in Selected Countries, 1964/65   182

Tables

10.1 Income, Investment, and Other Variables 201

11.1 1966/67 Viet Cong Tax Schedule 219
11.2 An Example Household's Taxable Capacity 220
11.3 Viet Cong Political-Economic Classification 221

B.1 Data on Rice Area Cultivated, Exports, and Prices 258

ix

Figures

1.1	Economic Indices	2
1.2	Map: Population Densities by Province, July 1964	6
1.3	The Mekong River Delta	7
1.4	Map of Than Cuu Nghia	10
1.5	Map of Long Binh Dien	13
2.1	The Settlement of Cochinchina	20
2.2	Cochinchina, 1868–1966: Area Cultivated, Rice Exports, and Population	22
2.3	Labor and Rice Production	26
3.1	Percentage of Land Area Rented (Mekong Delta Region)	54
3.2	Security and Rents Paid in Long Binh Dien	61
3.3	LBD and TCN Landownership and a Comparison of Landholdings of Delta Sample and Japan	73
4.1	Income Sources	76
4.2	Standard Vegetable Plot	85
4.3	The Crop Calender	89
6.1	Sample (LBD and TCN) Population Pyramid	124
6.2	Wages	127
6.3	Rice-Labor Demand	138
6.4	The Effect of the Labor Shortage on Efficient Plot Size	143
8.1	The Motor Pump	166

Figures

9.1 Long Binh Dien Yield Response to Fertilizer   184
9.2 Than Cuu Nghia Yield Response to Fertilizer   184
9.3 Returns to Fertilizer Use   190
9.4 The Subsistence Response   192

10.1 Family Net Income   200
10.2 Income, Investment, and Savings   202

Preface

From June through September 1966, on my first visit to Vietnam, I worked for the United States Mission's Economic Office, examining the problems of economic stabilization, refugee resettlement, economic warfare, and the general issues of economic development.

In October 1966, with the kind assistance of Richard Moorsteen and Charles A. Cooper of the White House staff, I decided to study the economics of the rural areas of the Mekong River Delta. The results of this study and of further research carried on in two additional trips to Vietnam, from January through April and June through September 1967, are presented here. In this study I received generous support from Willard D. Sharpe, Director of the Economic Office, and Charles Cooper, who from May 1967 until May 1968 was the United States Embassy's Economic Counselor in Saigon.

Intellectually, my debts are widely held. At Oxford, my supervisors Colin Clark, Professor S. H. Frankel, and C. B. Winsten were sources of constant guidance and encouragement. At My Tho, Mr. David Elliott of the RAND Corporation gave me the benefit of his abundant political knowledge of Dinh Tuong Province. At Tuy Hoa, Mr. Terry Rambo offered helpful survey research advice. Both in South Vietnam and in Cambridge, Massachusetts, I enjoyed the hospitality and intellectual persistence of Professor Arthur Smithies of Harvard University. In Oxford, my use of the KDF 9 computer was facilitated by the advice and assistance of Miss Ann Black of Nuffield College. I am particularly indebted to Tom Cotton, a fellow student at Nuffield College in 1967–1968, who over a period of six months served as a sounding board for and constructive critic of my ideas and analyses. None of these persons is in any way responsible for the views or shortcomings in the results reported here.

In the literature studied, two names stand out: Pierre Gourou for his meticulous recording of the facts of rural economic life in North Vietnam, and Bernard Fall for his ability, only infrequently abused, to go to the heart of the matter of Vietnam and tell us of our profound ignorance. I owe little substantive debt to either of these writers; I only hope that in method and in purpose, respectively, I have followed their examples.

Because of the stringencies of war, personal debts accumulate more rapidly in wartime than they do in peacetime. Therefore, I am particularly indebted to John Wilhelm, Ron Robichaud, George Laudato, John Holmes, and Paul London, all of the U.S. Agency for International Development in Vietnam, for the kind sharing of their My Tho and Saigon facilities and generous hospitality.

I received financial assistance from the Rhodes Trust, the United States Air Force, and indirect in-kind support from the U.S. Agency for International Development and Nuffield College. None of these organizations is responsible for the views expressed herein.

I am especially grateful to Nguyen Van Thuan, who for over ten years has been a student of sociological conditions in South Vietnam. His command of English and the local dialects of the Delta was vital to this project's completion, and his emphasis on the subtleties of the communications process enriched the entire research experience. Perhaps the best testimony to his concern for the problems of his country was his willingness to accompany an American into the less-than-secure rural areas.

Finally, my greatest debt is to the countless Vietnamese—farmers, landlords, merchants, laborers, and others—who, despite the persistence of my questioning, never became impatient with my curiosity and provided innumerable insights into their own activities.

It may be helpful to know beforehand my views on the wider issues of the war. In South Vietnam, it was common knowledge that so-called hawks arrived hawks and departed hawks, and doves arrived doves and departed doves. If it showed anything, my research demonstrated why this was so. Evidence was readily available to support either position.

I became more and more conscious of the good and the bad on one side and the good and the bad on the other. The tragedy of Vietnam was that the good and the bad were so evenly divided; thus the peasant had no clear choice.

The bloodbath arose from the fact that the closest side was always changing. Self-interest dictated neutrality, but, for the peasant, neutrality was seldom an option.

Robert L. Sansom

Oxford
June 1968

Abbreviations and Units

Abbreviations

AAC	Agricultural Affairs Committee
ASB	*Annual Statistical Bulletin* (published since 1957 by USAID, Office of Joint Economic Affairs, Saigon)
COSVN	Central Office of the National Liberation Front
GVN	South Vietnamese government
JUSPAO	Joint U.S. Public Affairs Office, Saigon
LBD	Long Binh Dien (a traditional rice growing village studied in the upper Mekong Delta)
n.a.	not applicable
NLF	National Liberation Front of South Vietnam (also referred to as Viet Cong)
NACO	National Agricultural Credit Organization (until May 1, 1967, then Agricultural Development Bank)
TCN	Than Cuu Nghia (a rice and vegetable growing village studied in the upper Mekong Delta)
USAID	United States Agency for International Development
USG	United States government
USOM	United States Operations Mission

Units

cong	one-tenth hectare
CU	Consumption Unit
gia	40 liters, or 19 to 21 kg, of paddy, often called a *thung* in the lower Mekong Delta

hectare (ha)	2.47 acres
kilogram (kg)	roughly 2.2 pounds
kilometer (km)	0.621 mile
mau	hectare
metric ton (MT)	1,000 kilograms (throughout this book, all figures in tons are metric tons)
piaster (V$N)	Vietnamese currency unit, valued at 60 piasters per U.S. dollar before June 1966 and at 118 piasters per U.S. dollar after June 1966

The
Economics
of Insurgency

I   Introduction

Scope and Method

THE PURPOSE OF STUDY
An examination of the possibilities of economic research in the Mekong River Delta revealed that the factors separating the economic problems of South Vietnam from seemingly similar cases were those related to the insurgent conditions in the rural areas. Therefore, throughout the research, an effort was made not only to focus on the theoretical issues of development economics, such as disguised unemployment, technical change, and investment decisions, but to examine as well the larger social and political implications of the economic changes observed.

Moreover, there was a close relationship between the considerations of war and the changes in economic indicators, a relationship superficially evident in Figure 1.1. After the intensification of the war in early 1965—represented by the number of U.S. troops in South Vietnam—the cost-of-living and rice price indices began to move to higher levels at changing rates. Expenditures related to U.S. troop deployment and to the expanded size of the Vietnamese army, which increased in size three times between 1963 and late 1966, caused prices to rise rapidly. Conditions of labor surplus were changed to those of labor scarcity. Capital became cheaper. New techniques of production became available both through aid programs and as a result of private activities of the Vietnamese. These developments, although they represented a major change from the traditional state, were the products of orderly economic change.

The implications of these changes, however, were more profound in

1

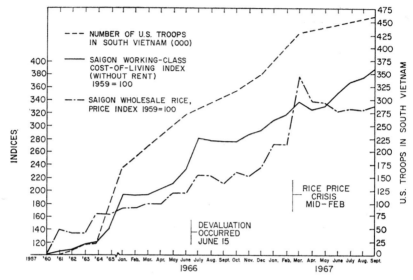

FIGURE 1.1 Economic Indices

both source and outcome than a cursory study would reveal. It is difficult to generalize about them except in the grossest terms. For the present, it is sufficient to say that social and technological changes in the context of the war were responsible for the transformation of the Delta economy in the 1960s.

THE THEORETICAL FRAMEWORK

Professor Schultz has postulated a dichotomy between traditional agriculture—consisting "of farming under a long-established economic equilibrium, which is attained during generations of farming, and the critical conditions on which it depends have remained virtually constant for generations"—and modern agriculture, in which change is the way of economic life.[1]

Three general explanations have been put forward to explain the differences between traditional and modern agriculture. One view finds that the values and motivations of the inhabitants of traditional econ-

[1] Theodore W. Schultz, *Economic Crises in World Agriculture* (Ann Arbor: University of Michigan Press, 1965), p. 13.

omies are distinct from those of the inhabitants of modern economies. An early exponent of this view was the former Dutch civil servant in Indonesia J. H. Boeke, who termed this distinction "social dualism."[2] More recently a similar view has been expressed by Professor E. E. Hagen, who has argued that the predominance of some personality forms, for example, authoritarian over innovational, may influence the rate of development.[3]

A second view is that of Professor Schultz and others who argue that traditional agriculture is distinguished from modern agriculture by differences that are easily discernible to those employing the tools of economic analysis. He maintains that traditional agriculture has not modernized because the opportunities for production that would justify additional investments have not yet appeared, either because markets have not been opened up or because highly productive factors have not been made available. To Schultz, "it is a matter of costs and returns."[4] He says: "The marginal returns to labor, to land, and to reproducible material capital are very low. Stated another way, the *price of increasing the capacity of traditional agriculture, as things stand, is high.*"[5]

The third view of traditional agriculture is that espoused by the structuralists.[6] This view was given a special emphasis by Balogh in a review of Schultz's 1964 book,[7] in which he vehemently rejected Schultz's view, saying that it ignored the vital *institutional* characteristics of traditional economies.[8] To Balogh and the structuralists, the causes of poverty in traditional agriculture are the feudal system of landholding, the control of money markets by moneylenders, and the con-

[2] J. H. Boeke, *Economics and Economic Policy of Dual Societies* (New York: Institute of Pacific Relations, 1953).

[3] Everett E. Hagen, *On the Theory of Social Change* (Homewood, Ill.: Dorsey Press, 1962).

[4] Schultz, *Economic Crises*, pp. 18–19.

[5] Ibid., p. 19; Schultz's emphasis.

[6] See Dudley Seers, "A Theory of Inflation and Growth in Under-Developed Economies Based on the Experience of Latin America," *Oxford Economic Papers*, vol. n.s. 14 (June 1962), pp. 173–195.

[7] Theodore W. Schultz, *Transforming Traditional Agriculture* (New Haven, Conn.: Yale University Press, 1964).

[8] Thomas Balogh, "Review" of Schultz, *Transforming Traditional Agriculture*, in *Economic Journal* (London), vol. LXXIV (December 1964), pp. 996–999; reprinted in idem, *The Economics of Poverty* (London: Weidenfeld and Nicolson, 1966), pp. 74–78.

3

trol of product and factor markets by a few merchants. The structuralists argue that these impeding institutions must be removed or severely modified before development can take place.

The object here is not to arrive at a general verdict, applying to all traditional agriculture, on these three views. (In fact, it is doubtful that such a general solution exists.) Nor, in the particular case of South Vietnam, is it intended herein to give special research emphasis to the motivational issues singled out by Boeke and Hagen. This approach was buttressed by the view of James B. Hendry, who studied the economy of the upper Delta in 1958/59. He wrote:

> Another factor which entered into things was my own preoccupation at the time, with the extent to which traditional agriculture was heavily influenced by the social setting. Although I satisfied myself that this influence was pretty marginal, it diverted my attention from looking more thoroughly into some of the more purely economic aspects of village life.[9]

In later chapters it will become clear that little evidence was found to dispute Hendry's conclusion.

Initial research objectives were formulated along the Schultzian lines discussed earlier; however, in the course of analysis, it became clear that the institutions of land tenure demanded additional study. This is not to reject the Schultzian view, which was found to be particularly valuable, but to argue that its emphasis is not placed broadly enough. Schultz has written:

> Similarly, such a basis ["for distinguishing between traditional and other types of agriculture"] is not to be found in the differences in particular institutional arrangements, for example in whether farms are under resident or absentee ownership, whether they are small or large, whether they are private or public enterprises, and whether the production is for home consumption or for sale.[10]

For the Vietnamese case, this framework is inadequate.

But an alternative to the institutional approach, one that would encompass the valid economic ingredients of Schultz's method, has not

---

[9] James B. Hendry, private correspondence dated November 30, 1966.
[10] Schultz, *Transforming Traditional Agriculture*, p. 29. In his later book, *Economic Crises*, p. 25, Schultz appears to have softened his view toward institutional matters.

been articulated. No existing framework can contain the evidence found by this study, which supports the institutional case on land tenure, rejects the structuralist position on money market control, and at the same time supports the central role played by technology, as argued by Schultz. Therefore, the results of the research presented in the following pages are best seen as an empirical dialogue between the market-technology view of development held by writers like Schultz and the structuralist-institutional view of writers like Balogh.

The Area of Study

THE MEKONG DELTA

The area studied was the Mekong River Delta, or that area in South Vietnam served by the Mekong River and its tributaries (see the maps, Figures 1.2 and 1.3), which consists of approximately 45,000 square kilometers of mostly alluvial soils. The Delta region contains slightly more than 25 percent of South Vietnam's land area and about 70 percent of the South Vietnamese population.

Extending from the tip of the Ca Mau Peninsula to an area 50 kilometers north of Saigon, the Delta can, for the purposes of economic analysis, be divided into the upper Delta and the lower Delta. The upper Delta extends from the southern banks of the Hau Giang River north to Saigon, excluding the Plain of Reeds. This area, which includes Dinh Tuong Province, is usefully distinguished from the remainder of the Delta by the fact that for ten to twelve months of the year fresh water is available in the natural waterways that interlace its area. In constrast, the lower Delta, which includes Bac Lieu Province, is served by man-made canals that contain fresh water for only the five to six months of the year during which they are filled with monsoon rains (otherwise, they contain saltwater). (By adding to the Delta area defined here 15,000 additional square kilometers to the north, one describes the area formerly known as Cochinchina.)

Field research was conducted at three levels. First, an intensive study was made of two villages in Dinh Tuong Province of the upper Delta. These two villages were selected to meet both economic and security criteria: One had to be representative of the traditional rice economy

5

and the other of the recently evident nontraditional economy; second, the villages were chosen to represent the most common security categories (described in the next section). After the village studies were completed, a study was made of economic conditions in Bac Lieu Province in the lower Delta, where different hydrologic circumstances

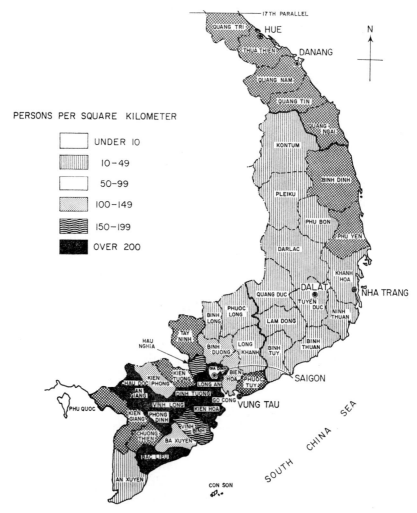

FIGURE 1.2   Map: Population Densities by Province, July 1964   Source: *ASB, 1966*

6

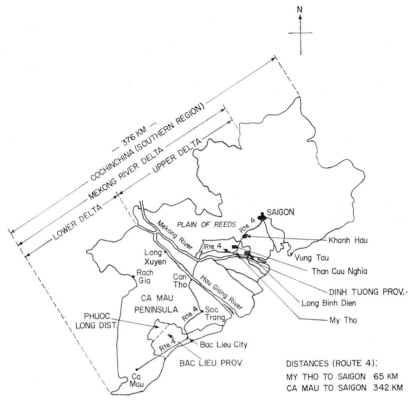

FIGURE 1.3 The Mekong River Delta

and different security conditions provided useful contrasts with upper Delta conditions. Finally, for additional perspective on general Delta economic conditions, three Delta-wide surveys were conducted: on rice production, rice marketing, and land tenure.

The selection of Dinh Tuong Province[11] as the primary area of study

11 Before 1658 Dinh Tuong was part of the Khmer (Cambodian) country of Chan Lap. In 1658, following the death of the king of Chan Lap, a conflict for the control of Dinh Tuong developed between his Cambodian successor, the Vietnamese king of Annam (Nguyen Phuc Tan), and the Chinese warlord Kwang-Si. In 1698 the Vietnamese gained control of Dinh Tuong only to lose it in 1750 to an invading Thai army. By 1831 the Vietnamese had regained control, at which time Dinh Tuong (with Vinh Long) became one of thirty-one provinces comprising the country of Vietnam, then governed from Hué. In 1858 French armies invaded the Delta, and by 1861 they controlled Dinh Tuong.

7

was dictated by three considerations. First, James B. Hendry and Gerald C. Hickey in 1958/59 studied the upper Delta village of Khanh Hau in Long An Province north of Dinh Tuong.[12] It was anticipated that these earlier studies would provide valuable comparative material. Second, the area was far enough from Saigon (55–65 kilometers) to be considered a rural economy representative of upper Delta conditions rather than an appendage to the urban economy. Third, Dinh Tuong was not in 1966–1967 a so-called priority area receiving the concentrated attention of Vietnamese government (GVN) and United States government (USG) officials.

VILLAGE SELECTION AND SECURITY

The selected villages had to meet certain minimum security criteria; foremost was that it would be possible to enter them in daytime, unarmed and unaccompanied, except by an interpreter, and to move freely in the fields and populated areas talking with the inhabitants. There could be no guarantee of complete security. Because of the diversity in security conditions in the Delta in 1966–1967, it was possible only to specify meaningful gradations of GVN or Viet Cong control of a village or hamlet. These security categories were as follows:

1. *GVN village:* The land and living areas were controlled by the GVN, and GVN officials and Americans could travel unescorted during the day and in most places at night.[13] Village officials lived in their homes.

2. *Semisecure GVN village:* The living area but not the land was controlled by the GVN. The ability of Americans and Vietnamese officials to move about in living areas or closely associated fields (within 3 km) in daytime depended on the continuous presence of the local militia (Popular Forces, Regional Forces, or Revolutionary Development Cadre Team). At night, free movement for such persons was restricted to that area enclosed by wire fortifications in the case of a fenced-in former strategic hamlet or to that area in the immediate vicinity of the village-

---

[12] James B. Hendry, *The Small World of Khanh Hau* (Chicago: Aldine Publishing Co., 1964), and Gerald Cannon Hickey, *Village in Vietnam* (New Haven, Conn.: Yale University Press, 1964).

[13] Landlords belonged in a slightly more constrained category than Vietnam government officials or Americans.

8

guard command post (usually the village office) for other such villages. Village officials could not live in their homes at night and slept in the closely guarded village office.

3. *Contested village:* Neither the living area nor the land was freely accessible to unescorted officials in daytime or at night. But since such villages were not the permanent residence of troops from either side, movement with only light (platoon) protection was possible. At night such villages were often subject to Viet Cong efforts to propagandize, entertain, draft (for labor or military purposes), or tax their inhabitants. In daytime similar pressures came from the GVN side.

4. *Semisecure Viet Cong village:* These villages were the permanent residences of Viet Cong militia and civilian officials. Their economies were usually isolated from GVN area markets because of roads cut by ditches or blown bridges. They were the frequent targets of GVN search and destroy missions during which the Viet Cong cadres, properly warned, withdrew to secure Viet Cong areas.

5. *Viet Cong village:* It contained a full complement of Viet Cong military and civilian personnel and frequently had not been entered by GVN or USG officials since 1946.

In the Delta in 1966–1967, probably half of the population and nearly half of the land were located in contested villages. In terms of population, the second most important category was the GVN semisecure village, which included only about 15 percent of the Delta's land but probably contained a quarter of its population.

To be representative of Delta conditions, the selected villages had to fall into the contested and semisecure GVN categories. In late 1966 several villages in Dinh Tuong had moved, for reasons of either diminished Viet Cong efforts or increased GVN attention, from the contested to the semisecure GVN category. Of these, Than Cuu Nghia village (hereafter referred to as TCN) was selected for research (see Figure 1.4) because no Vietnamese army battalions were stationed there and because general security conditions were relatively safe. The other village chosen was Long Binh Dien (LBD), located 10 kilometers east of My Tho. A semisecure GVN village since 1963, LBD was selected because it was passably secure and, unlike TCN, did not have the outward appearance of having changed economically.

9

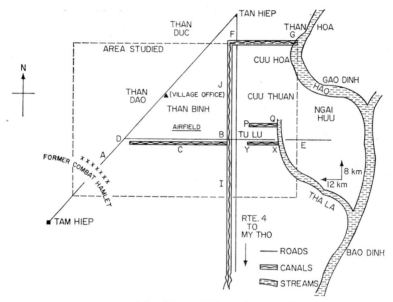

FIGURE 1.4   Map of Than Cuu Nghia

THAN CUU NGHIA

TCN is located 8 to 9 kilometers north of My Tho in Ben Tranh district. Local officials estimated that there were 8,734 inhabitants in the eight hamlets of the village. The survey was conducted in four of these hamlets—Than Binh and Than Dao west of Route 4 and Cuu Hoa and Cuu Thuan east of Route 4 (see map, Figure 1.4)—which contained an estimated 2,350 people. (The excluded hamlets were too insecure for unaccompanied entrance and had no GVN organizations.) The TCN village office was located in Than Binh (at ▲ on Figure 1.4). After January 1967 a Revolutionary Development Cadre Team (with about thirty members) was located in Than Dao hamlet.

In 1946 the Viet Minh seized control of TCN, only to relinquish control after the cease-fire of 1954. The Viet Minh organization was a small contingent of six to eight former political prisoners of the French. Opposing the large landowners and rich merchants, they redistributed land and lowered rents. After an interlude of five years of GVN control, in late 1958 and early 1959 the Viet Cong appeared in TCN and destroyed the Than Dao guardpost. By 1960, Viet Cong activities had greatly intensified. In that year they killed the Than Duc hamlet chief and the Than Dao information officer and arrested three to five people and held them prisoner for several months. They also began collecting taxes in Cuu Hoa and Cuu Thuan hamlets and implemented a small land redistribution in Than Dao hamlet. In early 1966 a portion of Than Dao became a Viet Cong combat hamlet. A palm-frond fence was built along the road, frequent propaganda meetings were held, and a community work project was organized to cut the road at point A with multiple manually dug trenches.

But TCN was not the object of a marked Viet Cong effort and had never been a major center of Viet Cong (or GVN) support. The Viet Cong judged TCN a poor village from an economic viewpoint. Viet Cong tax collectors described TCN as "an area where dogs have only stones to eat, and the chickens have to be fed with salt." Nevertheless, even in 1967, Viet Cong taxes were collected in Cuu Thuan and Cuu Hoa hamlets. Collections were made at night by small armed groups or during the day by a complicated messenger system that employed innocent villagers as collectors. In 1966, families in these hamlets paid 2,000–6,000 piasters in Viet Cong taxes, depending on their landholding and family size.

At TCN in 1961 the GVN built a short airstrip for light planes delivering passengers to My Tho and in August 1963 stationed a Vietnamese ranger battalion on the strip. With a nighttime attack in November 1965, the Viet Cong scored one of their three major pre-1968 Delta victories by overrunning the ranger outpost and killing at least forty soldiers and dependents. The airstrip was not used again until mid-February 1967, when a battalion of the U.S. Ninth Infantry Division was stationed there for one month. This unit was hit by a Viet Cong mortar attack on the night of February 27, 1967. (The nearby residents, having received a warning of the attack, had moved during the two previous nights to the nearby district capital, where they stayed for the duration of the attack.)

After four years in his post, the TCN village chief resigned in 1963, citing poor GVN security as the reason for his resignation. As village chief, he was forced to live in the fortified village office and was unable to emerge in daytime to cultivate his rice field. A new village chief was appointed by the GVN in 1966, and he circumvented the security problem by commuting daily from the more secure district capital where he lived. With the village chief not even a resident, the TCN village government was ineffective; it served only to pass requests for licensed purchases on to higher levels and to issue identification cards. The local militia, organized in 1966, was controlled by district officials. Even in 1967 the Viet Cong occasionally entered the village in daytime from the Plain of Reeds; one was arrested at noon in mid-July 1967, in the presence of the author. Usually local residents notified us when Viet Cong arrived in the area and suggested that we leave. As a general rule we were free to move about the village from 8:00 A.M. to 5:00 P.M.

LONG BINH DIEN

The other village selected for study was Long Binh Dien (LBD) in Cho Gao district. By official estimate its six hamlets (see Figure 1.5) contained 5,880 inhabitants. Security conditions permitted the study of only two hamlets, Binh Hanh and Long Thanh, which housed 1,875 inhabitants, including 170 post-1963 refugees from nearby less-secure hamlets.

Although the Viet Minh controlled LBD in the late 1940s and redistributed land, Viet Cong activities in 1966 were not of major importance. Viet Cong taxes had not been collected since the hamlets became strategic hamlets in 1963. In the evening the inhabitants felt secure in their fortified residential area; but in August 1967, on a night raid, a Viet Cong unit entered the village and shot all the dogs. This action appeared to the villagers as a prelude to future Viet Cong activities and, therefore, made the population uneasy. In daytime one could travel to the Ong Van market and into the fields of both hamlets. Generally, security conditions were better in LBD than in TCN.

In contrast to TCN, the LBD government controlled the local militia. The government itself was presided over by the village administrative committee, consisting of a chairman, a vice-chairman, and finance, youth, police, and information officers. This committee was responsible to the village popular council, a body of five members. In April 1967, LBD residents voted, from a limited slate of candidates, for new council members and selected three of the former appointed members.

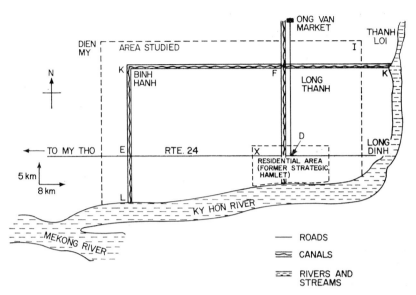

FIGURE 1.5   Map of Long Binh Dien

The Sample

SAMPLE SELECTION

Several methods of data collection were employed. For general economic information—such as production techniques, prices, and costs—interviews were conducted until the responses satisfactorily explained the item in question and multiple independent sources gave compatible replies. This procedure was followed in the villages, as well as in My Tho, Saigon, and other Delta locations as required. For example, research on the origins of the motor pump (discussed in Chapter 8) involved fieldwork throughout the Delta. However, the primary focus of the research effort was on two sets of interviews. The first, best described as a farm production interview, was administered to 120 farmers, 70 in TCN and 50 in LBD. The second set was conducted with 25 landlords (owners of more land than they farmed) in various cities in Dinh Tuong and Bac Lieu provinces as well as in Saigon. (Copies of both interviews are given in Appendix A.) The landlord interview also served as the basis of the Delta-wide survey of land tenure conditions conducted in July 1967.

The farm operator interview was the product of the research objectives of the study. In designing it, copies of similar questionnaires used in India, Pakistan, Syria, and Vietnam were examined and the relevant literature studied. After several revisions, the interview was field tested in Tan Tao village of Gia Dinh Province near Saigon in January 1967. During the course of this test it was revised twice.

In February 1967, a 25 percent sample was selected from among the TCN farmers. Such a large sample was taken because exact census data were not available. As it turned out, a smaller sample of 15 percent would have been adequate, for the political and economic changes of the 1960–1966 period had produced remarkably homogeneous production characteristics among households. In particular, the major economic variable—the size of the landholding farmed by each household—varied within a narrow range.

Security conditions prohibited the selection of specific households, since it was not safe to make appointments or to return again and again seeking to interview the same occupant (the risks involved were a consideration to members of the household as well as to the writer and his interpreter). Therefore, starting from the best census data available, which was an estimate of the number of households in the area studied (340 in TCN), it was assumed that four-fifths of the village households were farm households.[14] (Previous studies in Vietnam had shown that in almost all rural villages the farm population was less than 80 percent of the total population).[15]

In TCN, as noted, 70 households were interviewed. To obtain a random sample, two techniques were used. First, the housing area of the universe was divided into twenty-five subareas from which at least 2 interviews were to be conducted. Second, the surrounding fields of the village were divided into areas from each of which at least 2 interviewees were to be chosen. This dual procedure was dictated by two considerations. It was thought that, in choosing two households from each residential block area, certain types of farmers absent with their families in the fields might be excluded from the sample. Moreover, it

[14] Farm households were defined as those that cultivated at least one-tenth hectare (one *cong*) in any crop.
[15] See Robert H. Stroup, "Rural Income Expenditure: Sample Survey," mimeographed (Saigon: USOM, Economic and Planning Division, 1965), p. 23.

was possible that, because of recent population movements, certain fields in the village under cultivation by nonvillage residents would be unintentionally excluded from the sample. Actually the process worked as follows: Since it was found, after conducting 50 interviews, that two areas of farmland had not been covered, an additional 4 interviews were conducted in the fields of these areas. The final 16 interviewees were selected at random from those residential blocks already having only two households represented in the sample.

In LBD, the sample of 50 was selected in a similar manner for another 25 percent sample of farm operators. Interviewing in LBD began in March 1967, a month after the start of the TCN research, and was conducted on an irregularly alternating basis in both villages through July 1967. This procedure was followed because predictable repetitive trips to a single village involved unnecessary risks.

THE RELIABILITY OF THE RESPONSE

The typical approach was to encounter the farmers in the field, exchange pleasantries, and ask questions such as "How is your rice crop?" "Are you using insecticides?" Eventually, when the responses began to involve detailed information, for example, the amount and type of fertilizer used, the farmer was asked if he had any objection to the recording of his responses. There was never any objection.

It was typical for the farmer to invite us to his house or fieldside hut for tea. There we met his family and continued the interview. In the fields we often sat on a bund or on the floor or equipment in the fieldside hut. In his home we sat with the farmer and often a neighbor or an elder son at a table in the central (and often only) room in the house. The farmer's wife usually participated in the conversation, but she never sat at the table. She served tea and stood in the background as an attentive observer and frequent contributor. It was common for her to intercede when her husband could not recall a date or amount of purchase and to correct or amend his statements. Many women exhibited a more precise knowledge of the details of farm activities than the men. The children also stood in the background. Their wide-eyed but silent curiosity never seemed to diminish even after three hours of seemingly paralyzed concentration. Occasionally when their concentration did wane, for example, when a chicken or a pig disrupted the scene, they were quickly disciplined by their parents, who threatened to make them leave if they did not keep silent.

The interviews ranged from 140 to 210 minutes and averaged less than 165 minutes in length. Often only one interview was conducted in a day. The remaining time was spent on related research into general economic matters. Despite the heavy demands on their time—the farmers were always busy, even in the dry season—no compensation was offered, nor were any promises made. The farmers quickly became aware of the narrow focus of the interview and willingly provided the information sought. After several weeks in each village, the purpose of the project was widely understood and our almost daily presence was acknowledged, usually by a slight nod of recognition or a smile from the distant farmer, and occasionally with a voiced greeting or wave of the hand.

The farmer's knowledge of his own activities was, with few exceptions, amazingly precise. With his wife's help he recalled the necessary information on factor use and production. Frequently, to make a comparative point on fertilizer use, he could cite his purchases for several years past. General questioning showed that the older farmers recalled predepression rice prices and wages—not a surprising outcome if one considers how closely their survival was related to these two figures. People thought in terms of events rather than specific dates. It was typically "before the depression," "after the Japanese came," "after the 1954 agreements," and "before the Diem land reform." For more recent dates, taxes on purchases, and other information, it was not uncommon for the wife to leave the room and return with a well-wrapped box from which she produced the relevant purchase receipt or license.

In only two cases, one a farmer who was drunk and the other an illiterate, were the responses unclear. In the former case, the wife provided the information; in the latter, with the aid of long, detailed questioning and an examination of the family's records, the necessary information was obtained. For reasons of incomplete or unclear responses, five interviews were rejected in the field research stage.

LANDLORD INTERVIEWS

Landlord interviews were conducted, from the question outline in Appendix A, with landholders mentioned by the farmers as the largest owners in the district and provincial capitals of Dinh Tuong and Bac Lieu provinces. Whereas the farmers generally had work to do, the landlords, isolated in the towns by the Viet Cong, were anxious to talk at great length. The information provided showed that the landlords were not apologetic about the past; they felt that what they had done was socially acceptable. Most regretted that these activities were no longer condoned and said, "things will never be the same again." But they did not distort the past to meet present values. Even on matters like current rents collected, their reported receipts from the areas studied were in agreement with the amounts tenants claimed to be paying.

Outline

The next chapter reviews the economic conditions of the Delta from 1862 until the period of study. Its emphasis is on the evolution of rice culture and the institutionalization of a system of landlord control over the 1862–1945 period. Chapter 3 places the landlord problem in the context of Viet Minh, Viet Cong, Diem, and post-1960 GVN land policies. Chapter 4 surveys the production opportunities available in the 1960s, including transport and marketing conditions. Chapter 5 is a study of capital, which was in abundant supply in 1966 and 1967, and Chapter 6 examines conditions in the tight labor market, placing them in the perspective of the theoretical issue of disguised unemployment. Chapters 7 and 8 examine, in turn, the development of irrigation systems in the villages studied and the arrival of a new technology. The critical question of fertilizer use is analyzed in Chapter 9. Chapter 10 is a study of income and investment, and Chapter 11 discusses economic aid and Viet Cong tax and trade policies. The final chapter draws broader conclusions from the accumulated evidence and relates them to the policies of the Viet Cong, the Vietnamese government, and the United States government.

2 Land and Income: A Historical Inquiry

Introduction

The institutional changes implemented by the Viet Minh from 1946 to 1954 and the Viet Cong from 1960 through 1967 must be seen in the context of the changing conditions of tenancy and related economic well-being of the 1930–1940 period. During these ten years the landlord-tenancy system, which since the late 1860s had proved an efficient instrument for the settlement of the Mekong Delta, became, because of prevailing technological and economic conditions, the controlling influence upon Delta economic life.

As the population grew, production techniques remained unchanged, and the supply of new land was exhausted, the landlord acquired an institutional grip on the economic conditions of millions of Delta families. The landlord bought out small landowners whose Malthusian behavior placed them in his financial debt and forced them to become his tenants. By playing one tenant against another for higher rents and favoring larger tenant-farmed holdings, the landlord drove small tenants off the land into a rural proletarian class. This class, deprived of frontier-opening opportunities for employment and augmented in number by a falling death rate, grew rapidly. With the mass of the population in his institutional grip, the landlord pushed them to a lower economic state in order to serve the export market. By 1945 the institutions of tenancy had become rigid and elite-serving; they were economically unproductive for and socially unacceptable to the vast majority of the Delta's inhabitants.[1]

[1] In China before the communist-initiated land reform, conditions were not dis-

The Settlement of Cochinchina

Cochinchina is an anomaly in Southeast Asia. One-third of its 60,000 square kilometers ranks with the finest rice lands in the world. Yet, though located in one of the most densely populated and ancient regions of the world, it was until recently very sparsely populated.

In the mid-seventeenth century scarcely 40,000 families, predominantly farmers from Cambodia, inhabited the rich Delta.[2] The Vietnamese controlled the area by 1700, but disease and internecine fights kept them from populating and exploiting the land.[3] The shaded areas (of Figure 2.1) show when formal Annamite (Vietnamese) administrative institutions were established in the various areas of Cochinchina.

Efforts to expand the area under cultivation in the Delta usually failed. For example, in 1840 the Vietnamese emperor Minh Mang sent settlers to ten villages in the Plain of Reeds north of My Tho. The villages flourished briefly until four were abandoned in 1863 because of sickness, particularly a cholera epidemic, and pillaging by pirates.[4]

Before the Vietnamese could settle the Delta and after colonial overtures by the Portuguese, Dutch, British, and French, each seeking a trading base in the area, the French captured Saigon in 1859. By a treaty of June 5, 1862, Emperor Tu Duc ceded three eastern provinces of Cochinchina—Bien Hoa, Gia Dinh, and My Tho—to the French. Another treaty, on March 15, 1874, forced Tu Duc to recognize French sovereignty over Cochinchina. In the next sixty-two years, from 1868 until 1930, Cochinchina developed at a rate probably unmatched at any time in any area of the world.

Before the French arrived, the Mekong Delta of Cochinchina was inundated by saline water throughout most of its area in the dry-season

---

similar to those described here, which applied from 1930 until 1945 in South Vietnam. In his study of agrarian conditions in China in the early 1930s, Chen Han-seng concluded, "The present system of land monopoly in China can only bestow perpetual ownership to a selected few, and simultaneously force perpetual indebtedness upon an ever growing mass." See *Landlord and Peasant in China: A Study of the Agrarian Crisis in South China* (New York: International Publishers, 1936), p. x.

[2] See D. G. E. Hall, *A History of South-East Asia*, 2nd ed. (London: Macmillan & Co., 1966), p. 399.

[3] A group of Chinese fugitives also preceded the formal Vietnamese administration, settling near Bien Hoa and My Tho around 1679. See ibid., pp. 393–413, for a history of the settlement of Cochinchina.

[4] "La Plaine des Joncs et son exploitation agricole," *Bulletin Economique de l'Indochine* (Hanoi), October 1898, p. 114.

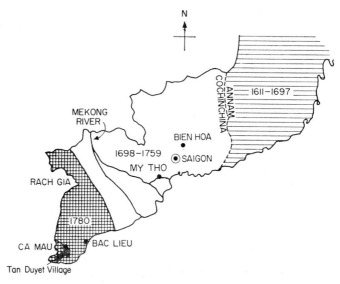

FIGURE 2.1   The Settlement of Cochinchina
Adapted from Le Thanh Khoi, *Le Viet-Nam*

months of January to April. During the rainy season, monsoon water stood in undrained flatlands, leaching the soil of needed nitrates, making it unfit for rice cultivation. Only those few settlers who could find high ground for houses and scattered rice fields lived in the area. Many of these were fishermen rather than rice cultivators. For them life was a constant struggle against death from cholera, plague, malaria, smallpox or attack from roving mercenaries.

To the north in Annam and Tonkin,[5] the tranquil existence of communalized village life was much preferred to the uncertainties of Cochinchina and the world beyond. But there was no choice. The pressures for expansion were great—particularly in the Tonkin Delta and the small coastal deltas of Annam, where the population could produce crops to meet only the minimum subsistence needs. In 1830 the Vietnamese emperor Minh Mang, in an effort to encourage expansion, granted a

[5] The region of Annam includes the area of Vietnam north from Cochinchina (see Figure 2.1) to a line just north of Than Hoa, now in North Vietnam. All the inhabitants of Vietnam were called Annamites by the French, a term whose origin lies in the fact that Vietnam was known to the Chinese as the Kingdom or Empire of Annam.

seven-year tax exemption to new villages.[6] For the Vietnamese, "the creator of a new village was held in higher esteem than the winner of a battle."[7] Yet, by a process of demographic percolation, the Vietnamese had moved, in one hundred years, only from Dong Hoi, now in North Vietnam, to Nha Trang (400 miles), settling each coastal plain along the way.

Arriving with needed engineering and medical skills, the French opened the era of expansion.[8] The settlement of the Delta can be seen in Figure 2.2 in terms of the number of hectares of rice in cultivation in Cochinchina. From 1868 until 1930 there was a rapid and steady rise in the area cultivated, from 215,000 to 2,214,000 hectares. It was possible for the writer in August 1967 to interview a landowner who recalled arriving in 1926 in the unsettled Ca Mau area of the Delta to establish Tan Duyet village (see Figure 2.1). With eight companions from Bac Lieu, this landlord constructed a small hut, after having climbed a nearby palm tree to survey the virgin land. Later he cleared and developed 1,600 hectares of land in this village 200 miles south of Saigon. But after 1930 there was no more new land to be cleared; the frontier had closed. The acreage cultivated continued to decline in the post-1946 hostilities and dropped again as the war intensified after 1965.

Meanwhile, the population of the area had increased from an estimated 1,679,000 in 1880 to 4,484,000 in 1931. After the closing of the frontier in 1930 the population continued to grow, reaching 5,578,000 in 1943 and 9,000,000 by the early 1960s.

The area cultivated and the population—respectively, engineering and demographic variables—were the exogenous determinates of Delta economic life. Between them and the dependent variable of economic well-being stood the institutions of landownership and the techniques of production. It was the interplay between the last two that determined the rice exports from the Delta and thus the residual production available for mass consumption. Therefore, the level of exports is of central importance. We see from Figure 2.2 that the general trend of exports was upward until 1907, remained, with fluctuations, at a high level until

[6] Joseph Buttinger, *The Smaller Dragon* (New York: Frederick A. Praeger, 1958), p. 281.
[7] Le Thanh Khoi, *Le Viet-Nam* (Paris: Editions de Minuit, 1955), p. 327.
[8] For a detailed assessment of the French role in the settlement of the Delta, see the appendix to this chapter.

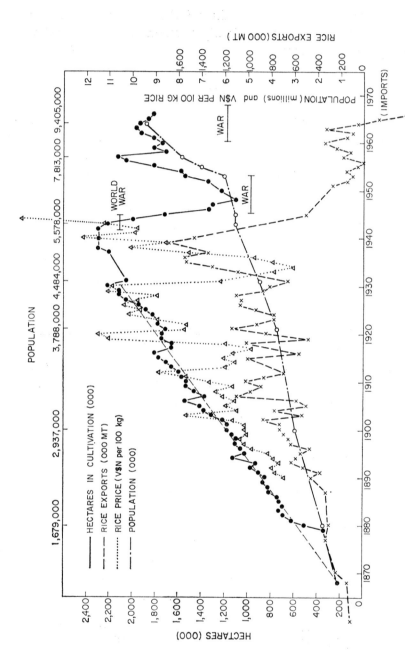

FIGURE 2.2 Cochinchina, 1868–1966: Area Cultivated, Rice Exports, and Population Source: Appendix B

the 1930s, and reached a peak in the 1935–1940 period, ten years after the frontier was settled. After 1940, exports declined steadily into the rice deficit years of the mid-1960s.

Tenancy as a Means of Development

The opening of the Delta for cultivation was not simply an engineering accomplishment of historical dimensions; it was also a major organizational achievement. The development of an extensive canal network—marked by the opening of the Cho Gao Canal in Dinh Tuong Province in the 1870s, the Rach Gia–Cai Lon Canal to Kien Giang Province in 1903, and the Can Tho–Soc Trang Canal between Phong Dinh and Ba Xuyen provinces in 1905—had to be followed by intensive land development work requiring large labor inputs before rice could be produced. Men skilled in mobilizing capital and labor were needed.

One such land developer was Truong Binh Huy, who in 1925 owned 70 hectares of land. In that year he bid against four competitors for the right to own and develop 650 hectares of land. His winning bid was equivalent to 0.61 metric ton of paddy per hectare; at that time the land was yielding nothing, yet it had a potential yield of about 1.6 metric tons per hectare.

Using hired labor and starting on a small portion of the landholding, Huy first drained the land by digging ditches that connected to the large canals. Next he cleared the land and burned the brush, leaving the ashes to enrich the leached soil. His "most difficult problem" was recruiting settlers. The first people to come were friends and relatives. Additional tenants were brought from other areas after Huy paid off their creditors for their release. Beginning with twenty to thirty people on 60 hectares, he expanded the cleared area by steps to 200, then 400, then 600 hectares. Tenants were free to take as much land as they could cultivate; the average family took 7 hectares, a small family 3 to 5 hectares, and a large family 10 hectares. According to Huy, there was "no limit" to the size of the holding occupied. He estimated the cost of clearing the land at 50 piasters per hectare in 1925 and 25 piasters per hectare after the depression. At 1925 prices, 50 piasters purchased 1.2 metric tons of paddy, meaning that his total outlay to purchase (0.61 metric ton) and to clear (1.2 metric tons) was 1.81 metric tons of paddy.[9] But the normal yield of 1.6 metric tons per hectare was not obtained until three years after cultivation began. Meanwhile, the annual market rate of interest was 50 to 60 percent, which provided a short-run financial justification for the land developer's demand for up to 70 percent of the crop in rent. This rent was in turn often used to develop additional acreage in the holding. The high cost of settlement was largely attributable to the cost of digging the canals and ditches (necessary to drain off the excess water) and building the dikes (necessary to block the dry-season ocean tides), without which, according to Huy, "you could not recruit tenants."

Later, in 1929 and 1933, Huy purchased two other concessions. One, costing 35,000 piasters, was obtained in 1929 by agreeing to pay off in ten years a debt of the same amount that the previous owner had with a real estate firm. This individual had attempted to develop the concession from Saigon, using a local manager, and had failed.

Huy's case is similar to that of the largest landowner in Cochinchina: Tran Trinh Trach owned 28,000 hectares of land at the time of the 1957 Diem land reform, when 26,000 hectares were confiscated. He came from a poor Chinese family. In the 1880s, when French schools were opened in Bac Lieu, the children of the wealthy Vietnamese sought to avoid mandatory attendance. Trach accepted money to be a substitute for one such Vietnamese child and learned French. Later, in 1898, he got a job as a government clerk and served as an interpreter between the Chinese merchants and the French administrators. Soon he had saved enough from his commissions as an intermediary to establish himself as a moneylender.

At the age of 30, in 1903, he was able to quit government work altogether and enter business for himself as a moneylender and land developer. He received no free land concessions, although he later served on the administrative council of the French Governor General, but acquired his land through purchase from various holders who were unable to develop their land and needed financial help. By the time of the depression he owned 15,000 hectares and in the 1930s acquired 10,000 more.

[9] When harvested, rice is in paddy form, unhusked. The rice product of the milling process weighs about 60–65% of the paddy weight, depending on how finely it is milled.

The cases of Huy and Trach were not untypical of the successful side of the development effort in the Delta. But for every success there were many who failed. During an era of expansion, failure was tolerable. Jobs were plentiful; one could become a tenant on a large plot or an agricultural worker. But around 1930 the economic prospects for the nonland-owning classes began to diminish. The institutions of tenancy, which had served for over fifty years as an efficient mechanism for development, within a few years became the mechanism for widespread economic exploitation and social abuse.

Tenancy as a Means of Exploitation[10]

By the early 1930s the over-all economic picture in the Delta was one of a fixed land frontier, static techniques of production, unchanging market opportunities, and a high rate of population growth. The structural implications of these conditions were momentous, though hardly predictable.

THE PROCESS OF MALTHUSIAN EVICTIONS

The dynamics of this structural process can best be seen at the micro-level. The attitude of both tenants and landlords toward landholding was not a simple one of maximizing the rate of return on invested capital, although revenue maximization was an important objective. In Figure 2.3, which relates labor input to farm output for a given size of farm-holding, line OD represents the subsistence requirements for the family, which increase at a constant rate related to the family size or labor input. (If the subsistence requirements were less than OD, say, at OE, and more family members existed than were required at labor input L_A, they would remain idle or share the work at L_A rather than apply more labor for marginal returns of zero beyond L_A).[11]

---

[10] The word "exploitation" is used advisedly. As the argument develops, it will be seen that the profit-maximizing landlords were exploiters to the extent that their profits were put to consumption uses without giving due attention to the development of new investment opportunities. Implicit in this reasoning is the assumption that the landlords, as the rulers of the country, had some social responsibility for the economic state of the people whose labor they employed. Therefore, even if new production opportunities were not found after due effort (which was never made), then some sort of income redistribution would have been in order.

[11] The author's view of this issue has been influenced by R. S. Eckaus's discussion

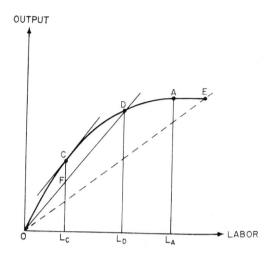

FIGURE 2.3   Labor and Rice Production

Curve $OCDE$ is a production function relating labor input to farm-plot output. We assume that the available technology is fully utilized or that the production function cannot be shifted upward. A family of profit-maximizing size L_C would have a surplus of CF. The Malthusian family would be limited in size to L_D on subsistence line OD. Since profit considerations are a priori not the single determinant of family size, one would expect various-sized families between O and L_D.

In Vietnam the family would probably have approached size L_D because a household head views his income earning potential and survival needs on a lifetime basis. He views his first years after marriage as the most productive; he is able to work long hours at the strenuous tasks of rice growing and earn more than his subsistence requirements on his plot. Looking beyond this period to the time when he is over fifty or sixty years old, he realizes that his declining physical condition may render him unable to earn income for his subsistence needs. Tending grazing buffalo, a common pursuit for older people, would not provide a subsistence income. By choice he might wish to become a fruit grower (a shift to a new production function), but the high capital outlay and

in "Notes on Invention and Innovation in Less Developed Countries," *American Economic Review*, vol. LVI, no. 3 (May 1966), pp. 98–109.

the long gestation period associated with this investment placed it beyond most farmers' financial reach. Moreover, landlords often demanded the entire product of fruit crops. Therefore, limited investment opportunities—not limited credit availability, for even the family at L_D could borrow funds if a new production function were financially feasible—forced the farmer to venture toward the Malthusian margin, for he saw in his children the hope of a prosperous old age. He reasoned that the more children he had the greater the likelihood that they would be able to sustain him in retirement.

However, in the short run, families at L_D ran a risk, either as tenants or small owners, vis-à-vis families at L_C or anyone with a financial surplus. If the Malthusian family suffered an unexpected crop failure or one of its members suddenly became ill, it was forced to go into debt to a family in the profit-maximizing-size range (near L_C) or to anyone with surplus cash balances. Conversely, the family L_C that sought investment opportunities for its cash surplus but found itself frustrated by the high costs of additional cash flows seized the opportunity to loan money at a high interest rate to family L_D. It was by this process that landholdings became larger as the population on a fixed land area continued to grow after 1930. A family at L_D first became indebted, then another crisis or its failure to earn a surplus forced it to give up its landholding. But even for non-Malthusian tenants one would expect landholdings to become more fragmented as families divided their land among male and often female heirs who married landless peasants.[12]

From the dynamics of tenancy and ownership discussed here, we surmise that small Malthusian landowners and tenants were evicted by large landowners and tenants. It is likely that between 1930 and 1945 the share of land farmed by owners fell and, conversely, the share farmed by tenants rose. (Because of the opposing influences of increased fragmentation of tenant holdings due to land being passed to successive generations, and the landlord's preference for large and "solvent" tenants, it is not clear whether the average tenant holding became larger or smaller over the period; it is highly probable, however, that the median holding did increase.)

---

[12] Primogeniture is not a practice in Vietnam, except in some cases of "cult," or ancestor worship, land.

Writing in 1937, Jean Goudal noted the expected owner-tenant dichotomy when he wrote:

> It will thus be seen that agriculture in Indo-China has gradually evolved . . . to a position in which there are two very distinct elements: on the one hand the large and medium-sized landowners—Annamite or French—who exercise their influence through the authority of the mandarins, the local councils and chambers of agriculture, etc., their associations, the press and the credit system; on the other hand, the working masses: small-holders, tenant-farmers, share farmers, wage earners, all more or less subject to the other group. . . .[13]

THE ACCUMULATION OF LARGE LANDHOLDINGS

Typical of the method of acquisition of large holdings was the case of Le Ngoc Chieu, a large landowner in the upper Delta. Chieu was not a mandarin but began as a farmer on 30 hectares of land inherited from his parents. By using his profits he purchased land from other owners, eventually acquiring 1,500 hectares. He owned land in Go Cong, Long An, and Kien Hoa provinces when, in 1957, 1,305 hectares were confiscated by the government. Ngo Quoc The, another upper Delta landowner, who inherited 15 hectares and eventually built it into a holding of 80 hectares, explained, in an interview with the author, the method of acquisition:

> Land was very scarce *before* the depression in Dinh Tuong and one could not purchase it from large owners but only from small holders who came under financial hardship.[14] They became indebted to you; eventually they could not pay cash so you acquired their land.[15]

After 1930, conditions changed but the method remained the same. Landlord Tam Vy explained how he purchased 100 hectares: "It was easy to get land in the depression years when the paddy price had fallen from 0.5–0.7 piaster per *gia* to 0.2–0.3 piaster per *gia*. The land came

[13] Jean Goudal, *Labour Conditions in Indo-China* (Geneva: International Labour Office, 1938), p. 193.

[14] The emergence of these conditions in Dinh Tuong before 1930 is a reflection of the earlier completion of the upper Delta's settlement in the 1920–1922 period. However, because upper Delta workers could migrate for work to the still-developing lower Delta until 1930, completely static production conditions did not prevail until that date. Nonetheless, the Malthusian process had begun.

[15] The legal basis of this process—the mortgage loan—was authenticated by a government decree of March 22, 1919, although the practice had existed earlier.

from the poor farmers who got into debt and had to sell to the *Doc Phu* [mandarin] district chief—who had their land as collateral." Vy in turn purchased his land from a mandarin in 1931/32 and later in the 1930s from creditors who acquired land in the depression but did not desire to become landowners. Vy was in the business of taking rice from tenants as rent and selling it on the export market in Saigon; like many large landowners, he owned a rice mill and rice warehouses in several locations.

THE LANDLORD-TENANT RELATIONSHIP

Before 1945 the relationship between the landlord and the tenant (both of whom were usually Vietnamese) was not one that is easy to judge. Despite the fact that conditions since 1945 have altered this relationship, often to the extent of completely reversing it, its basis and workings are still etched in the minds of tenant and landlord alike. It was first of all not simply an economic relationship but a social and political one as well. This was reflected in the landlord responses to one particular question: "Did your tenants ever approach you in an effort to buy land and did they ever actually purchase land from owners?"

This question prompted one landlord to rise and leave the room; he then reentered mimicking a tenant approaching his landlord—kowtowing, with his chin almost to the floor, a servile smile on his face, and a chicken or duck as a gift in his arms. The most complete response is quoted in detail:

> In the past, the relationship between the landlord and his tenants was paternalistic. The landlord considered the tenant as an inferior member of his extended family. When the tenant's father died, it was the duty of the landlord to give money to the tenant for the funeral; if his wife was pregnant, the landlord gave money for the birth; if he was in financial ruin the landlord gave assistance; therefore, the tenant *had* to behave as an inferior member of the extended family. The landlord enjoyed great prestige vis-à-vis the tenant. For this reason, a tenant who proposed to purchase land from his landlord would have risked *condemnation* by the "father." There were cases when a landlord in need of money sold to a tenant, but in such cases there had to be an intermediary. It was not possible for the tenant to converse directly. For the landlord the intermediary was necessary to avoid a "loss of face." A proposition directly from the tenant to the landlord

would imply that the tenant wanted or wished the landlord to be in a state of financial ruin.

The landlord acted not only as owner and lessor of land but as an informal administrator, like the chief of a small state. All disputes between tenants were judged first by the landlord. Only if the landlord failed to resolve such a dispute did the parties go to the government—the village council. There was an unwritten code administered by the landlord; it applied first. For example, if there was a case between tenants involving violence or animosity, the landlord would come down to their houses with twenty or thirty armed followers to settle the dispute. Occasionally there were difficult cases. At such times the landlord would gather the eldest tenants and set up a committee, serve them a meal, and obtain their advice. The landlord would enforce his own type of discipline, including corporal punishment for the men and detention for the women. Often the guilty party would be beaten with three, seven, or ten strokes. The tenants considered their landlord as their protector and as a good father; they would dare not ask to purchase land.[16]

This statement surpasses that of other landlords only in style and completeness. In every case the paternalistic relationship, the fear that a request by the tenant to purchase land would risk a costly loss of face to the landlord, and the need for an intermediary if such a transaction were to occur between a landowner in financial distress and a tenant were very clearly stated. The sanction on this relationship was equally evident. Since there was vigorous competition (after 1930) among the members of the working class to obtain land from the landowners, a tenant who fell into disfavor with his landlord could be readily replaced by another paying an equal or even higher rent. Landowners recalled that at any given time there were several prospective tenants, each offering to pay them a "transfer fee" and higher rents for the opportunity to replace those tenants occupying the landlords' land.

Before 1945, tenants had to provide the landlord with two days of free labor each month. Often this labor was used to dig or clear irrigation ditches, but it could be used for any task from constructing the landlord's house to serving at a ceremonial occasion. During festive periods

[16] From an interview on August 18, 1967 with Mr. Truong Binh Huy of Bac Lieu City. Huy was 68 years old.

tenants were expected to deliver chickens, ducks, or glutinous rice[17] as gifts to the landlord.

The tenant had to obtain the landlord's permission to dig a canal or ditch for irrigation or for the household water supply. Landlords in Dinh Tuong Province said they provided no financial or in-kind assistance on such projects, although permission was usually granted. In less densely populated Bac Lieu Province the landowners often provided assistance in the form of meals, but it was rare for them to pay wages as well. In the upper Delta, owners seldom provided investment or consumption credits to their tenants. Credit appears to have come from a separate moneylending class of Vietnamese and Chinese. In the lower Delta, however, landlords often loaned funds to tenants.

The landlord's attitude toward matters of production, after the land had been cleared and settled, was passive. No effort was made to devise new methods to raise productivity. Landlords were product- rather than production-oriented.

RENTS: MAXIMIZING REVENUES

The attitudes of the landlords on matters of production and estate management were determined by their efforts to maximize the rent output from their fields while minimizing the administrative costs of estate management and rent collection. The landlord commonly took 40 to 60 percent of the annual rice crop in rent.[18] Rice was an ideal crop for a landlord. It matured every year at a predictable date, its yields did not fluctuate greatly, and it was easy to collect and store.

Since yields were stable, the rent was fixed not as a share of the crop but as a share of the normal yield on the field. The size of the "normal yield" was determined by agreement between the owner and tenant and, because of the keenness of the competition for land and the landlord's social and political power, was usually above the average yield.

[17] High-quality glutinous rice is a special variety grown for use on festive or ceremonial occasions.

[18] Among historical sources there is no disagreement on this figure. For example, Paul Bernard, *Le problème économique indochinois* (Paris: Nouvelles Editions Latines, 1934), pp. 22–23, uses 50 percent; Yves Henry, *Economie agricole de l'Indochine* (Hanoi: Imprimerie d'Extrême-Orient, 1932), p. 193, 0.8–1.2 MT per ha on yields of 1.5–2.2 MT per ha. The landlords surveyed in 1966/67 recalled similar figures.

The rent was commonly 1.0 metric ton per hectare on an average yield of 1.5–2.0 metric tons.

In the case of a crop failure, the tenant was not automatically relieved of his rent burden; he had to obtain "tolerance" from his landowner. If this was not granted and the yield fell to 1.2 metric tons per hectare from an average of 2.0 metric tons, for example, the rent share rose from 50 to 83.3 percent.

Landlords preferred large tenant holdings to small holdings because they then collected rents from fewer people. Moreover, a bad crop for a tenant on a small plot implied starvation and a dramatic appeal for "tolerance," whereas a larger holding allowed the tenant to spread his risks and made it less likely that the landlord would be bothered by numerous appeals from tenants. As one former tenant recalled, "*Potential solvency was the decisive consideration one needed to gain a landlord's permission to farm his land*" (author's emphasis).

By the 1930s the landlords were moving out of the rural areas, a development indicating that it was administratively feasible to collect rents from Saigon or a provincial capital.[19] They hired agents who, by sampan, at the appointed time of the year visited the villages to collect in-kind rents. Many landlords had rice storage warehouses in several villages and owned rice mills.

THE DETERMINATION OF EXPORTS

The landlord did not take rents for his consumption use, for his family's consumption needs were an insignificant portion of his rent revenues. He was primarily an exporter of rice from the Delta to Saigon or, in the case of larger owners, from Saigon itself.

It is unlikely that international prices affected the share of a yearly crop sold for export, except perhaps during the depression. In a good crop year with low export prices, exports rose. In a bad crop year with high export prices, exports fell, although not to the extent of the crop failure,

---

[19] See Goudal, *Labour Conditions in Indo-China*, p. 208, or Charles Robequain, *The Economic Development of French Indo-China*, trans. I. A. Wood (London and New York: Oxford University Press, 1944), p. 193, for descriptions of this development, which appears to have been precipitated by the obsolescence of the landlord's role in the rural areas after settlement had been accomplished. It is clear that this exodus was taking place *before* the application of political and military pressures by the Viet Minh after 1945.

because tenants frequently were unable to obtain tolerance. In a bad crop year with low export prices, perhaps tolerance was more readily granted, but this is doubtful, except during the depression. Such was the case because the landlord did not forgo the opportunity to profit on higher rice prices six to eight months after the time of harvest or rent determination simply because prices were low. Also, the costs of rent collection did not vary with the share collected from each farmer. For reasonable export price fluctuations, therefore, the landlord had a constant incentive to obtain the largest possible share of his crop in rent. As long as the variable costs of collection were covered, the difference between rents of 15 and 50 percent was a net positive gain to the landlord, whatever the export price level. By taking a larger share of the yield, he spread his fixed costs over high volume with constant unit variable costs and profited from the declining average total costs of collection.

In the model implied by this analysis, exports are seen to have been primarily structurally determined; that is, *the extent of tenancy and the degree of competition among prospective tenants for the right to farm land determined the share of the crop taken in rent.* Competition among agricultural laborers for the rights of tenancy varied directly with the size of the population, inversely with the amount of land in cultivation, and inversely with the amount of land being brought into cultivation. It follows then that the role of the rice price was of secondary importance as an export determinant.

This is not to say that international prices played no role. In 1931 the rice price declined 43 percent from the 1930 level, and exports were down 19.3 percent. Yet this change can be partly attributed to a 7.4 percent decline in the cultivated acreage between these two years. When the international market collapsed, 163,000 hectares of marginal land were removed from cultivation. This change, however, was not typical. More typical are the comparisons in Table 2.1 between the 1920–1922 and 1935–1937 periods. In these years (selected because of the reliability of the available export data and their similarity in terms of general economic conditions—see Appendix B) there was no evident relationship between rice prices and exports.

A priori the argument that in the short run higher prices bring greater exports appears no stronger than the converse—at lower prices the land-

TABLE 2.1   Rice Prices and Exports

Year	Area Cultivated (000 ha)	Exports (000 MT)	Saigon Rice Price (V$N per 100 kg)	Price (francs)
1920	1,752	840	11.53	134
1921	1,714	1,138	7.77	53
1922	1,780	920	7.63	51
1935	2,200 (est.)	1,530	3.96	39
1936	2,200 (est.)	1,560	4.74	47
1937	2,200	1,350	7.59	76

Note: Exports from one year's crop are shipped the following year. Piasters were converted at exchange rates reported by Banque de l'Indochine à Saigon in *Annuaire statistique de l'Indochine, 1939–1940*, p. 279. Price and export movements for the period of study are given in Appendix B.

lords may be less tolerant with their tenants. Scatter diagrams relating prices and exports (lagged and unlagged) showed no relationship between these variables. Nor were Vietnamese rice exports a large enough share of world rice exports to allow Vietnamese conditions to determine world prices.[20] For these reasons, the sale price was not the primary export determinant except in the severe case of the depression, when export prices did not cover the variable costs of production.

The Export Model

BASIC DATA

We have seen that, while the Delta's population continued to grow, the area under cultivation actually declined over much of the 1931–1964 period and never again reached the 1931 level (see Figure 2.2). Between 1921 and 1931 the population density of Dinh Tuong Province rose from 130 to 164 per square kilometer; in 1964 it was 316 per square kilometer. The population density of less intensively cultivated Bac Lieu Province

---

[20] Over the 1934–1938 period, rice exports from Vietnam averaged 1,285,000 MT per year. Total annual world exports during this period were 9,250,000 MT, with Vietnam the third leading exporter, behind Burma and Thailand. Vietnamese rice exports were 13.3% of total world rice exports for the 1924–1928, 1934–1938, 1950–1952, and 1957–1961 periods, inclusive. See Food and Agriculture Organization (FAO), *The Economic Relationships Between Grains and Rice* (Rome, 1965), pp. 62–70.

rose from 31 to 64 per square kilometer between 1931 and 1964. Meanwhile, in 1931 there was more than twice as much rice land per capita in Bac Lieu Province than in Dinh Tuong, yet by 1964 the rice area available per capita in Bac Lieu was less than that available in Dinh Tuong in 1931 (0.405 hectare per capita versus 0.421 hectare per capita). For all of Cochinchina the rice area cultivated per capita remained stable from 1921 until 1931, when it began to fall; by 1964 it was less than one-half its 1931 level.

If the amount of productive land per capita declined after 1930 and if the techniques of production remained unchanged or became more labor intensive, this would be evidence—barring the availability of new employment opportunities outside the rice economy—that per capita incomes declined. We know that the productivity of the land was constant or declining over the 1879–1951 period: By accepting the most pessimistic evidence (in the following section) available (see Appendix B), we use a yield of 1.6 metric tons per hectare for the 1879–1936 period and 1.4 metric tons afterward (except for 1.3 metric tons in 1950), a decline due largely to the expanding extensive margin of cultivation, which brought the poorer lands of the lower Delta into cultivation.

EXPORT MODEL

With this evidence on yields and population densities, we arrive at a simple export model, which—using data from Appendix B and recognizing the preeminent role that rice occupies in the Vietnamese diet (discussed in the next section)—shows a rather startling decline in real incomes for Delta inhabitants sometime before 1936 and continuing at least until 1940. This decline followed a rise in income levels over the earlier period of settlement.

By taking as an example the 1920–1922 period from Table 2.2, the residual method of calculation can be demonstrated. For 1920–1922 the three-year average of the area under cultivation is multiplied by the indicated yield. The average paddy exports for the 1921–1923 period and the seed required to plant the average 1921–1923 crop (20 kilograms per hectare) are subtracted from the result. The residual paddy available is then divided by the average 1921–1923 population and adjusted by an estimated loss figure of 10 percent. Data from the succeeding year (1923 instead of 1920) were used because the annual rice crop was

TABLE 2.2 Rice Export Model

	1879–1880	1899–1901	1920–1922	1929–1931	1935–1937	1950–1952
Area cultivated (000 ha)	435.5	1,169	1,749	2,136	2,200	1,291 (1)
Yield (MT per ha)	1.6	1.6	1.4	1.4	1.4	1.3 (2)
Paddy exports[a] (000 MT)	490	1,140	1,560	1,195	2,385	326 (3)
Population (000)	1,679	2,937	3,788	4,484	4,616	5,750 (4)
Seed requirement (000 MT paddy): (1) × 0.02	9	23	35	43	44	26 (5)
Total paddy (000 MT): (1) × (2)	697	1,870	2,448	2,990	3,080	1,680 (6)
Residual paddy for consumption (000 MT): (6)−[(3)+(5)]	198	707	853	1,752	651	1,329 (7)
Kg paddy available per capita: (7) ÷ (4)	119	241	224	392	141	230 (8)
Adjusted for 10% loss in production-consumption cycle (kg)	107	217	202	353	127	207 (9)

Source: Appendix B.
[a] One should not conclude from the data for 1935–1937, for example, that all exports were the outcome of the rent collection process, i.e., that rents were at a 74.1% level. The larger-scale tenant farmers frequently sold over half their crops, and these sales would eventually make their way to the export market.

harvested between December and February; therefore, exports, seed requirements, and consumption from the 1922 crop were determined by 1923 conditions.

The use of a three-year average is intended to minimize the problem of rice stocks, on which data are unavailable. Rice grown in one year is generally removed from warehouses and rice mills within a year of harvest, a practice encouraged by yearly price cycles; the price of rice exhibits a 12 to 25 percent drop at harvesttime each year. It is also encouraged by the peasants' distrust for older rice, which in about a year becomes discolored. (Although wealthy owners occasionally stored glutinous rice—used for special festive celebrations—for longer than a year, few rice consumers fell in this category.)

The years selected for Table 2.2 were those coinciding with reliable export and census data. Census estimates were made in 1880, 1898, and 1960; 1921 was the year of the first general census, and 1931 was the year of the first census based on individual returns. Between these observations, large-scale immigration precludes projections based on unknown population growth rates. The rice export data for these years are also the best available.[21] Among the years selected, only 1931 is not typical in terms of crop cultivation and export conditions; no years of severe drought are included.

According to the results in line (9), residual paddy per capita consumption rose from 107 kilograms in 1879–1880 to 217 kilograms in 1899–1901. By 1920–1922, consumption had not changed significantly, but it rose dramatically in 1929–1931, fell sharply by 1935–1937, only to rise again in the 1950–1952 period. Because of the likelihood that stock spoilage in the depression period was above normal levels, or even that some fields went unharvested, it is probably best to discount the 1929–1931 results.

THE ROLE OF RICE IN THE VIETNAMESE DIET

The relevance of these results to the issue of fluctuations in the level of economic well-being of the Cochinchinese is a derivative of the role of rice in the Asian diet. Rice has a particular status among Asians that is not analogous to the role of wheat in Western diets. Asians at very low income levels rely on starchy roots—tubers, manioc, and sweet potatoes—for caloric intake; Vietnamese peasants consuming only 107 kilograms of paddy in 1879–1880 or 127 kilograms in 1935–1937 instead of the necessary 240 kilograms[22] probably ate such items. But as soon as

---

[21] There is some question whether or not Cambodian exports through Saigon are included in the export statistics. In 1900, 1936, and 1951 it could be determined that they were not included. In other years, sources were unclear on Cambodian exports; in either case, on the basis of data from years in which they are specified, the share exported from Cambodia through Saigon was not large (see Appendix B).

[22] This per capita figure is equivalent to 156 kg of rice per year and is within the range of results obtained in a study by the Vietnamese National Institute of Statistics

incomes permit, paddy consumption will rise to a level of about 240 kilograms (150 kilograms of rice) and remain stable there, even at much higher income levels, to the exclusion of barley, maize, and wheat, which are available on a comparative price-calorie basis.[23] In Japan, only at the income levels reached in the 1950s did rice consumption begin to fall, and then only after rice had been unfavorably priced compared with wheat, which received a government subsidy.[24]

This characteristic of Asian rice consumption makes it an ideal food for calculations of the type being considered. At higher income levels, the richer Vietnamese, although they may move to better-quality rice, will maintain a relatively constant rice consumption level in quantitative terms. We conclude then that, because of this strong preference for rice,[25] Vietnamese rice consumption would rise immediately as income or wages rose from low levels.

---

in the Delta in 1962/63. It is higher than the 1959–1961 average figure for Burma, 130 kg; Taiwan, 137 kg; and Hong Kong, 112 kg (see Food and Agriculture Organization, *Economic Relationships*, p. 18); but it is justified by the fact that the population is rural and dependent on cash sales of rice for subsistence nonfood needs. See also Colin Clark and Margaret Haswell, *The Economics of Subsistence Agriculture*, 2nd ed. (New York: St Martin's Press, 1966), pp. 49–53, who use a similar figure. The caloric equivalent of 240 kg of paddy is 1,530 calories per day. If supplemented from other food sources, one arrives at a general Asian standard of 2,100 to 2,300 calories per day (see Harry T. Oshima, "Food Consumption, Nutrition, and Economic Development in Asian Countries," *Economic Development and Cultural Change*, vol. 15, no. 4 [July 1967], pp. 387–388). That the 240-kg figure had local importance is supported by the fact that the Viet Cong used it as the base from which to calculate tax deductions.

[23] Initially, rice and wheat consumption displaces coarse grain and starchy root consumption. "Experience tells us that the tendency is [as incomes grow] to shift away from starchy roots or coarse grains and toward rice or wheat which are almost universally regarded as 'superior' cereals" (Food and Agriculture Organization, *Economic Relationships*, p. 39). Later, "At high incomes, therefore, the elasticity of demand for rice would remain fairly stable (and may rise in expenditure terms) whereas demand for wheat tends to decline" (ibid., p. 40).

[24] Ibid., p. 51. Because Japan imports both rice and wheat, the wheat subsidy was intended to give the rice-oriented Japanese an incentive, greater than the import price differential, to consume more wheat. In terms of caloric content, the world price of rice was almost twice that of wheat, meaning that a wheat-consuming Japanese population would save foreign exchange.

[25] A National Institute of Statistics (Saigon) survey in Saigon and six other areas of South Vietnam, conducted from April 1962 to March 1963, showed a daily per capita rice consumption figure of 318 grams in Saigon and 440 grams in the rural areas. These figures give an annual rice consumption rate among the highest in the world. See U.S., Agency for International Development (USAID), Office of Joint Economic Affairs, *Annual Statistical Bulletin* (hereafter cited as USAID, *ASB*), 1966, p. 108.

CONCLUSION: FALLING INCOMES

The results obtained from the export model show that after prices and exports had recovered to predepression levels or above in the 1935–1937 period, these benefits were not passed on to the vast majority of the people, that is, to the tenant farmers and laborers who were living at less than subsistence consumption levels. Instead, the export market was served at the expense of domestic consumption.

This conclusion is strengthened by the fact that not only did the three-year 1920–1922 and 1935–1937 periods show a fall in consumption, but exports in the 1920–1922 period were at or above the general level of the 1920s and in the 1935–1937 period were no higher than those of 1939–1940. In terms of the model, this means that, if anything, 1920–1922 consumption was lower than for the 1920s in general and that the 1935–1937 figure was probably not lower than that of the postdepression to pre–World War II era. Therefore, considering the constraints imposed by population and export data as well as those arising from exogenous factors (the depression and World War II) and abnormal years (1938 was a year of drought), the periods chosen are representative of the 1920s and 1930s, respectively. One can be less confident about the pre-1920 trend, although the dramatic income jump between the 1879–1880 period and the 1899–1901 period, which was not reversed in 1920–1922, indicates that Delta rice incomes did rise over the period of settlement.

Next, contrast the low level of residual consumption of the 1935–1937 period with the results for the 1950–1952 period. It appears that the landlord's flight from the countryside in 1945–1946 and the related institutional controls enforced by the Viet Minh denied the landlord his one-half share of the crop in rents—leaving that share to the tenant, who consumed a portion of it. Exports continued to decline after the war even though the Delta exporters again had access to the world market. For the first time since the depression, rice consumption in Cochinchina began to move upward in a significant way.

Wages: Another Indicator

Changes in rural wages serve as another useful indicator of changing economic conditions over the 1862–1945 period. After the lower Delta was opened for cultivation, there was a shortage of labor, particularly at times of peak demand. This demand was met by seasonal migrants from the more densely populated upper Delta provinces of Gia Dinh, Long An, Dinh Tuong, and Go Cong. Henry has described how the later maturing dates of rice in the lower Delta provinces allowed workers to begin with the upper Delta harvest in November and work southward, finishing work as late as March in Bac Lieu and Rach Gia.[26] By the early 1930s, however, after the frontier had closed and while the population continued to grow, this opportunity vanished; by the 1950s there was no seasonal migration worth noting.

While the opportunity for migration existed, an ambitious worker might find employment for up to 250 days a year, although most farm laborers probably worked fewer days. In the early 1930s, however, a prominent French economist found that the average annual income of a farm laborer in Cochinchina was 55 piasters at a wage rate of 0.3 piaster a day.[27] By this accounting, he worked approximately 184 days. Although the figure of 200 days a year may overstate the work opportunities available between 1930 and 1960 (therefore overstating the income of a wage earner in this period), it will be used in all of the calculations to follow because, if anything, it will bias the results against the anticipated decline in incomes.

DECLINING WAGES

The data in Table 2.3 show the calculated real wage of a farm laborer in selected years from 1898 through 1958. Over the period, there was a trend of rising wages from 1898 until 1929, after which wages fell sharply in the 1930s, only to rise again in the war years, then fall in 1958 to the 1915 level. Notably, the fall in the wage rate relative to the price of rice during the depression was not recovered by 1938, even though the price of paddy had risen to predepression levels.

The last column of Table 2.3 (7) shows the per capita paddy income for a family of five living on the wages of a single wage earner. The results demonstrate that such a family's economic position improved dramatically between 1898 and 1925, only to level off by 1930 and fall

[26] Henry, Economie agricole de l'Indochine, p. 50.
[27] Bernard, Le problème économique indochinois, pp. 23–24.

TABLE 2.3 Wages

Year	Daily Rural Wage (V$N) (1)	Paddy Price (V$N per gia)[a] (2)	Margin (4)−(2)÷(2) (percent) (3)	Saigon Wholesale Paddy Price (V$N per gia) (4)	Paddy per Day (1)÷(2)×20 (kg) (5)	(5)×200 Days (kg) (6)	Per Capita, Family of Five (kg) (7)
1898[b]	0.2	0.4	50	0.6[f]	10.0	2,000	400
1915[c]	0.3	0.5	46	0.73[f]	12.0	2,400	480
1925[c]	0.7	0.7	69	1.18[f]	20.0	4,000	800
1929–early 1930[c, d]	0.8	0.8	75	1.4[f]	20.0	4,000	800
1931[c, a]	0.18	0.27	185	0.77[f]	13.3	2,660	532
1938[c]	0.3	0.9	47	1.32[f]	6.67	1,334	267
1940–1943[c]	1.0	1.2	25	1.5[g]	16.7	3,340	668[h]
1958[e]	30.0	50.0	23	61.6	12.0	2,400	480

[a] One gia of paddy is 20 kg; annual calculations are on the basis of the Delta paddy price.
[b] "La culture du riz à Gocong," Bulletin Economique de l'Indochine, March 1899, pp. 303–307.
[c] From interviews.
[d] Yves Henry, Economie agricole de l'Indochine (Hanoi: Imprimerie d'Extrême-Orient, 1932), pp. 50–52.
[e] James B. Hendry, The Small World of Khanh Hau (Chicago: Aldine Publishing Co., 1964), pp. 83, 135.
[f] Annuaire statistique de l'Indochine, 1939–1940 (Hanoi, 1942), p. 290.
[g] 1941 figure.
[h] During the war years, rice exports fell, and occupying Japanese troops consumed only a part of the amount additionally available for domestic consumption. According to Buttinger, Japanese troops consumed annually a million tons of rice from Indochina. In 1941–1942 Japan took 80% of Indochina's rice exports, having taken almost none before 1940; after 1943, exports fell as transport to Japan was interrupted by war. See Joseph Buttinger, Vietnam: A Dragon Embattled (New York: Frederick A. Praeger, 1967), p. 239.

markedly in the 1930s. Because of vanishing employment opportunities after 1930, this result was expected.

If one recognizes that tenants could become laborers and laborers could become tenants by outbidding existing tenants for the rents they were willing to pay (that is, there was perfect mobility in the labor market among the employment opportunities), then these declining wages in the 1930s are indicative of the general decline in Delta economic conditions during that period. This wage evidence confirms the results arrived at with the export model.

Harvesting Techniques

A change in harvesting techniques that took place in the upper Delta region in the late 1920s and early 1930s provides additional evidence to support the contention that the farmers' level of income was declining during that time.

Originally throughout the Delta's upper and lower regions, a single harvesting technique was used: Farmers cut the rice stalks in the field at midlevel with a sickle and transported the stalk, with head attached, in ox-driven carts to central gathering points where it was threshed by buffalo or oxen treading around a stake or pulling a stone roller. This technique was employed because it allowed the farmer cultivating 5–10 hectares of land to remove the grain from the fields in the short period necessary to avoid damage from floods or rain or loss from pillaging and haul it immediately to safe, high ground near his house. If the farmer had not employed this procedure, choosing a more labor-intensive one instead, he would have been unable to harvest as much land; therefore, he would earn on a smaller plot a smaller net product than obtainable if he had used a buffalo to assist on a larger holding. In 1966–1967 in the lower Delta, this capital (animal)-intensive harvesting technique was still being used.

By contrast, in the upper Delta, where settlement and the ensuing land fragmentation occurred approximately two generations earlier than in the lower Delta, the farm family could no longer afford to use a buffalo team for harvesting. The buffalo was replaced by a new technique that made intensive use of human labor on the smaller plot. The harvester cut the stalk close to the ground and threshed it in the field, using a flailing movement against a wooden lattice covering a bamboo sledge. The rice straw was left in the field and the paddy transported by shoulder pole to the farmer's home plot.

For the villagers, adopting this new technique was seen as progress, and they welcomed the innovation.[28] But that it signaled a decline in the level of income is evident in Table 2.4. Listed in ascending order of labor intensity are the harvesting techniques employed in the upper and lower Mekong Delta, the Tonkin Delta as reported by Gourou in 1936,[29] and on the islands of Java and Bali as witnessed by the writer in 1967.

The labor intensity of the technique employed is closely associated with the population density on the land. The most capital-intensive technique is that employed in the lower Mekong Delta both in 1931 and today. It is followed by the upper Mekong Delta method currently employed. Next, Gourou found that farmers in the Tonkin Delta cut the rice plant near the head in the field and carried it with shoulder poles to their home plots for threshing by various labor-intensive processes.[30] He reported that a few Tonkinese farmers employed the flail method of threshing but that most used a rope attached to two bamboo poles, which the worker used to strike the ears of the grain violently against a stone.[31] Some threshing was done by laborers pulling a stone roller over the grain or by treading the grain underfoot. Even more labor intensive was the method employed in Java and Bali in 1967, where harvesters used a small hand knife to cut the stalk near the head and transported and threshed it by methods similar to those employed in the Tonkin Delta.

Besides the change in the upper Mekong Delta in the 1925–1935 period, when the population density was approximately 150 per square kilometer, changes moving toward more capital-intensive techniques have been observed. Swift,[32] an anthropologist studying a Malayan village in the 1950s, noted that between 1955 and 1956 the harvesting

[28] James B. Hendry, *The Small World of Khanh Hau* (Chicago: Aldine Publishing Co., 1964), p. 237.
[29] Pierre Gourou, *The Peasants of the Tonkin Delta*, trans. Richard R. Miller (New Haven, Conn.: Human Relations Area Files, 1955), pp. 414–417.
[30] Ibid.
[31] Gourou found that some plowing in Tonkin was done by workers who hitched themselves to a plow (ibid.).
[32] M. G. Swift, *Malay Peasant Society in Jelebu* (New York: Humanities Press; London: Athlone Press, 1965).

TABLE 2.4 Rice Production Techniques

Location, Date	Harvesting	Threshing	Transport, Field to Home	Population Density (per km²)
1. Lower Mekong Delta, 1920–1967	by small sickle at base of stalk	by buffalo treading or pulling stone roller over stalks and heads at central gathering point	by buffalo cart hauling stalk and head	31 (1931) 64 (1964)
2. Upper Mekong Delta, pre-1930	same as 1	same as 1	same as 1	164 (1931)
3. Upper Mekong Delta, 1930–1967	by V-shaped cutting blade at mid or lower stalk	by hand flailing against sledge in field	by shoulder pole, carrying only rough grain	164 (1931) 316 (1964)
4. Tonkin Delta, 1936	by knife or sickle near head	rope and bamboo-throwing device on stone; man pulling stone roller or treading with feet at home-plot area	by shoulder pole, carrying sheaves of grain	430
5. Java and Bali, 1967	by hand knife near head	same as 4	same as 4	504 (Central Java)

Sources: See text.

method changed from a "traditional" one similar to that used in the Tonkin Delta and in Bali and Java, with each stalk being cut separately below the head, to one similar to that employed in the upper Mekong Delta, using a sickle and threshing by the flail method. Finding that only two farmers employed this technique in 1955, whereas in 1956 everyone used it, he writes, "I cannot explain this sudden change."[33] The farmers' explanation was that the "new method was quicker." But Swift later tells of the sudden labor shortage in the rice fields that had been the result of "rubber-madness" and an increase in the price of labor due to the Malayan emergency; he also noted that marginal land was removed from production.[34] Doubtless it was this labor shortage that caused the farmers to reject the hand-knife cutting technique, a method more efficient in terms of the grain preserved for consumption but more labor- and time-consuming than the flail method. (Generally it takes about 20 man-days to harvest a hectare of rice land using the flail method; using the hand-knife cutting technique requires at least 30 man-days per hectare.)

From this analysis of techniques we conclude that, around 1930, labor conditions in Cochinchina forced upper Delta farmers to employ a more labor-intensive harvesting technique. This finding is another indication that incomes began to decline during this period.

Conclusions
It could hardly be a coincidence that the evidence presented in this chapter on residual rice consumption, wages, and production techniques —gathered from diverse sources and analyzed from different viewpoints, using pessimistic assumptions with regard to the expected outcome—has given compatible results. In every case the results indicate that the economic conditions of the rural Delta declined in the post-1930 period after having risen sharply during the preceding period of settlement. It seems clear that economic conditions were deteriorating; furthermore, this development was the expected outcome from the prevailing institutional conditions: As the population grew, landlords were able to prevent the rural population's near-subsistence needs from supplanting production going to the export market; therefore, economic conditions became progressively worse.

[33] Ibid., p. 47.
[34] Ibid., pp. 47, 51–52, 60.

Appendix to Chapter 2:
Historical Footnotes

There is no obvious need to reconcile the evidence presented here with other evidence of secular changes in the income level in Cochinchina, for, in the analytical sense, no such evidence exists. Nonetheless, the Marxist view of exploited colonies, and what can be called the conventional American view of the French as the responsible agents for many U.S. post-1954 Vietnam problems—both views in the Indochina case being largely and paradoxically the same—cannot be reconciled with the evidence presented here, that is, the finding that from 1862 until at least the early 1920s the indigenous population of the Delta enjoyed rising incomes.

THE PRE-FRENCH LEGACY

The conventional American view, exemplified in Buttinger's recent tome,[35] that the French disrupted the idyllic communal life of the peasant without providing anything better,[36] does not describe the changing conditions in Cochinchina over the 1862–1954 period.

The basic error in this view is its starting point. While it is true that the communal arrangements of Tonkin were conducive to a more considerate treatment of the poor, it is naïve to view life in these communes as a healthy one, free from poverty, disease, and social unrest. Even a brief survey of the available historical sources shows that almost every practice later condemned and often described as French in origin—the corvée, arbitrary treatment of the peasants by government or village authorities, usury, and other alleged shortcomings—had its origin in pre-French practices. Further, even those practices of later origin, such as the landlord's role, were Annamite practices devised by the Annamites to deal with the new conditions brought by the French.

For example, although land-mortgage loans were officially sanctioned by decree in 1919, this was not the origin of the practice. Buttinger himself has observed that, under the Annamite code, creditors

---

[35] Joseph Buttinger, *Vietnam: A Dragon Embattled*, 2 vols. (New York: Frederick A. Praeger; London: Pall Mall Press, 1967).

[36] It was President Franklin D. Roosevelt's view that the French had controlled Indochina for a hundred years and had "milked Indochina dry"; he reasoned that the people "are entitled to something better than that." See Bernard B. Fall, *The Two Viet-Nams*, 2nd ed. (London: Pall Mall Press, 1967), p. 53.

had a right to seize a debtor and hold him in bondage until he paid off his debt with labor.[37] Surely it is progress when one's land instead of one's self is used as collateral.

Another example of the less-than-ideal conditions in pre-French times was the unequal distribution of political power. Virginia Thompson wrote: "The notables made the laws and executed them, and there was no check upon their power. In theory it was age and ability, but in practice solely property which qualified them for this office, so naturally they governed in the interest of their own class."[38] On the allocation of village land, André Dumarest wrote: "It seemed as though this system ought to have assured a certain level of riches; in reality, the distribution was undertaken by the Council of Notables in charge of the administration of commercial affairs, who favored above all the powerful."[39]

A serious weakness of many of the historical accounts of Indochinese conditions is that they have relied too heavily on official statements— decrees of the emperor or later of the French colonial government— which often did not reflect what actually took place. In 1966, for example, one could receive official assurance that there was no corvée and that government officials did not collect rents; but an investigation of actual conditions showed that official decrees were seldom implemented.

Some writers were aware of these inconsistencies. Virginia Thompson wrote that the general corvée was abolished in 1898, and purchased exemptions were allowed. Then she found that between 1900 and 1914 the corvée was "legally abolished," only to be "unconditionally abolished" in 1937. Then, in describing actual conditions, she wrote, "Village notables arbitrarily selected their victims who were perennially the same. Villages were deserted at the approach of a traveller who might have a permit to requisition assistance."[40]

THE FRENCH SUCCESSES

An understanding of the conditions that were to play such a significant role in the post-1945 developments in the rural areas is not complete if

---

[37] Buttinger, *Smaller Dragon*, p. 146.

[38] Virginia Thompson, *French Indo-China* (New York: Macmillan Co., 1937), p. 35.

[39] André Dumarest, *La formation des classes sociales en pays annamite* (Lyon: Imprimerie P. Ferréol, 1935), p. 38.

[40] Thompson, *French Indo-China*, pp. 162–163.

it encompasses only the basic Annamite habits that the French willingly or unwillingly allowed to persist. In many ways the French contribution to the settlement of Indochina was vital and beyond the reasonable capacity of the native Vietnamese. First, the French provided the engineering skills necessary to drain the Mekong Delta and open it up to investors, who then recruited tenants to settle it. One writer has rightly placed this engineering feat "among the great works of modern civilization."[41] In 1860 there was only an "inadequate and neglected" river system around Saigon.[42] But in the 1890–1900 period an annual average of 824,000 cubic meters of soil was excavated; this figure rose to 7,233,000 cubic meters between 1920 and 1930, and by 1930 as much as 165,000,000 cubic meters had been excavated in Cochinchina.[43] This total is comparable to 260,000,000 cubic meters excavated in the construction of the Suez Canal and 210,000,000 in the excavation of the Panama Canal.

The second development vital to the settlement of the Delta was a medical achievement. In the 1890s, Dr. H. A. E. Yersin founded a branch of the Pasteur Institute at Nha Trang, where successful efforts were made to combat the plague, cholera, malaria, smallpox, beriberi, and tuberculosis. Work stoppages like that caused by a cholera epidemic among laborers on the Cho Gao Canal in 1875 became less frequent, although in 1927 it was still possible for an epidemic to kill 27,000 people.[44]

The French could be ambitious and often overzealous in constructing public works such as railroads and canals. After a government study had shown that roads were a cheaper method of transport than railroads, roadbuilding became almost a government obsession; by 1936 Robequain could describe the road system in Indochina as one of the best in the Far East.[45] In 1920 there were 10,000 kilometers of year-round, non-asphalt roads; in 1926 there were still no asphalt roads, yet by 1933 there were 3,200 kilometers of asphalt roads and 16,600 kilometers of non-asphalt all-weather roads in Indochina.[46] The number of automobiles on

---

[41] Goudal, *Labour Conditions in Indo-China*, p. 200.
[42] Robequain, *Economic Development of French Indo-China*, p. 105.
[43] Goudal, *Labour Conditions in Indo-China*, p. 199.
[44] Thompson, *French Indo-China*, pp. 280–281.
[45] See Robequain, *Economic Development of French Indo-China*, pp. 97–100.
[46] "L'automobile en Indochine," *Bulletin Economique de l'Indochine*, March 1934, p. 1363.

these roads rose from 350 in 1913 to 31,000 in December 1933.[47] Even in 1966–1967 this road system, basically unchanged since 1945 and damaged by over a decade of war, was remarkably efficient.[48]

The wider implications of a mobile society, standing in marked contrast to the often-assumed cloistered, communal attractiveness of village life, were anticipated by Virginia Thompson in the following words written in the mid-1930s:

> Everyone uses roads, from bonzes to peasants. The roads have quickened their feeling of life and power. It has sufficed only the briefest contact with the road to dissolve the tradition of centuries that made for inertia, isolation, and detached contemplation. If the Annamite is taken more swiftly from his native village, he can also return more easily. He fears journeys less, and departure for him no longer means death. The whole country is united by this living cordon. Products hitherto deemed unsalable find purchasers. A new sense of human dignity comes from this conquest of nature which is shared alike by those who build and those who use the roads. Egalitarian sentiments flourish.[49]

Even the educational efforts of the colonial government, although belated, were in the end successful in raising the literacy rate to the high levels found by Hendry in 1958 and this writer in 1966. In 1940 in North and South Vietnam there were 525,000 children in 7,164 schools; in 1944 this number had risen to 960,000 attending 13,384 schools; and in 1955, the first year of peace, there were 1,077,000 children in 8,905 schools.[50]

THE FRENCH FAILURES

The downfall of French economic policy, evident by the 1930s, can be traced to two notable failures in the French economic role. First,

[47] Ibid.
[48] See Table 4.1.
[49] Thompson, *French Indo-China*, p. 213.
[50] From Bernard Fall, *Two Viet-Nams*, p. 466. Buttinger's assertions that "in regard to education, French intervention so far had been remarkable only for its shockingly negative results"; that "precolonial Vietnam had been famous for its system of free general and higher education"; and that "at least 80 per cent of the people were literate to some degree" (*Vietnam: A Dragon Embattled*, p. 46) cannot be accepted. His argument that, by simply knowing a few Chinese characters, the people acquired a firm "ethical and moral outlook" (ibid., p. 456) is neither relevant nor important. The French provisions for Annamite education were inadequate, but whether this was the case relative to pre-French efforts is doubtful.

the French employed a technology that was implicitly static. When the frontier was settled, the dredges lost their value. Efforts to establish the Office du Riz in 1930 were not only belated but inadequate. Technology had not been brought to the rice culture; it had been brought only to the land. Yields were either static or declining despite marked tendencies to the contrary in nearby countries such as Japan and the Philippines. The controlled development of high-yield rice varieties was not a French skill. Small-scale irrigation devices suited to Delta conditions were not developed.[51] There were no extension service programs nor was any high-level applied agricultural education available for qualified Vietnamese. After the 1930s, French technology did not have the capacity to raise labor productivity, but French medical technology combined with Vietnamese demography was capable of lowering it.

The second and most important French economic shortcoming deserves more detailed treatment. As we have seen, the actual settlement of the Delta region was a task performed largely by the Vietnamese. Although the infrastructural contributions of the French were vital, the recruiting of tenants, clearing of land, and digging of secondary and tertiary canals were Vietnamese accomplishments.

We must dispel the belief that the French owned a large portion of the cultivated rice land in Cochinchina. A French decree of 1874 initiated the free land concession, granting the right to develop land to those who requested it, and permitting them to acquire ownership in three years if they had the land in cultivation and were paying land taxes. In 1880 the size of the free concession was limited to 500 hectares. During this period other concessions could be purchased at low prices. The *Bulletin Economique de l'Indochine* in December 1899 reported that as of March 1, 1899, 187 concessions (107 free, 80 purchased) had been recorded, covering 62,404 hectares of which 13,968 hectares were in cultivation—11,936 of these in rice. Therefore, of 1,143,000 hectares

---

[51] These comments are aided by hindsight. Three technological improvements assisted in the Vietnamese agricultural revolution of the 1960s: fertilizer, high-yielding rice varieties, and small-scale irrigation mechanisms. In the late 1930s fertilizer was introduced in the Delta, but its high price and the unresponsiveness of the available rice varieties precluded its widespread use. Sometime after 1940, a new, quick-maturing rice variety became available, probably from Japan; but its impact was slight until its use was facilitated in the late 1950s by a faster-growing primary variety and in the 1960s by new irrigation developments.

of cultivated rice land in 1899 only 1 percent was French owned.[52] (The fact that only 22.6 percent of the land conceded was in cultivation in 1899 made it unlikely that large concessions were composed of land already in cultivation, thereby denying ownership to small holders who had settled before the French arrived.)[53]

By June 1921, concessions of only 184,000 hectares had been granted. By 1931, 606,500 hectares had been granted,[54] a reflection of the land boom of the 1920s and the establishment of rubber and tea plantations. Of these 606,500 hectares, 253,400 were cultivated in rice—11.5 percent of the total rice land in cultivation in 1930. It has been estimated that, of a French population of 16,000 in Indochina in 1931, 2,000 were naturalized Vietnamese.[55] This means that the 11.5 percent figure may be too high because it includes land owned by Vietnamese naturalized as Frenchmen. On the other hand, Henry estimated that in 1931 an additional 133,000 hectares were owned by Europeans (French) who had purchased land on the open market.[56]

By any accounting, it is doubtful that Europeans owned more than 15 percent of the cultivated rice land in 1930. On September 10, 1958, when the Republic of Vietnam received from the French land formerly owned by French citizens in the Cochinchina area, the amount was 224,000 hectares,[57] or about 10 percent of the cultivated rice land. Although we may absolve the French of responsibility for being the primary agents of landlord abuse, one must conclude with Gourou that, "all things considered, there is no doubt that the French administration has unconsciously favored the development of large land holdings."[58] It was this permissive policy toward landowners that was to negate the economic benefits the French brought to the Delta and signal their final failure as a colonial economic power in Cochinchina.[59]

---

[52] *Bulletin Economique de l'Indochine*, December 1899, pp. 70–71.

[53] This was a fault of the concession system in the already settled Tonkin Delta.

[54] Thompson, *French Indo-China*, p. 229.

[55] Buttinger, *Vietnam: A Dragon Embattled*, p. 527.

[56] Henry, *Economie agricole*, p. 224.

[57] J. L. Cooper, "Land Reform in the Republic of Vietnam," mimeographed (Saigon: USOM, 1966), p. 6 and associated Appendix E.

[58] Gourou, *Peasants of the Tonkin Delta*, p. 383.

[59] It would be more than a historical coincidence if, as chap. 12 suggests, the failure of many U.S. policies in South Vietnam can be traced to a similar permissive attitude toward landlords.

CONCLUSION

The basic problem, one soon to come into focus after the French withdrew, was that the Vietnamese, who had proved so efficient and cooperative in settlement, were unqualified for the task of economic development. Just like the technology, the landed oligarchy was static in attitude and motivation. It seemed to combine the aversion to technology of the pre-French mandarins with the isolation of the French bureaucrat or administrator. Living in Saigon or the larger provincial cities, the landlords had little knowledge of the problems of the peasants on their land and a negligible desire to solve them. Their only concern was to collect rents. These rents, which in earlier days had provided the funds for investment in land development, became the vehicle for indulgent consumption.

3 Recent Conditions of Land Tenure

The problem of land is of decisive importance.
Vo Nguyen Giap[1]

From 1945 to 1960

In the Delta from 1946 to 1954, the conditions of land tenure changed markedly, but these changes were obscured by the issue of independence and the withdrawal of the French. During the interregnum of 1954–1959, the social-institutional accomplishments of the Viet Minh were held in abeyance or (often) reversed. In 1960 the Viet Cong instituted the second phase of this struggle, and by 1967 they had achieved a major institutional transformation.

THE SCOPE OF THE PROBLEM

The primary areas of research into land problems were Bac Lieu and An Xuyen provinces (representative of the lower Delta wet-rice area), Dinh Tuong Province (representative of the upper Delta wet-rice area), and An Giang Province (representative of the floating-rice area). (See Figure 3.1.) Not only were these areas representative of the economic conditions of the Delta but they were also typical of the contrasting political-military conditions. Tan Duyet village of An Xuyen Province and Phuoc Long district of Bac Lieu Province were representative of areas under continuous Viet Minh and Viet Cong control since 1946. An Giang was the only Delta province that could be considered to have been GVN secure throughout the period. Security conditions in the villages studied in Dinh Tuong ranged from GVN semisecure to contested.

---

[1] Denis Warner, *The Last Confucian* (New York and London: Macmillan Co., 1963), p. 59.

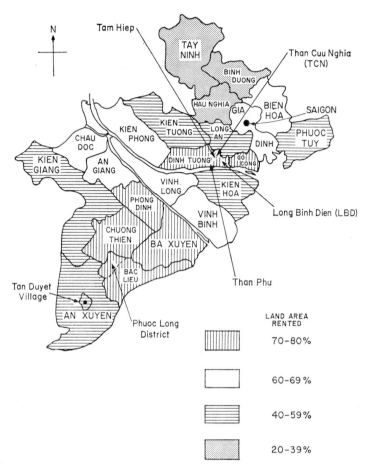

FIGURE 3.1   Percentage of Land Area Rented (Mekong Delta Region)
Source: *Census of Agriculture, 1960–1961*

For the Delta as a whole, approximately 2,000,000 hectares were under cultivation over the 1946–1967 period. The Delta was farmed with an average holding of 1.5 hectares;[2] that is, there were roughly 1,330,000 farmers, at least 77 percent, or about 1,000,000, of whom were tenants.[3]

[2] Republic of Vietnam, Ministry of Agriculture, Agricultural Economics and Statistics Service, *Census of Agriculture, 1960–1961* (Saigon, 1964), p. 80.
[3] Ibid., which showed that 47% of the farmholdings were on rented land, 30% on owned and rented land, and 23% on owned land.

With an average family size of 6 (Hendry found 5.5 in 1958/59,[4] this writer 7.7 in 1966/67), considerations of tenancy were relevant to approximately 6,000,000 persons. Add to this an additional 2,000,000 landless peasants who were the potential recipients of redistributed land, and one sees that land tenure issues were of immediate economic concern to 80 percent of the Delta's 10,000,000 inhabitants.

THE VIET MINH

The Viet Minh recognized the social and economic importance of land. After seizing control of large areas of the Delta in the 1946–1954 period, they conducted an intensive campaign of terror against landlords and government officials, usually the same persons. The gradual retreat of landlords to the cities that had begun in the 1930s for reasons of role and preference, in the 1946–1948 period became a panic-stricken exodus to escape intimidation, assassination, or trial and probable execution by the Viet Minh.

In Tan Duyet village in 1946, Viet Minh threats caused the largest owner (of 1,600 hectares, or almost the entire village) to flee to Bac Lieu City. Backed by the Viet Minh, only one-half of this owner's tenants paid any rent from 1946 through 1948, and those who did paid much less than the pre-1946 rate of 40 to 60 percent of their crops. In 1949 a Viet Minh tribunal sentenced the owner to death, in absentia, and redistributed his land, allocating 5 hectares to each family. He received no rents between 1949 and 1954. Similarly, in nearby Phuoc Long district of Bac Lieu Province, landlords who owned more than 100 hectares had by 1950 retreated to the district capital. Owners of 500 to 3,000 hectares moved to Saigon. In neither area by 1967 had the landlords or the GVN reasserted the control they lost in 1946 except for a brief period— and then only partially—from 1955 until 1958, when some rents were collected from those the landlords termed "faithful" tenants. Parallel events occurred in many areas of Dinh Tuong Province, where the Viet Minh executed a program of rent reduction and land distribution after seizing control in the 1946–1948 period.[5]

---

[4] James B. Hendry, *The Small World of Khanh Hau* (Chicago: Aldine Publishing Co., 1964), p. 12.

[5] On July 14, 1949, the Viet Minh government of Ho Chi Minh decreed a rent reduction program. On April 12, 1953 a new decree was promulgated, applying to

However, in An Giang and other areas of the lower Delta over which the Viet Minh had never exerted control, the tenancy system was not modified, and pre-1946 Delta-wide conditions prevailed throughout the 1950s and 1960s.

THE VIET MINH AND THE VIET CONG

Viewing the Viet Minh's programs from the vantage point of post–Viet Cong developments, landlords were unanimous in their preference for the Viet Minh compared with the Viet Cong. They recalled that the Viet Minh struggle was simply a resistance movement against the French and not a conflict with the landlords, whereas for the Viet Cong, according to one landlord, "it is a class struggle and no landlord dares live in his home village." Landowners pointed out that the Viet Minh redistributed land to everyone, while the Viet Cong gave preference to families of National Liberation Front (NLF) members. The Viet Minh tolerated the landlord's presence as long as he agreed to the redistribution, accepted lower rents, and paid Viet Minh taxes. They were also more tolerant of the large-scale cultivator, allowing farmers in the upper Delta to farm 5 hectares compared with the less than 2 hectares permitted by the Viet Cong.

THE GENEVA PEACE

After the peace of 1954, the Viet Minh threat to the landlords was never completely removed from the Delta. A few of the smaller landlords returned to their villages, but most did not. Instead, they relied on returning GVN officials or hired agents to collect rents. The social status quo ex ante was not reinstituted.

Irretrievable power had slipped from the landlord to the tenant. For this reason plots distributed by the Viet Minh were rarely repossessed. Rents, although they did rise again above the legal level (that is, 25 percent), never attained pre-1946 levels: In the 1954–1959 period rents were in the 25 to 40 percent range instead of the 40 to 60 percent range common before 1946. Despite these improvements, however, the tenant's gains over the 1946–1954 period were threatened; his tenure status was less comfortable and less secure.

---

the whole territory of Vietnam. See Allan B. Cole, ed., *Conflict in Indo-China and International Repercussions* (Ithaca, N.Y.: Cornell University Press, 1956), p. 151.

Isolated in fortified outposts and district towns, Vietnamese government officials recognized, as early as 1953, the importance of land reform as a political program. On June 4 of that year, Bao Dai's premier, Nguyen Van Tam, decreed that rents be limited to 25 percent or less and that the size of landholdings not exceed 100 hectares for any owner. This decree was never implemented by the Tam government, which fell in December 1953.

Later, on January 8, 1955, Ordinance Two of the Diem government established a rent minimum of 15 percent and a maximum of 25 percent. It further protected the farmers' tenancy rights by guaranteeing three- to five-year contracts, which were intended to prevent the competitive evictions of the past. Diem's Ordinance Seven of February 5, 1955 guaranteed additional rights to tenants on abandoned land. The effect of these decrees has not been clearly established. However, in 1958 Hendry found that rents averaged 25 percent; that is, many tenants paid more than the legal maximum.[6] In general, where supply-and-demand conditions prevailed unaffected by Viet Minh pressures, rents often exceeded the maximum allowed, and the Diem ordinance was ignored.

The major land reform decree issued by the Diem government was Ordinance Fifty-seven of October 22, 1956. It limited an owner's holding to 100 hectares, plus 15 hectares for the family's cult or ancestor worship land, and an additional 30 hectares if the farmer cultivated it himself. By February 28, 1957, under this law, 2,600 owners had declared themselves the owners of 1,075,000 hectares. From this amount approximately 740,000 hectares, roughly 30 percent of the rice land in South Vietnam, were available for redistribution.[7] But by 1965, only 440,678 hectares had been expropriated and only 247,760 hectares redistributed to 115,912 farmers.[8] This left approximately 817,000 tenants (87.5 percent) who did not benefit from Ordinance Fifty-seven.

[6] Hendry, Small World of Khanh Hau, pp. 36–41.

[7] Price Gittenger, "Agrarian Reform," in Richard W. Lindholm, ed., Viet-Nam: The First Five Years (East Lansing: Michigan State University Press, 1959), p. 205.

[8] Republic of Vietnam, Ministry of Agriculture, Agricultural Economics and Statistics Service, Agricultural Statistics Yearbook, 1965, p. 183. As of September 27, 1958, 258,969 ha had been allocated to 97,229 tenants. The cost of the Diem reform was $2.2 million over the first three years.

Under the Diem reform, tenants paid for the land they received, a fact that acquires significance when contrasted with the Viet Cong reforms under which land was given to the farmer. The landlords argued that they were inadequately compensated for their land. In the upper Delta the market value of the land, for which landlords received 1,000 piasters per hectare, was 2,000 piasters, and throughout the Delta the prices paid were about one-half or less of the market value. On the other hand, tenants reported that many landlords were able to re-distribute land to relatives and close friends before the confiscation was implemented. One landlord during his interview said that local officials had simply missed his name on the land register, an easy mistake since officials had to compare many land registers from different villages and districts.

Nonetheless, for the Diem government and for the landlords the Diem land reform was a revolutionary step, but for the tenants it was much less than that: It was only a positive indication that the Diem government could be interested in their welfare. Landlords still view the Diem reform with shock; it was the first time a government had moved against the landlords' interests in any major way. The Diem reform was a significant step in the right direction, but no additional steps were taken. At most, 10 percent of the tenants were affected.

Moreover, in some cases the Diem reform was accompanied by abuse. In one village studied, over 30 tenants, farming 58 hectares of land received from the Viet Minh, were evicted by GVN police, who claimed to be implementing the Diem reform. The farmers were each given 500 piasters ($8.33) per hectare as compensation, and their land was sold to the highest bidder. The son of one of the evicted farmers recalled that this incident as well as his enforced labor in President Diem's strategic hamlet program caused him to join the Viet Cong. (Before deserting the Viet Cong he had been a senior political officer in Dinh Tuong Province.)

Viet Cong Reforms

The Viet Cong land reform program possessed the universality and mass appeal that the Diem land reform lacked. It was implemented to please the tenant rather than to ease the pain to the landlord and was executed by a widespread program of terror and assassination against the landlords. The Viet Cong program pursued three related objectives: land redistribution, rent reduction, and higher wages for rural workers. Small tenants and landless peasant workers were the beneficiaries. Large landowners and large-scale tenants were the objects of Viet Cong terror and economic pressure.[9]

THE SANCTION OF TERROR

In over 90 percent of the Delta's villages, sometime during the 1960–1966 period, the following events transpired. The Viet Cong entered one or several hamlets in the village and issued a word-of-mouth threat to the large resident landlords. As in TCN, selected officials, usually landowners, were assassinated, intimidated, and arrested; others fled to the nearby district town, to secure hamlets in the village, to the provincial capital, or to Saigon. The Viet Cong then ordered tenants not to leave the village for the purpose of paying their rents. Instead, landlords had to come personally to collect rents, or in the words of one tenant: "Landlords had to find their tenants." Reportedly, hired rent-collecting agents were killed. If the absentee landlords acquiesced and did not return, the Viet Cong exerted no pressures against them. Often absentee landlords received token rent payments from their "faithful" tenants, who in most cases were simply hedging their positions by secretly sending their landlords a small monetary payment in case the GVN reasserted control over their villages.

Landlords who refused to accept nonpayment either relied on government officials for rent collection or brought their tenants to court. Few landlords chose the latter course, however, and their fate served as a lesson to many who might have considered legal action. For example, a TCN landlord residing in Tan Hiep, when asked to be specific about his reluctance to press for court action against delinquent tenants, replied by citing what had happened to two large landowners who in 1964 had sought court action against their tenants for nonpayment of rent. The respondent recalled that "because of this, in 1965 the Viet Cong entered their homes and killed them." Or, as a Dinh Tuong land-

---

[9] For a chronicle of events similar to those described here but which took place in China in the 1940s, see William Hinton, *Fanshen: A Documentary of Revoluton in a Chinese Village* (New York: Random House, Vintage Books, 1966).

lord who had fled to Saigon saw it, "according to the Viet Cong law, he who collects rents will be killed."

For smaller owners (less than 25 hectares) who remained in their hamlets in contested areas or in GVN semisecure areas, the Viet Cong's policies were more discriminating. Often, verbal persuasion was sufficient to convince them to lower their rents to about 10 percent. One owner of 30 hectares said he collected "whatever rents the tenants are willing to pay." In his case these amounted to less than 5 percent of the crop.

INSECURITY AND DECLINING RENT PAYMENTS

By 1966 the benefits of the Viet Cong land program, initiated with the 1960 General Uprising campaign, were manifest. Approximately 817,000 tenants in the Delta were apprised of a single overriding fact: Rents paid on land in the Delta were determined by the Viet Cong and the market; they were not affected by Vietnamese government regulations or laws.

Where the Viet Cong exerted little or no control, that is, in GVN secure areas, market considerations dictated rents of 25 to 40 percent, without regard for the legal limit of 25 percent. In these areas tenants sought GVN contracts to lower their rents, but landlords refused to sign them. In contrast, in areas over which the Viet Cong exerted control, even including GVN semisecure areas, rents fell well below the 25 percent limit. Here it was the landlord who sought to secure a GVN contract, and it was the tenant, backed by the Viet Cong, who refused to sign one; these conditions prevailed over 70 percent of the Delta's land.

In Figure 3.2, compiled from data collected in LBD, a semisecure GVN village, the rent-security relationship is distinctly seen. The plotted numbers are interview numbers. Numbers 15, 2, and 36 were landlords collecting rents from land in the designated areas. The rents collected from 5 kilometers and beyond by these LBD landlords were at the same low level as those reported by the 25 respondents in the separate landlord sample. (The distances are accurate within 0.05 kilometer.) The vertical axis represents the percentage of crop paid in rent; the horizontal axis represents the distance from the secured GVN road (Route 24; see map, Figure 1.5). Because Viet Cong influence increased and GVN influence decreased in direct proportion to the distance from the road (which was patrolled by Vietnamese army forces in daytime and dotted with static defense guardposts), the plot of observations shows clearly that as Viet Cong influence increased, the rents paid by tenants to their landlords decreased.

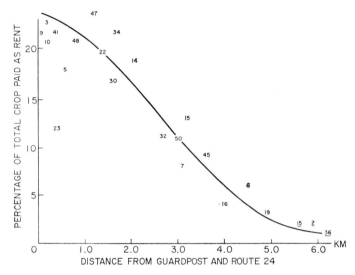

FIGURE 3.2   Security and Rents Paid in Long Binh Dien

In contrast, two surveys conducted in An Giang Province, one in March and another in August 1967, showed that tenants in this GVN secure area paid rents of 25 to 40 percent of their total crop. For the Delta as a whole, in 1966–1967 the average rent paid by tenants was between 5 and 10 percent, compared with 40 and 60 percent before 1946 and more than 25 percent from 1954 to 1959.

LAND VALUES AND THE RETURN TO LANDOWNERSHIP

In Table 3.1, data are presented showing the marked influence of the structural changes previously discussed on land values and the return to landownership. We see that the real price of land (1) in the upper Delta almost doubled between 1899 and 1930. Because crop yields and the rent share were relatively unchanged over this period, the price-yield ratio and the price-rent ratio rose. That is, the profits from landholding declined markedly between 1899 and 1930, reflecting an increased demand for land, one of the few opportunities for investment in an environment deprived of new opportunities and techniques for production.

The 1958 and 1967 entries in (3) of Table 3.1 show a dramatic reversal of the earlier trend, reflecting the changes implemented by the Viet Minh and Viet Cong in their campaigns against the landlords.

TABLE 3.1   Upper Delta Land Prices

Year	Price per Hectare (MT of paddy) (1)	Yield per Hectare (MT of paddy) (2)	Price-Yield Ratio (1) ÷ (2) (3)	Land Price– Rent[a] Ratio (4)
1899[b]	4.44	1.80	2.46	4.95
1930[c]	8.50	1.60	5.30	10.62
1958[d]	8.00	2.40	3.34	13.31
1967[e]	4.00	2.50	1.60	12.50

[a] Rent as percentage of crop: 1899 and 1930, 50%; 1958, 25%; 1967, 20%.
[b] *Bulletin Economique de l'Indochine*, March 1899, pp. 304–307 (Go Cong Province).
[c] Yves Henry, *Economie agricole de l'Indochine* (Hanoi: Imprimerie d'Extrême-Orient, 1932), p. 165 (Dinh Tuong Province).
[d] James B. Hendry, *The Small World of Khanh Hau* (Chicago: Aldine Publishing Co., 1964), p. 48 (Long An Province).
[e] My estimate (Dinh Tuong Province).

Land prices had fallen by 1958, and by 1967 the real price of upper Delta land had halved compared with 1958; this outcome is a direct reflection of the decrease in the percentage basis for rent collection between the periods. Moreover, as one would expect, the price-rent ratio in 1967 was not different from that of 1958 or even 1930. The Viet Cong cut rents, and the price of land fell accordingly.

LAND REDISTRIBUTION

In addition to a rent-suppression program, the Viet Cong, like the Viet Minh, implemented a program of land redistribution. The Viet Cong "suggested" to farmers cultivating plots larger than 2 hectares[10] that

[10] The exact size varied from 1 to 2 ha, depending on the soil's fertility and the family's size.

members of the working class be permitted to farm a portion of their land; this failing, they applied the pressure necessary to accomplish the land redistribution. Redistributions were implemented in both LBD and TCN. For example, one farmer owning 50 hectares had 33 hectares confiscated and redistributed to two former laborers.

After gaining control of a hamlet or village, the Viet Cong were immediately able to allocate the land abandoned by the families of GVN officials, army members, and large owners. In one village surveyed, the confiscated land went first to those who had received it from the Viet Minh but who had lost it following the return of the GVN after 1954; next, it was given to the families of the Viet Cong, allowing them to sustain themselves while their breadwinners served the NLF (and providing an incentive to poor peasants to join the NLF); as a third priority, land was redistributed to families with many dependents. Generally these priorities were adhered to, and land was allocated to the extent that it was available and there was a demand for it. Occasionally there were abuses, for example, when the village party members received a disproportionate amount of land, but these were not widespread.

In Chapter 6 we shall see that the Viet Cong followed other economic policies designed to encourage the redistribution. They used boycotts and raised the harvest wage rate to make it difficult and costly for the large-scale farmer to hire labor. As a further dissuasion to large-scale farming, Viet Cong tax policies allowed a per capita subsistence exemption beyond which earnings were taxed at a highly progressive rate. The effect of these policies is seen in the fact that in 1966 a farmer in TCN who worked only 2.6 hectares of rice land was labeled by other farmers a "big rice grower."

THE PHILOSOPHY OF THE VIET CONG REFORMS

The land policy guidelines issued from the Central Office of the National Liberation Front (COSVN) were not specific, and the local policies implemented in the villages exhibited a remarkable flexibility in response to local economic conditions (soil productivity, the supply of and demand for land) and institutional conditions (a predominance of very large owners, small owners, large tenants, small tenants, and so on). The flexibility allowed by COSVN directives is evident in the "Agrarian Policy of the Party," a document captured in Long An Province in 1965.[11] The document began with a statement on the goal of agrarian policy, which was to "reinforce the peasants' support for the patriots' fight for rural unification." It then outlined the policy principles of (1) rent reductions, (2) protection of farming rights, (3) "confiscation of land from the U.S. imperialists and South Vietnamese government and landlords who bear a blood resentment toward peasants," (4) redistribution of confiscated lands, (5) recognition of land possessions of landlords who "neither serve the GVN nor bear a blood resentment toward our people," and (6) protection of land rights of medium landowners, churches, temples, and families of the Council of Notables. The document went on to suggest the following guidelines:

> a. Rent decreases are fixed according to the number of landless peasants, lands possessed, strength of the revolutionary movement, and productivity of the field.
> b. Automatic rent reductions are allowed for natural disasters.
> c. Special treatment is to be given to landowners with sons in the Viet Cong.
> d. Landowners are not permitted to take back land unless the tenants willingly give it back; and the occupying tenant must be given the first option to purchase any land put up for sale.

The implementation of these policies was to be based on "negotiations" between the interested parties. The document said that "torture and terrorism are not to be used."

Because this document also dealt with conditions on rubber and tea plantations and with Montagnard affairs, items not relevant to Long An or the Delta, it can be interpreted as a copy or immediate by-product of a COSVN directive. The document reflects the changed conditions of the war in 1965. At that time often up to half of the farmland was idle in Viet Cong areas because of the mass exodus to GVN areas to escape hostilities. The document's tone implies a liberalization of earlier policies. It specified that "from now on, dividing lands of medium owners is forbidden," and added, "If dividing land does not cause resentment of medium landowners, then the procedure should continue." Moreover, the emphasis on negotiations and reconciliation rather than terror constituted a significant change from past policies. Yet, "strong

[11] Dated December 15, 1965; published as a mimeographed document by USAID, September 6, 1966.

persuasion is to be used in cases where big landowners object to having their lands divided." It concluded: "Promises to return their land are not to be made. Cleverness in persuasion is necessary to preserve rural unity."

The tone of this document is not one of confusion but one of flexibility. In effect, it says, "Meet the local situation with a land policy that will get the most support and the greatest production." Of wider importance, in the words of a student of Viet Cong organization and techniques, "Around land and on the solutions of land tenure problems, the NLF built its indoctrination system. . . . Cadres were instructed to turn every issue into land terms."[12]

THE BENEFITS OF VIET CONG LAND POLICIES

The peasants' view of Viet Cong land policies (and the land policies of the Vietnamese government) was not determined by their consistency or ultimate aim to achieve larger objectives (for example, collectivization, communism, capitalism, or whatever) but by their immediate effect. The peasants had had over twenty years on which to base their judgment of Viet Minh and Viet Cong land policies.

In terms of their economic welfare, these policies were, for the vast majority, very effective. It is difficult to overestimate the extent of these reforms. Every landlord in the Delta, including those in GVN secure areas, was conscious of Viet Cong policies, interests, and desires. Those who collected rents above 10 to 15 percent did so at the risk of their lives. In contrast to previous years, tenants found landlords anxious to give "tolerance" on the rent demanded in poor crop years. One tenant, who over the 1963–1966 period had paid an average rent of less than 5 percent to his Saigon landlady, said, "My land is located in an insecure area so my landlady is ready to give tolerance. She is afraid of getting killed, but I am an honest tenant and never thought of being delinquent in my payments." From all the benefits it brought to the peasantry, it can probably be said that the impetus behind the Viet Cong land reform was not in the general case terror but the sanction of implied force supported by the general will.

[12] Douglas Pike, Viet Cong (Cambridge, Mass.: The M.I.T. Press, 1969), p. 276. For some reservations on Pike's broader conclusions see chap. 12.

The Vietnamese Government's Response

The Vietnamese government response to the Viet Cong land reform program was one of opposition. At the village level, for example, in TCN in 1959–1960, those who accepted land redistributed by the Viet Cong were arrested. At the Saigon level, the ability of the GVN to separate itself from landlord interests—a capacity clearly demonstrated by the Diem land reform—diminished as the Viet Cong threat grew and the shortsightedness of those who opposed the Viet Cong on ideological grounds prevailed. Therefore, complicity with landowners at the lower government levels, where officials and army officers were often land-owners, determined the government's policies.

The peasants, however, supposedly the object of the GVN reforms, judged the government on land matters from two of its roles: as a tax collector and as an agent collecting rents for nonresident landlords. In itself, tax collection was hardly important. In 1966 the assessment on average-quality rice land was only 110.5 piasters (less than one dollar) per hectare, which included a basic assessment of 85 piasters that went to the national government, 17 piasters (20 percent of the base) to the provincial government, and 8.5 piasters (10 percent of the base) to the village government. In 1966 the total land tax assessment for LBD village was 145,000 piasters, of which 35,000 piasters were actually collected. Of this sum the village government kept 10 percent (that is, 3,500 piasters).[13]

The relevance of the land tax was twofold. First, if the landlord had left the village for Saigon or My Tho, the village finance officer collected this tax from the tenant, who, it was reasoned, would deduct it from the landlord's rent. From this administrative precedent it was an easy step for local governments to begin rent collection for absentee landlords. If the government was going into the insecure fields with troops to collect taxes, why not collect rents at the same time? Second, there was a financial motive. Conditions of insecurity in the early 1960s, coupled

---

[13] A 1963 study of rice-land taxes in South Vietnam found that of a total assessment of V$N 85,289,000 on 2,469,860 ha of rice land, only V$N 30,924,000 were collected. Countrywide property tax (urban and rural) collections fell from V$N 109,867,000 in 1960 to V$N 79,278,000 in 1965. Over this same period the value of the piaster had declined to about 40% of its 1960 level. See R. E. Davis, "An Analysis of the Property Tax in Vietnam," mimeographed (Saigon: USOM, March 1965).

with a fixed land tax assessment and rising prices, caused village revenues, both piaster and real, to fall sharply. Local officials were paid from these declining revenues. By 1963 the TCN village chief could no longer afford to maintain his office or family; therefore, he resigned. Other local officials were more enterprising—or security conditions were more favorable. They made agreements with absentee landlords to collect rents for them, charging a fee of 30 percent on the amount collected.

RENT COLLECTION BY VILLAGE OFFICIALS

Thus began, for reasons of the common identity of landlord and village official, administrative ease, and financial necessity, a practice that has continued to plague the Vietnamese government in its relationship with tenants: rent collection by village officials. Of the 25 landlords interviewed, 11 had, at one time or another since 1960, employed local village officials to collect rents.

The procedure was a straightforward one. The absentee landlord made an agreement with a village or district official under which that official agreed, for the 30 percent fee, to collect rents on designated land. After the harvest, this official reached a separate agreement with a local military officer to share the fee, and the officer employed his local troops to collect the rents. In general, 10 percent of the amount collected went to the troops involved, 10 percent to their commanding officer, and 10 percent to the entrusted village official.

At the village level, in 1966–1967, information on this practice was readily available. Tenants reported it, local military officers reported it, and village officials reported it—each with complete openness. After a conversation with the LBD village chief and two of his predecessors, I obtained a list of those landlords who had made these arrangements with the village chief, the police officer, and the finance officer. No rent was collected from half of the tenants listed because their fields were too insecure. Similar arrangements were made at the district level; for example, the largest Dinh Tuong landlord hired an army officer to collect the rents on his fifty hectares in Cho Gao district.

In Phuoc Long district of Bac Lieu Province, the district chief, in his fortress surrounded by Viet Cong territory, was quite candid about the whole procedure. He regretted that the need for secrecy on military operations prevented him from giving the resident landowners in his town the advance notice that would enable them to follow his operations and collect rents. He noted with satisfaction, however, that his *chieu hoi* (open arms, or returnee, program) chief and the police chief, who because they were not only landlords but part of the official party on these military operations, were able to collect rents.

Inquiries at higher levels brought less candid responses. Nevertheless, in both Dinh Tuong and Bac Lieu provinces the land service chiefs admitted that the practice continued—in the words of one, "although it is informal and illegal." Officially, a circular issued by the Minister of Agriculture in December 1965 (Official Circular no. 11.000–BCN/-KH/4G) had prohibited military units from taking part in the collection of back rents from tenants in non-GVN or formerly non-GVN areas. This circular was reissued over the signature of Prime Minister Ky (Official Circular no. 61–TT/XD) on March 28, 1967. But even if implemented, this directive did not prohibit the collection of *current* rents by village officials and officers; therefore, it overlooked the basic problem.

The tenants, knowing nothing of the legality or illegality of the practice, reported that they paid the rent to soldiers (the *nghia quan,* or local militia) who came to collect it. Some landlords were satisfied with the arrangement, but most found it unsatisfactory. Several reported that local officials were too afraid of the Viet Cong to collect rents; another noted that he had never used the procedure because the village officials would "cheat" him.

RESURRECTING THE DIEM REFORM

The balance of the Vietnamese government land program consisted of attempts to resurrect the Diem reform and to point out land problems in Viet Cong areas while ignoring the more serious ones in GVN areas.

In March 1967 the GVN issued permanent land titles to replace the temporary ones granted during the Diem reform ten years earlier (and which had been the source of some Viet Cong propaganda). By the end of 1967, because of the insecure conditions and a slow response on the part of the recipients, less than 10 percent of these titles had been distributed. This program amounted to an attempt to repeat, as a paper transaction, the Diem reform, which, as we have seen, covered less than 10 percent of the tenant-farmed area. Prime Minister Ky's circular dated March 28, 1967 also contained instructions on the disposition of lands repossessed from the Viet Cong, and these sought to grant certain rights to tenants who had received land in the Viet Cong distributions. Yet the circular conveniently ignored the blatant abuses in GVN secure areas where many tenants paid rents in excess of the legal 25 percent limit.

APPLYING TECHNOLOGY

In An Giang Province, the Vietnamese government was assisting the U.S. government in an exercise of technological self-deception on the issue of land reform. Under a project run by the U.S. Army Corps of Engineers, a photographic survey was made of the province's lands for the purpose of "land identification." The objectives of this program are evident in the following excerpt from a Joint U.S. Public Affairs Office "Guidance Paper" (no. 34, dated March 20, 1967) entitled "Psyops Aspects of GVN Land Title and Land Tenure Programs":

> GVN and USAID technicians are working side by side in An Giang Province to create a national demonstration area that will set the pace for land development and agricultural productivity in other provinces. As a part of this pilot program, land is being surveyed using aerial photography and checked by surveyor teams on the ground using the most advanced methods, to provide exact data on landownership. This will permit speedy issue of permanent official titles to prospective land-owners and provide accurate land records at the village, province, and national level. The An Giang demonstration project will provide over the next two years a testing ground for measures to be adopted by the GVN as part of a determined long-range effort to improve the lot of the rural population throughout South Vietnam, and encourage individual farmer initiative.

This program amounted to an unintentional effort to ignore the whole land reform problem by obscuring it with technology or, in the words of this JUSPAO release, "military technology." The farmers knew exactly where the boundaries of their fields were located. At issue were the disposition of the crop from and the ownership of already well-defined areas of land. A low-level USAID official in An Giang Province recognized this when, on August 20, 1967, he reported that "the land identification project is gaining momentum at the provincial technical counterpart level [that is, the Vietnamese were helping with the project], but there is little indication and indeed signs to the contrary that the provincial administration is committed to any meaningful effort in the direction of land reform."

One GVN institution—the village Agricultural Affairs Committee (AAC)—contained at least the beginnings of a productive GVN land policy effort. These committees were instituted under the Diem government but were not effective in representing the tenants' interests because they were controlled by landlords.

In 1966–1967 such a committee was operating in LBD (one of the few actually functioning in the Delta), and a brief look at its activities points up the possible role such a body might play in resolving land disputes. The LBD committee functioned from 1957 until 1963 when, after the fall of Diem, it was dissolved. In 1966 it was reinstituted with the help of the provincial land affairs office. Its objective was to settle disputes relating to land and rent payment. Serving on the committee were three representatives of the tenants in the village (elected at a meeting of twenty-five tenants in 1966), three representatives of resident landowners (elected at a meeting of ten owners in 1966), the chief of the village popular council, and the chief of the village administrative council. Members of this committee reported that it dealt mostly with cases of tolerance.

For example, in 1966 a tenant, observing that his yield was low, notified the village AAC and his landowner of this fact before harvesting his crop. The landowner, a village resident, examined the field, and the village AAC designated a subcommittee to do the same. The tenant requested 100 percent tolerance because he anticipated a 50 percent crop loss, which under both Vietnamese government and Viet Cong regulations allowed him to pay no rent. This particular tenant had also failed to pay his rent in 1965. The village AAC met and recommended that the tenant be granted 100 percent tolerance for 1966 and pay full rent for 1965. Both parties accepted the ruling.

Villagers recalled that only once in the 1960–1963 and 1966–1967 periods had the village AAC failed to resolve a dispute. In 1963 a landowner of two hectares of land located in a less-than-secure area of the village wanted to take back her land from two women who rented one hectare each. The tenants, both of whom had sons fighting with the Viet Cong, refused. Their landlady sought a ruling from the village AAC and received the recommendation that the tenants be allowed to continue farming the plots. The landlady found this ruling unacceptable; the case was sent to the district AAC, where a similar ruling was made —and again rejected; finally it went to the provincial AAC, where again the village AAC's ruling was upheld. The landlady again rejected it, but the tenants continued to farm the land.

LBD tenants and landowners alike were satisfied with the committee's rulings. Its strength lay in the fact that landowners had to accommodate themselves to what one farmer termed "the threat of an alternative government." In another farmer's words, "the only effective judgment or settlement is the one made by the Viet Cong."

The preceding statement is clarified if one examines the composition of the village AAC. Theoretically it was possible for landlords to control the committee since the landowning group with the support of either of the village officials (usually landowners) controlled the majority of votes. But the landowners' strength was weakened by the absence of nonresident landlords when their representatives were elected. Therefore, only those landlords who had already acquiesced in the land reforms participated in the elections. In LBD one landlord representative was actually a former tenant representative who, having paid for land received in the Diem reform, was elected as an owners' representative. In the LBD village AAC, therefore, power had shifted from large landowners in the 1950s to tenants and small landowners (and farmers) in the 1960s. Members of the committee openly acknowledged that the Viet Cong were responsible for this shift.

In organizations similar to the village AAC—which had no need for an elaborate photographic survey of village lands—lay the potential for a thorough Vietnamese government land reform, had such organizations only received, in provinces like An Giang, the backing of a reform-minded Saigon government that could have substituted legal sanctions for the makeshift sanctions applied in LBD and other nonsecure villages by the Viet Cong.

Landholdings and Land Use

A TREND TO SMALLER HOLDINGS

Data are available (see Table 3.2) to establish that in the area studied the size of landholdings owned diminished markedly between 1931 and 1962. In 1931 in TCN, 27.4 percent of all landlords owned more than 5 hectares; by 1962 this figure had fallen to 10.6 percent. In LBD village, the fragmentation was more marked than in TCN; in LBD 18.3 percent of the holdings were in excess of 5 hectares in 1931 compared with 3 percent in 1962. This greater fragmentation in LBD resulted partly from the effects of the Diem land reform program of 1967, under which 34 LBD farmers received landholdings ranging in size from 0.2 to 2.8 hectares.

TABLE 3.2 Distribution of Landholdings by Size

		Number of Land- holdings	Percentage of Sample Owning					
			0–1 Ha	1–5 Ha	5–10 Ha	10–50 Ha	50–100 Ha	100–500 Ha
LBD	1931	1,787	43.1	38.5	12.1	5.9	0.3	(0.01)
	1962	414	63.0	33.1	2.9	0.1		
TCN	1931	1,313	20.1	50.5	20.5	6.9		
	1962	311	34.0	55.3	9.3	1.3		

Sources: 1931 figures are from Yves Henry, *Economie agricole de l'Indochine* (Hanoi: Imprimerie d'Extrême-Orient, 1932), p. 164, for districts in which the villages of LBD and TCN comprise over one-third; 1962 figures are from records of the Provincial Land Service, Dinh Tuong Province.

The distribution of land by size of holding is shown in Figure 3.3 (a). The data are from the 50 owners in the complete sample of 120, representing the 27 farmers (54 percent) of the LBD sample and 23 farmers (31 percent) of the TCN sample who owned land. The average holding for the 50 owners in the sample was 2.0 hectares, and 18 of the 50 resident owners also rented land (on a median holding of 1.3 hectares).

Figure 3.3 (b) compares the size of the holding farmed by the sample's owners and tenants with the results from a 1960 Japanese survey of farm-size holdings. Because the Vietnamese sample combines data from both villages, the figures disguise a major difference: In LBD there were no farmholdings smaller than 0.3 hectare; in TCN 30 percent of the holdings were in this group, a reflection of the fact that garden vegetable

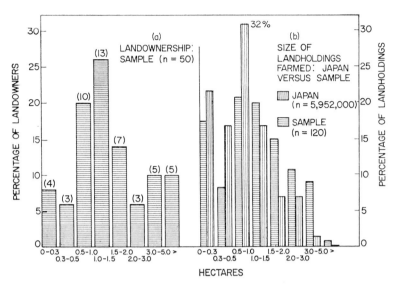

FIGURE 3.3   LBD and TCN Landownership and a Comparison of Land-holdings of Delta Sample and Japan   Sources: Mekong Delta sample and B. A. Stout, *Equipment for Rice Production*

growers in TCN were farming smaller plots. Generally a rice holding of less than 0.3 hectare was not a viable production unit. Nevertheless, after all holdings are grouped, the comparison with Japan shows that the average-size holding of the sample (1.5 hectares, median 1.2 hectares) is still larger than that common in Japan in 1960. Without the 21 vegetable growers in TCN, this difference would have been wider. The comparison serves to point out that further fragmentation, if accompanied by the utilization of more labor and capital-intensive techniques similar to those used in Japan, could be the source of higher levels of income for Vietnamese farmers.[14]

LAND UTILIZATION AND AVERAGE PRODUCT

In the sample, 81 percent of the farmed land was cultivated in rice, 12 percent in fruit, and only 7 percent in vegetables. Irrespective of the allocation of land, Table 3.3 also shows that on the basis of sources of village revenues, rice land accounted for 36 percent, fruit for 5 percent,

[14] Because the area studied is as densely populated as any in the Delta, this conclusion applies Delta-wide.

and vegetables for 35 percent of income from all sources. The final
column states this result in another way, showing that the average
revenue product of vegetable land was more than ten times that of
fruit or rice land.

TABLE 3.3   Land Utilization and Average Product

	Area Farmed (ha)	Average Farm Area (ha)	Number of Farms	Total Revenues (V$N 000)	Per Hectare Average Product (V$N 000)
Sample total	182.8	1.5	120	7,594	41.54
Rice	147.4	1.5	97	3,588	24.34
Fruit	22.5	0.4	57	525	23.33
Garden vegetables	12.9	0.2	59	3,481	269.84

ATTITUDES TOWARD LAND

Land was treated as a family possession, more immobile than the family's
labor supply, much in the manner of an artisan family's heritage of
skills and reputation: nontransferable, but the basis on which were
determined the family's economic activities and, for the case at hand,
its economic well-being. For a complex of reasons discussed earlier, there
was no market in land and only rarely was land transferred between
tenants. In the two villages studied, representing over 2,000 hectares of
land, no more than two land transactions had occurred in the previous
seven years and no more than seven in the previous twenty years. Inquiries regarding the price of land brought puzzled expressions, an occasional reserved smile or chuckle, but usually no reply.

4 The Production Opportunities of the 1960s

The range of production opportunities open to the farmers surveyed in 1966–1967 was, at first glance at least, impressive. Not only was rice grown but, to varying degrees, vegetables and fruits of many varieties, sugarcane and corn, fish, animals such as oxen, buffalo, pigs, rabbits, and fowl—chicken, ducks, and pigeons—were raised in the two villages studied. In addition, various household enterprises, ranging from hat and basket weaving to the merchandising of farm products, were important sources of income. Yet, all these opportunities considered, the income position of each farm family was subject to two restraints: Families not having properly located or irrigated land were often physically limited to producing only a few of the wide range of products grown in the Delta, and the available production opportunities could be exploited only to the degree permitted by scarce low opportunity cost factors of production.

The two major sources of income were rice and vegetables. Seventy-one percent of the calculated income of the sample came from sales or the value imputed to in-kind consumption of these two items (Figure 4.1). For the sample, rice and vegetables are of equal importance, while between LBD and TCN their roles differed. In LBD only 7.3 percent of the income was attributable to vegetable production, compared with 45.2 percent for rice. In TCN vegetable production was a major activity, providing 54.0 percent of all income, compared with 29.5 percent for rice. The villages differed in other respects as well. In LBD, fruit sales and nonagricultural wages (mostly salaries to part-time government military and civilian employees) were important secondary sources of income,

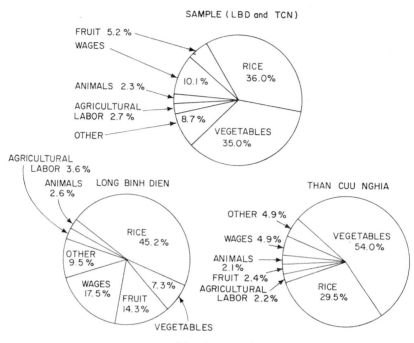

FIGURE 4.1   Income Sources

while neither played a major role in TCN. In both villages income from animal sales and agricultural labor was small, while the "other" category shows a larger role for household enterprises and fish merchandising in LBD than in TCN.

LBD's economy was typical of the rice-growing villages of the upper Delta. TCN, in contrast, was a village that between 1963 and 1966 experienced an economic transformation by moving from a monoculture in rice to a rice and vegetable based economy.

Primary Agricultural Activities

RICE PRODUCTION: THE PRIMARY CROP

Every farmer in LBD and 67 percent of the farmers in TCN grew rice. In terms of income and land utilization, rice was the major product of the farmers interviewed. Before the advent of vegetable growing in the early 1960s, a description of the village economy of the Delta was that of a monoculture in rice. Planting began after the arrival of the southwest monsoon in May, following four months of rainless weather. The traditional rice varieties were planted in seedbeds located in the lower first-flooded areas of the rice fields. After eight to ten weeks, when the seedlings had grown to a height of eighteen inches, they were transplanted in July or August to the primary growing areas. Then, four to five months later, in December or January, the crop was harvested, having taken the complete rainy season to reach maturity. In years when the monsoon was cooperative, the farmer whose timing was precise could harvest his crop from dried fields at the termination of the rains. But the natural constraints of the monsoon allowed little maneuverability. If the rains arrived late, the farmer planted late, hoping for a long monsoon; if the rains arrived on schedule but remained longer than expected, he salvaged what crop he could from the flooded fields. Using a man-powered waterwheel, some attempt was made to control flooding and drainage, giving the farmer better water control and perhaps two additional weeks for growing.

One method of escaping the limitations of the economic conditions was to cultivate a second rice crop, thereby moving to a new production function on which yields per hectare could be doubled. Until the 1950s three obstacles prevented the growing of a second crop: First, water conditions were inflexible outside the boundaries set by the monsoon; therefore, the growing season could not be lengthened; second, the available rice varieties required the full monsoon period to mature; and third, the natural fertility of the soil could sustain a single crop only if it were allowed to lie fallow for five months of the year.

NEW CONDITIONS

By the late 1950s the second and third conditions had changed. Widespread fertilizer use enabled the soil to support a second crop, and varietal improvements shortened the growing period for the first and second crops. Still, these improvements were of only minor benefit to the farmers until supplemented by new irrigation works and a new irrigation device—the motor pump—which in the 1960s gave the farmer an additional four to eight weeks of water control and permitted him to grow a second crop without risking the first, on which his family's subsistence needs depended. By 1966, 40.7 percent of the sampled farmers grew a second rice crop, 38.0 percent in LBD and 43.8 percent in TCN. These farmers planted the seedbed for the first (and secondary) crop in early May, transplanted it six weeks later in mid-June, and harvested it by mid- or late August. Meanwhile, the second (and primary) crop's seedlings had been planted in early July, transplanted in late August, and harvested in December or January of the next year.

The selection of the proper rice variety could mean crop yield success, adequate family supplies, and market sales at high prices; an improper selection could bring crop failure because of insect or water damage and sale at low prices; farmers on adjacent fields choosing different varieties obtained very divergent results under the same conditions. But at planting time in May or August, the proper or improper alternatives were far from obvious. In the two villages studied in 1966, 25 varieties were grown, but only 8 were widely grown.

A farmer raising two crops selected for the initial crop a variety that matured in approximately one hundred days. The first variety to meet this criterion and gain general acceptance was the *so mo rang* variety, of unknown origin, which became available in the mid-1950s. Until the introduction of the motor pump in the 1960s, this new variety gave the greatest impetus to second-cropping; yet in the late 1950s less than 5 percent of Delta land was double-cropped. The first crop became known as the *so mo* crop, but the variety itself was not preferred by consumers; also the *so mo* plant, being taller than most, had a tendency to lodge. In 1966 a new early variety, termed *tieu*, which was shorter and more acceptable to consumers, was grown by 80 percent of the farmers, whereas only 10 percent had grown it in 1965. This rapid change in varieties planted was dictated by differing weather conditions. In 1965 the rains arrived late, and most farmers planted the *sami lay* variety that matures in two and a half months; in 1966 the timely arrival of the monsoon prompted farmers to use *tieu*, which matures in three months. Had the rains arrived even later than in 1965, the *xae xiem* variety, which matures in two months, could have been grown.

The farmers' attitudes toward the main crop varieties were not as flexible as they were toward the secondary or first crop. In 1964 the government distributed the *soc nau* variety to selected farmers, and by 1965 over 70 percent grew *soc nau*. Yet in 1966 only 17 percent grew *soc nau* and 62 percent grew a new variety called *nang tra*. This dramatic switch was prompted by two below-average crops in 1964 and 1965 caused by poor weather and a disease known as *tiem*. The change was made because farmers sought higher yields (for home consumption) despite the fact that *soc nau* prices were generally 30 percent above *nang tra* prices.[1]

Farmers spoke of the need to switch rice varieties every three to four years to avoid "soil familiarity." This belief led them to raise a particular variety until its yield began to fall, then to seek a new variety, often returning again three years later to the one previously grown. Although the exact reasons for such rotation were not clear (the farmers said that after the soil became familiar with a variety it became susceptible to insect damage), as a rule of thumb, three-year rotation was followed.

High labor costs in the 1960s were another factor in varietal decisions. Several farmers phased the maturing dates of their crops by growing different varieties on the same field in order to divide the harvest into two periods and avoid the high cost of hiring nonfamily labor. For example, a 60-year-old woman heading a household of fifteen members (which did not include men between 16 and 60 years of age) cultivated 2.4 hectares in the normal crop, 1.4 hectares in *nang tra*, the early-maturing variety, and 1.0 hectare in *soc nau*, which matures late. By phasing her planting, she was able to harvest the *nang tra* before most fields matured and the *soc nau* after the general harvest was complete. In her words, "the use of two varieties was intended to avoid failure in getting enough labor on the rush days of the harvesting season." Her efforts were successful: In 1965, harvest costs took one-fifth of her crop compared with one-seventh in 1966.

In changing varieties, particularly in adopting varieties not previously available in the village, the farmers' source of information was the experience of others. Nang tra was available in TCN in 1963 and in LBD in 1964,[2] but since it was less favorably priced than the more widely grown *soc nau* and *tan huong* varieties, few grew it. However, its success in 1964 and 1965 in yielding a good crop despite the failures of the

---

[1] The new high-yielding rice variety IR8, developed at the International Rice Research Institute at Los Banos in the Philippines, was not introduced to Delta farmers until late 1967.

[2] Gerald Cannon Hickey, *Village in Vietnam* (New Haven, Conn.: Yale University Press, 1964), p. 300, lists *nang tra* as a variety grown in Khanh Hau village in 1958.

more popular varieties led to a reappraisal. One farmer said: "I was un-lucky and found out too late that *nang tra* was a better variety; I per-sisted in thinking there was more money in *soc nau*." Another farmer who switched to *nang tra* in 1965 did so because "*nang tra* is more economical for the family." Other farmers were slow to switch to *nang tra* because they preferred to wait until it was given a thorough test by its pioneer users. Those who waited the longest suffered the most.

THE PIONEERS

Nang tra was introduced into LBD in 1964 by a then 62-year-old woman who as a tenant farmed 0.8 hectare of rice land. Late-arriving rains in 1964 caused her to look for a quicker-maturing variety. She considered planting *nep* (glutinous) rice, which matures fifteen days earlier than the common varieties, but was unable to locate any in LBD. She visited some relatives in adjacent Song Binh village, who persuaded her to try *nang tra*, saying it matured early. She tried it, and in 1964, when many farmers experienced crop failure, she was successful. In 1965 and 1966 other farmers visited her home to discuss her experience and often bought seed for their own crop. By 1967 most farmers had switched.

OLD BOTTLENECKS

By 1966, with new rice varieties and mechanized irrigation devices, the farmers were freed from the rigid constraints of the traditional cropping cycle. No longer were all fields planted, transplanted, and harvested at the same time. In 1966–1967, from June until September, one saw in the fields on any short trip in the Delta every production process in progress, from seedbed preparation, first plowing, transplanting, to (by August) harvesting itself. The shortage of labor had encouraged this diversification,[3] and technological and varietal changes permitted it to take place.

Nevertheless, although constraints on production became less binding between Hendry's study in 1958 and the present one, important tradi-tional techniques remained bottlenecks. The techniques employed in plowing, transplanting, and harvesting—the three most labor-demanding

[3] See chap. 6.

tasks in rice cultivation—were largely the same in 1966 as they were in 1958.[4] The changes discussed here affected the phasing of these operations, not the processes themselves.

FIELD PREPARATION

For one hectare of rice land cultivated in one crop, the seedbed (0.1 hectare) was plowed twice and the main field once. Plowing was the task of a buffalo (*trau*) or ox (*bo*) team (often led by a young child) pulling a metal-bladed, wood-framed plow guided by a plowman. The buffalo team was favored because it was more powerful and maneuverable than an oxteam, especially in a partially flooded field. The seedbed was harrowed (by a team pulling a rakelike wooden harrow) five to seven times and the rice field twice. Often a team-drawn roller was used to level the ground.

Farmers made various arrangements to accomplish these tasks. Much preferred was to have one's own oxteam, which enabled a farmer to be confident of having plowing services when they were needed, for example, on the arrival of the first rains. One woman described her husband's attitude in the following terms: "He wants to be an independent worker, not dependent on other people, so he wants to be 'equipped.' " Moreover, hired labor was considered less efficient and more difficult to supervise than home labor. Despite these advantages, however, many did not own a team; one might be too expensive, the farmer having no children or elderly parents to "guard" the grazing animals, or the farmer's field might be too small to support a team. Thirty-four percent of the rice growers in LBD and 56 percent in TCN owned buffalo or oxen, but some of these were raised for breeding purposes and others were too young for work in the fields.

Most farmers hired the services of a team. Plowing, harrowing, and rolling a rice field of one hectare was a five-day task for a good buffalo team working six hours a day. An oxteam might take eight days. In 1966 it cost 250 to 300 piasters for the services, with plowman, of a buffalo team for a six-hour day. The plowman himself received only 100 piasters of this sum. Total plowing costs per single-cropped hectare were 1,000 to 1,500 piasters in 1966, although most farmers hired ser-

[4] See James B. Hendry, *The Small World of Khanh Hau* (Chicago: Aldine Publishing Co., 1964), pp. 52–90.

vices on a daily basis. Less common was a package purchase of all the animal services—plowing, harrowing, rolling, and seedling transportation —necessary for cultivation. Those who farmed a second crop did not plow the field a second time, although seedbed preparations were again necessary.

Besides plowing, labor was required to prepare the rice field for planting. After flooding, 2 to 3 man-days of work per hectare using a wooden hoe were necessary to build up the bunds that had collapsed during the dry season and to corner the field by hoeing the areas a plowing team could not reach. But these tasks, as well as those of weeding (6 woman-days), seedling replacement (2 woman-days), fertilizer application (2 man-days), and insecticide spreading (1 man-day), could be met from family labor sources. Because they could be performed when convenient by family labor without cash expenditure, they were not seen to be financially constraining.

SEEDLING TRANSPLANTING

On the other hand, the labor-consuming tasks of transplanting and harvesting could not be stretched out for the application of family labor. Failure to obtain labor for transplanting when the seedlings matured or for harvesting when the crop matured meant a partial or total crop loss to the family. Transplanting was a two-stage process that had to be completed in one or two days. First, for a field of one hectare, three or four men began uprooting the seedlings by pulling them gently from their flooded seedbed and tying them in bundles of twenty to thirty each with a piece of rice straw. As they were doing this, another man, using a shoulder pole supporting a carrying platform, transported the seedlings to the rice field and set out the bundles at spaced intervals in the newly plowed and slightly flooded (to approximately six inches) field. If the field was large, the seedlings were transported by a buffalo team pulling a *cai van ma*, or seedling plank, loaded with bundles. Buffalo transport was common in the lower Delta in 1966–1967, but in the upper Delta, where the rice fields were small and seedbeds often adjacent to the field itself, human transport was employed. In the rice field, the women, working in teams of eight to twelve, placed the seedlings in the soil. Perfectly timed and with abundant labor, the transplanting process on one hectare formerly could be accomplished in one eight-hour day; but in 1966–1967, with labor in short supply, the task took two days.

HARVESTING

Like transplanting, harvesting was a bottleneck labor operation in 1966–1967. Despite the labor shortage, a capital-intensive technique was not available. The solution was to pay labor a larger share of the crop. This market tendency, evident by 1965, was preceded by subtle Viet Cong pressures to raise rural wages (see Chapter 6).

Harvesting was a two-step process, reaping and threshing, both of which were performed in the field. A three-man team—the farmer and one or two hired laborers, depending on the number of young men in the family—could harvest a field of one hectare in six or seven days of eight hours each. The reaper employed a sickle, cutting the rice stalks near the ground, while a second worker carried them to a threshing sledge that had been brought from the farmer's home. A third laborer or thresher grasped the stalks in a handful-size bundle, raised them with both hands above his head, and swung them, striking the heads against a wooden lattice device covering the sledge. After several swings the grain was separated and the stalks discarded to one side. The laborers rotated among the three tasks, changing jobs when the thresher became tired. At the end of each day the newly harvested paddy was divided between harvester and farmer, with the hired laborer getting a sixth of the portion he harvested.

After the crop ripened, it had to be harvested within approximately five days. Therefore, under ideal circumstances the farmer himself might have harvested one-fourth hectare without the assistance of hired help. But the strenuous task of threshing made it difficult for a man to sustain the activity for long periods in a day.

The acute labor shortage brought a significant change in harvesting practices. Before 1965/66, women had assisted in the harvest only by cutting rice stalks, and even this was not a common practice. But by 1966 some women, finding themselves more capable physically than the older men and children in some households, took part in the threshing operation itself. There was no social stigma attached to their doing this; in the past they had refrained because sufficient male labor was available. New labor conditions prompted them to assume a new role.

THE USE OF CAPITAL

Items of capital employed in rice production such as the hoe, rake, sledge, plow, roller, harrow, and sickle were inexpensive and had a long life. The most expensive traditional capital item was the buffalo (discussed earlier). A few farmers owned an oxcart.

A pressure insecticide sprayer, manually operated, was owned by one farmer in LBD and by thirteen farmers in TCN, where vegetables were grown. Most farmers spread insecticides on rice with a dried areca-nut flower, using it with scooplike motions from a pail. Two kinds of mechanical sprayers were available: one produced in Saigon selling for 2,000 piasters and another imported from the United States with foreign exchange provided by the AID Commodity Import Program, which cost 4,000 piasters. The farmers preferred the imported type because the domestically produced sprayer often had only one-fifth the life of the imported model.

The factor supply conditions of 1966—high labor costs and low capital costs—were ideal for capital substitution; however, the unavailability of the needed items limited such substitution. A hand-carried fertilizer spreader or a Japanese rice weeder would have sold well, but none were available. The supply of sprayers was inadequate. Only the motor pump, a new irrigation device (see Chapter 8), was available in adequate quantities, and it sold rapidly. Farmers in the lower Delta were importing tractors. As a general rule, however, the bottleneck tasks requiring much labor—planting, transplanting, and harvesting—were those in which, with the existing technology, capital was not substitutable for labor. Those who sought to save labor had to resort to a rephasing of tasks to spread the peak demand for labor over a longer period, using the old techniques rather than substituting capital for labor.

VEGETABLE CULTIVATION

Garden Vegetables The motor pump, a major agricultural innovation, opened up the new production opportunity of vegetable cultivation. Although the development of new markets in Saigon was an important stimulus to this change, such new markets were neither necessary nor sufficient to precipitate the change itself. Before 1963 the vegetable demand in Saigon was met by imports from the highland city of Dalat slightly more than 200 kilometers to the north.[5] (Dalat continued to supply vegetables to Saigon in 1966–1967.)[6] Its climate and soils were more suitable for vegetable cultivation than were conditions in the Delta area nearer Saigon, but its outstanding advantage was the availability of a year-round water supply from upland rains and mountain streams.

The motor pump, which allowed farmers to draw on the available fresh-water supply in the Mekong River, made vegetable cultivation

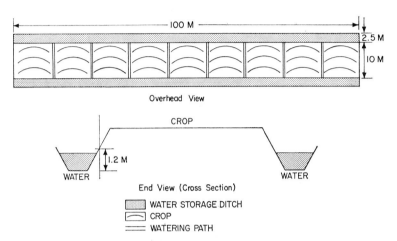

FIGURE 4.2   Standard Vegetable Plot (0.1 Hectare)

possible in TCN. Every few days, farmers pumped fresh water from newly constructed canals into storage ditches adjacant to their vegetable plots. Figure 4.2 shows a standard-size vegetable plot of 0.1 hectare. The average family vegetable holding was two *cong* (0.2 hectare), but most families started with one *cong* and expanded their scale of operations as they gained the necessary experience and capital.

[5] Dalat was developed as a vegetable growing center in the 1920s with the aid of a rail link with Saigon that enabled vegetables leaving Dalat in the late evening to arrive in Saigon the next day at 7:15 A.M. See "Le commerce de légumes de Dalat," *Bulletin Economique de l'Indochine*, 1935, pp. 1027–1034. The records of the Dalat vegetable cooperative show that from 1958 until 1963 vegetables in amounts ranging up to 1,000 MT a year were exported to Singapore from Dalat.

[6] *The New York Times* reported on June 18, 1967 that 10% of the vegetables produced in Dalat were purchased for U.S. military consumption and were transported by air to U.S. bases in Vietnam.

After a prospective vegetable farmer found a tenant or owner willing to sublease or lease land, an agreement was reached—usually verbally—about the conditions of tenure. The arrangements varied slightly. Under the most common one, covering a period of three years, a tenant agreed to pay a yearly rent of ten *gia* (200 kilograms) of paddy (in money or kind) per *cong* at the end of the year. Often this rent would decline in the second and third years to eight or six *gia* as the soil's fertility deteriorated. Because the land initially was physically prepared for rice cultivation and the tenant planned to ditch and mound it (see Figure 4.2), the lessor required some guarantee that, after the tenant had terminated his contract, the land would be reconverted into its original state. Even if the lessor planned to lease the land again for vegetable farming, reconversion was necessary if the land was to regain its fertility. To fulfill this requirement the tenant had to make a deposit (*tren ke*) of 2,000 to 4,000 piasters per *cong*, which was returned to him at the end of the three years if the land was reconverted as agreed. (Conversion costs from vegetable to rice land in 1968 were from 5,000 to 7,000 piasters.) If the tenant rented from a relative or friend, a deposit was not always required.

The farmer who had acquired land converted it for vegetable farming as shown in Figure 4.2. To dig the two water-storage ditches required 90 man-days of labor, costing 120 piasters per man-day in 1966. This implied a cash outlay of between 5,000 and 10,000 piasters, depending on the portion of the work the farmer did himself. The task involved digging the storage ditches to a depth of 1.2 meters and throwing the soil into the center, where it was later leveled into small rows for vegetable planting. The size of the ditch was uniform in the village and resulted from a compromise between water-storage requirements—two to four days' supply—and the land needs of the crop.

The median holding was 2 *cong* (range 1 to 5) made up of two standard units arranged sideways or endways. From the air the vegetable plots appeared as a group of carefully laid-out islands connected by narrow dirt paths. About twice a week the farmers pumped water into their storage ditches. The crop was watered two or three times a day—often by a young family member—with a sprinkling bucket, which the worker emptied as he walked between the rows, refilling it at each end.

Onions, cabbage, lettuce, peppers, and mint[7] were the items commonly grown, using the garden vegetable methods previously described. Depending on the product, $1\frac{1}{2}$–$2\frac{1}{2}$ months was the growing period per crop, providing the average farmer with four crops each year. Typically, farmers grew two or three different types of vegetables simultaneously. The reasons given for this diversification were: first, it protected them from crop failure due to insect damage on one type of vegetable; second, the risks of a market price collapse for any one product at harvesttime were lessened; and third, growing different vegetables at the same time allowed farmers to spread the limited amount of labor available over the differing labor-demand schedules for the various products. One farmer who grew 1 *cong* of onions and 2 of peppers, when asked why he did not grow more onions—the more profitable crop—replied: "Because the onion crop requires more continuous watering while peppers do not. There are only three of us [his wife and 15-year-old daughter], and we could not water three *cong* of onions."

The financial attraction of vegetable cultivation resulted from its efficient use of a small plot of land, its use of otherwise unemployable and easily managed family labor instead of hired labor, its rapid turnover period of two or three months, and the high prices the products obtained. Yet to begin as a vegetable farmer required an investment of between 10,000 and 15,000 piasters before the first crop was harvested. The average farmer was not likely to recover these costs from the revenues of the first sale. The cash costs were as follows: 4,000 piasters for land rent; 5,000 for land conversion; 7,000 for fertilizer, insecticides, and irrigation expenses; and perhaps 1,000 piasters for hired labor to supplement the available family supply. Average gross revenues were 18,000 piasters per crop or 72,000 piasters per year, for a net return of 12,000 piasters per *cong*. On 0.2 hectare several farmers netted as much as 60,000 piasters per year, but the average net return on this most common holding was about 24,000 piasters per year.

Field Vegetables There was another alternative for rice farmers who wanted to farm vegetables as well as rice. Either they could grow *garden*

---

[7] For a complete list of the vegetables grown in the upper Delta, see Hickey, *Village in Vietnam*, pp. 300–303.

vegetables and rice or they could grow field vegetables in their rice fields during the off-rice season.

Fourteen percent of the interviewed farmers grew field vegetables, which could be grown on idle rice fields without the costs and inconvenience of the land conversion necessary to farm garden vegetables. The most common field vegetables were melons, squash, and tomatoes. Like garden vegetables their cultivation began only after the invention of the motor pump in 1962. The difficulty of identifying the exact origin of a farmer's participation in this (or any other) new opportunity is exemplified by the following reply to the question of why one particular farmer had not farmed field vegetables earlier: "There was no water, no motor pump, no land available, nor was the price of field vegetables high enough." Another farmer responded: "I lacked the experience or knowledge available from other villagers."

The first farmer to grow field vegetables in LBD was a recent immigrant from Long An Province (north of Dinh Tuong). A week before Tet in 1963 he was instructed by the Diem government to move into a fortified, or strategic, hamlet. He refused and moved to LBD instead, bringing the knowledge of the method of field vegetable cultivation learned in his former village.

Crop Calendar The crop calendar (Figure 4.3) shows the improvements in land utilization made possible by the second rice crop, garden vegetables, and field vegetables. Of the factors employed in 1966, land, more than labor or capital, was the constraining factor barring larger-scale farm operations. The developments described earlier, because they allowed the farm family to make more intensive use of the land available to it, permitted a major increase in the level of family incomes.

Secondary Agriculture

FRUIT CULTIVATION

Fruit cultivation had a special significance to the farmers: It was considered the ideal activity for a couple in retirement after their children had grown, married, and set up separate households; it offered the older farmer an opportunity for high income with little effort during his

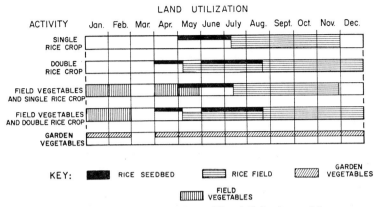

LAND UTILIZATION

ACTIVITY   Jan. Feb. Mar. Apr. May June July Aug. Sept. Oct. Nov. Dec.

SINGLE
RICE CROP

DOUBLE
RICE CROP

FIELD VEGETABLES
AND SINGLE RICE CROP

FIELD VEGETABLES
AND DOUBLE RICE CROP

GARDEN
VEGETABLES

KEY: ■■■ RICE SEEDBED   RICE FIELD   GARDEN VEGETABLES

FIELD VEGETABLES

FIGURE 4.3   The Crop Calendar   Note: The full horizontal bar represents
one hectare of land.

retirement years. But few farmers achieved this retirement objective.
First, fruit cultivation was land-intensive, requiring at least one-half
hectare to make it, by itself, an adequate source of income for the small
retired family. Second, its technical characteristics made it a feasible
alternative only for the landowner, not the tenant. Third, the prospective
fruit farmer had to be financially able to generate a surplus for one or
two years, not only to support his family but also to make the necessary
investments to begin fruit cultivation; meanwhile, he would get no
income from his land. For example, fruit trees require at least two years
in cultivation before they begin to yield a substantial income, and few
farmers could afford such a long period without a source of income.

Mainly grown were bananas, coconuts, Malayan apples, mangoes, areca
nuts, milk apples, and papaya. Less common were oranges, jackfruit,
tangerines, limes, sugarcane, and grapefruit. Few families had orchards
in the formal sense of the word. More commonly the home plot contained a few types of trees bearing fruit for home consumption and for
small-scale sales of less than 5,000 piasters a year.

Fruit growing on a formal basis began only in the late 1950s, when
it was the object of a large government aid program. Villagers were
shown how to dig irrigation ditches and phase the planting of several
varieties in order that the family could enjoy the revenues from bananas
and papayas in the short term while the coconut, mango, and other
longer-maturing varieties reached crop-bearing age. Phasing was also

necessary to obtain protection for the more delicate plants (mango) by the larger, stronger plants (Malayan apple) in the early growing period; the farmers also learned to grow the fruits that yield year-around (coconut, areca nut) with those that yield seasonally (such as the orange, lime, and mango). The government had played a major role in acquainting the farmers with this opportunity. Hickey has described a UNESCO project in Khanh Hau, which in 1958 tested and demonstrated these techniques.[8]

The war had created obstacles for the fruit grower. The Vietnamese army, finding that the foliage of orchards offered a cover for the Viet Cong, discouraged fruit cultivation. Its efforts were largely verbal but included the destruction of crops (particularly bananas) along Route 4 in TCN. In 1966, however, despite the army's efforts to persuade them otherwise, several farmers raised bananas.

Another obstacle to fruit cultivation was landlord opposition, since tenants growing fruit were more difficult to evict and the costs of conversion from fruit to rice land were prohibitive. Therefore, repossession of leased fruit land for rice growing, by a grown son, for example, was problematical. Landlords also preferred to have their tenants grow rice, because its cultivation simplified the rent collection process and made rent avoidance more difficult. Last, orchards were susceptible to pillaging. To protect his crop a farmer needed to have his fruit land located near his home plot; otherwise, passersby could steal the ripened fruit. Because living areas were commonly congested, such proximate land was in short supply.[9]

OTHER SECONDARY ACTIVITIES

Fish Production   One could hardly find a better example of the joint production function so common in traditional agriculture than the fish production function. Fishponds were always located near the family's house to ensure that no nonfamily member drained the pond and

---

[8] Ibid., pp. 153–154.

[9] Any counterinsurgency program that concentrates the population in a limited area, as did the strategic hamlet program in Vietnam, rules out the production of crops like fruit (and fish) that require close watching by the grower, thus denying the farmer these production opportunities.

carried away the fish. A 63-year-old woman with no adult male in the household had a fishpond near her house but had not raised fish since 1965, when her son was drafted, because "there is no male adult to keep strangers from stealing the fish at nighttime." The local and roving military troops were frequently cited as a source of this problem.

The food supply for the fishponds was generally human excrement if the products were for market sale. Those who raised fish for home consumption abstained from this practice, feeding their fish rice bran, bindweed, banana stalks, and food scraps. The only large-scale fish raiser in TCN had a public toilet located over his pond, which was in part the irrigation ditch for his orchard. Fish raising was possible because he used no insecticides (which killed the fish) on his fruit trees. All vegetable growers used insecticides, making fish raising impossible in their storage ditches.

For the villager who had a ready-made fishpond (for example, he had been forced to dig out an area to obtain dirt with which to build a platform above flood-water levels for his house) and a food supply (the public toilet), fish raising could be very profitable. But few farmers were in this position, and the cost of digging a pond (approximately 50,000 piasters) under the prevailing 1966–1967 conditions of scarce labor was financially prohibitive.[10]

Buffalo and Ox Production   Water buffalo and oxen were common in the villages. A third of the surveyed farmers owned them. These animals were in demand primarily for their plowing services, which cost a farmer 1,000 to 1,500 piasters per hectare.

Moreover, the farmer could plow ten hectares for others, earning an additional 12,000 piasters. He could also earn up to 10,000 piasters during the harvest season by providing transport services, although this opportunity was vanishing in the face of competition from the large number of motorized transport vehicles (motor scooters with pull-carts, and Tri-Lambrettas) coming into use in the rural areas. However, few buffalo owners seriously pursued these cash opportunities, arguing that too much work would weaken the animals and shorten their lives and potential usefulness on the household plot.

---

[10] Nighttime fishing, a popular occupation before 1960, had ceased completely because of the insecurity in rural areas.

One reason buffalo and oxen were not more widely owned was their susceptibility to the whims of war. They made good targets for Vietnamese army soldiers, the Viet Cong, and American armed helicopters. Also, with mortar and artillery shelling threatening their own shelters, few families could afford to build shelters for their buffalo.

The profitability of oxen and buffalo production depended to a large extent on how much of their food requirement was met from low opportunity cost sources such as one's rice field. But this in turn, in an environment without enclosures, depended on the supply of family labor available to graze the animals. "Guarding" consisted of herding the animals slowly from vacant field to vacant field in the village, where they could gather what foliage was left in the fields after the harvest, and of guiding them along irrigation ditches and bunds where grass was often available. The guarding task fell to either the very old or the very young. It was not uncommon to see an old man serenely tending a grazing buffalo, or a child between six and twelve years old riding one along the village paths to graze it in the nearby fields.

Initial cost was also an obstacle to greater animal ownership, although in 1966 it was not the major obstacle that Hendry found it to be in 1958.[11] A grown animal cost 20,000 to 30,000 piasters, a young one 6,000 to 10,000 piasters. A farmer who had not raised a buffalo before 1965, saying he was "too poor and lacked the money," purchased two cows in 1965 from money earned as a construction worker.

Buffalo and Oxen as a Store of Wealth   These animals, outside of land itself, were the major items of rural wealth. They played a special financial role: By allowing the family to convert idle labor and food resources by small increments into a valuable commodity, the expenditure was often seen as a saving rather than as an investment. One farmer planned to build up his herd to five or six, hoping to "sell them at one time and get a large enough sum for an important investment." Such an investment could be that necessary to start growing vegetables or to purchase a small concession, store, or Tri-Lambretta. Alternatively, the family faced with a financial crisis, for example,

[11] Hendry, *Small World of Khanh Hau*, p. 117.

needing money to meet unexpected medical expenses or consumption needs in bad crop years like 1964 and 1965, sold its animals to meet the expenses.

In 1965, a bad crop year, Dinh Tuong Province exported 9,330 animals, while in 1966, a good crop year, exports fell to 6,530. Gourou, studying the records of a district in Tonkin, found that in 1928, a good crop year, the buffalo-oxen population rose by 6,158, while in 1927, a poor crop year, it fell by 1,214.[12] In short, these changes in savings assets are analogous to the upward and downward movements of savings accounts in an advanced economy in times of boom and depression.

Pig Production   Many of the same considerations that apply to buffalo applied to raising pigs. Efficient use of idle family resources such as table scraps and the "guarding" capacities of young children and older family members made it a "savings device" more than an investment opportunity. Since a pig required a small initial outlay (1,000 to 1,500 piasters for a one- to two-month-old piglet), unlike a buffalo, it was a production opportunity within every family's financial capacity. Sixty-two percent of the families surveyed raised pigs.

If one purchased a piglet weighing 10 kilograms for 1,000 to 1,500 piasters, it could be sold after eight months, weighing 70 kilograms, for 6,000 piasters. Adding in the cost of rice bran to feed the pig (400 piasters per month), the net revenues were low, even without accounting for the more than 25 percent losses due to disease. But these calculations were not relevant to most pig owners. Instead, the feed costs to the household with two or three pigs were not more than 500 to 1,000 piasters per pig over this same eight-month period; most of the feed needs were met from family food scraps and mixtures of fruit, for example, bananas rejected from the family's orchard.

To the farmer, pig raising on a small scale was an ideal "savings device." Farmers said that the food purchases made for pig feed removed the temptation to spend idle small change on gambling or small consumption items. One farmer stated that when he had 100 to 200 piasters of surplus pocket money it was better to buy rice bran

---

[12] Pierre Gourou, *The Peasants of the Tonkin Delta*, trans. Richard R. Miller (New Haven. Conn.: Human Relations Area Files, 1955), p. 618.

than a food snack or sweet. The farmers agreed that, because of the high bran price and high disease incidence, pig raising beyond the scale suited to the family's leftover food, small cash surpluses, and idle labor supply was unprofitable. In one farmer's words, "pig raising is a money-saving device, not a profit-making enterprise."

Chicken Production   Slightly more than 75 percent of the surveyed households raised chickens. As traditional household items in Vietnam, chickens were used often as gifts or for ceremonial purposes, especially at Tet, and were an important source of meat in the family's diet. Again, as with pigs, the scale of the family's chicken-raising activities was limited by the high rice-bran price and costly disease losses.

Disease was the most important obstacle to expanded production. Of the 2,270 chickens owned by the surveyed farmers in 1966, nearly one-half, or 1,085, had died of disease; however, since these were eaten after they died, they were not a total loss. The farmers discussed this problem among themselves and tried to apply the advice available from the government, but the problem persisted. The various medicines, shots, and powders were used without any noticeable impact. These disease losses were a result of the increased density of the population in housing areas, a phenomenon attributable to the strategic hamlet program and the general search of the villagers for the security of central living areas. The villagers maintained that, while diseases had been a problem in the past, those farmers who had had larger plots away from the major living areas were able to raise large numbers of chickens without fear of disease losses.

Several farmers said they were afraid to raise chickens because it was the habit of the Vietnamese government troops in the area to steal them or, alternatively, to catch them and ask for them as a donation.

Transportation

THE TRANSPORTATION SYSTEM IN THE DELTA

The case of the Mekong Delta in Vietnam lends little support to those who would argue that transport in itself can do much to bring the traditional economy from its backward state: Despite the existence of a highly efficient transport system, the Delta remained, until the 1960s, an economy still characterized by the traditional techniques and resulting low productivities of the early twentieth century.

In the process of draining the Delta for rice cultivation in the late nineteenth century, a system of canals was constructed, providing efficient bulk transport to and from Saigon and to export markets. Between 1881 and 1886 the first railroad in Indochina was constructed from My Tho to Saigon. A financial failure from the beginning, it was dismantled in 1954.[13]

The basic road system in the Delta in 1967 was an impressive network, completely adequate for current development needs even though it had not been altered significantly or received more than the minimum necessary upkeep for over twenty years. Only off the major primary and secondary routes and within particular villages, where the Viet Cong had destroyed bridges and cut roads by ditching to keep out the Vietnamese government and American troops engaged in sweep and destroy operations, had the road system's capacity fallen behind requirements.

In the Mekong Delta in 1966–1967 one rarely saw an oxcart used for transport except at harvesttime between a family's rice field and home drying place. Most commodities and passengers traveled between major cities by bus and truck, between district towns and the larger villages by Tri-Lambretta, and between smaller villages and within villages by a motor bicycle towing a two-wheeled cart. The effect of this almost complete motorization on transport costs is seen in Table 4.1. At distances beyond those short hauls within the village that required smaller vehicles working with smaller loads on lower-quality roads, transport costs fell sharply. Over longer distances, vegetables, which need careful loading and unloading and are bulky, were more costly to transport than rice, fertilizer, or the self-loading and unloading passenger. The close relationship between passenger and vegetable transport costs by Tri-Lambretta (no. 4) reflects the fact that the driver of these privately owned vehicles had an option to carry either vegetables or passengers. Comparing no. 10, calculated

[13] See Joseph Buttinger, *Vietnam: A Dragon Embattled* (London: Pall Mall Press, 1967), p. 31.

TABLE 4.1 Transportation Costs, 1966/67

No.	Between[a]	Distance (km)	Mode	Item	Cost V$N per Kg	Cost V$N per Ton-Km	Current Paddy Price (V$N)	Kg Paddy Equivalent per Ton-Km
1.	Rice field and house	1.0	laborer and oxcart	paddy	0.25	250	10	25
2.	Vegetable field and Tu Lua collection point	2.0	motor bicycle with trailer	vegetables	0.4	200	10	20
3.	Rice field and house[b]	2.5	laborer	paddy	0.3	120	7.5	16
4	TCN to My Tho[e]	12.8	Tri-Lambretta	vegetables	0.5	39	10	3.9
				passenger	7.0ea[d]	9.1	10	0.91
5.	LBD to My Tho[e]	9.6	bus or Tri-Lambretta	passenger	10.0ea[d]	17.4	10	1.74
6.	Saigon to My Tho[e]	61.0	truck	fertilizer	0.38	6.23	10	0.623
7.	Tu Lua to Saigon[e]	64.0	truck	vegetables	0.6	9.38	10	0.938
8.	My Tho to Saigon[e]	72.0	truck	rice	0.35	4.86	9	0.540
9.	My Tho to Saigon[e]	72.0	bus	passenger	40.6ea[b]	9.26	10	0.926
10.	Tan An to Saigon (1958)[d]	50.0	truck	rice	0.1	2.00	2.5	0.800
11.	Can Tho to Saigon[c]	170.0	truck (1 day)	rice	1.0	5.89	11	0.535
12.	Can Tho to Saigon	170.0	barge (2–3 days)	rice	0.9	5.30	11	0.481

[a] See maps, Figures 1.2 and 1.4.
[b] December 1965.
[c] On paved roads.
[d] Assume passenger weighs 60 kg.
[e] From James B. Hendry, The Small World of Khanh Hau (Chicago: Aldine Publishing Co., 1964), p. 124.

on the basis of Hendry's results of 1958, with no. 8, we conclude that transportation costs declined between 1958 and 1966.

Comparisons of Vietnamese and non-Vietnamese transportation data are difficult since definitions differ. For example, the data from Vietnam in Table 4.1 include unloading and loading costs, which reflect the high cost of labor rather than the high cost of transportation.[14] But studies available from other countries, such as those surveyed by Clark and Haswell, do not specify whether loading and unloading costs are included, nor in most cases do they specify the type of commodity.[15] Even including the high labor cost, however, the transport costs in Vietnam are markedly below most of those cited; for example, in Nigeria a 70-kilometer motor vehicle journey, carrying an unspecified commodity, cost 0.75 kilogram per ton-kilometer grain equivalent,[16] which is most suitably compared with item no. 8, showing 0.54 kilogram per ton-kilometer for a similar distance in Vietnam. Haswell[17] found that it cost 1.55 kilograms of paddy per ton-kilometer to transport paddy by oxcart 7 kilometers in India in 1961. This figure compares favorably with the short-haul items in Table 4.1, probably because such animals are sacred objects in India as opposed to military targets in South Vietnam. She also found, however, that the radius of operation for the oxcart was 11 kilometers,[18] making it difficult to transport commodities to distant markets. For truck transportation, her 0.97 kilogram paddy per ton-kilometer over a distance of 30 kilometers is best compared with items no. 8 and no. 6, to its slight disadvantage.

Therefore, regardless of high labor costs, low transportation costs were an important asset to the rural economy of the Vietnamese villages studied.

---

[14] By comparing no. 3 with no. 1, both transport costs using human labor, one can see the effect of rising labor costs.

[15] Colin Clark and Margaret Haswell, *The Economics of Subsistence Agriculture*, 2nd ed. (New York: St Martin's Press, 1966), Table 34, pp. 160–163.

[16] From *United Africa Company Statistical and Economic Review*, March 1967, cited in ibid., p. 163.

[17] M. R. Haswell, *The Economics of Development in Village India* (London: Routledge & Kegan Paul, 1967), p. 22.

[18] Ibid., p. 79.

Transportation costs even had a bearing on the insurgent conflict. In TCN village, the main transportation route was impassable from early 1966 until February 1967 because the Viet Cong had established a combat hamlet and cut the road. In January 1967 the writer talked with several farmers selling vegetables at the point of blockage. They observed that only those close to the passable portion of the road could market vegetables; beyond the break, transport costs became prohibitive (motorized transport was not available), preventing competitive growing for the Saigon market. Two weeks later, while the road was being opened by a Vietnamese army engineering battalion, several farmers nearer Tam Hiep stated that they were already planting vegetables with the prospect that local transport services (Tri-Lambrettas) would soon be extending their routes into previously cutoff Tam Hiep. This belief was substantiated; by May 1967, even regular bus traffic was serving Tam Hiep. The fact that Tam Hiep farmers were, until early 1967, denied access to the high returns of vegetable cultivation provided (along with the associated insecurity) an important incentive for farmers to move the 3 to 5 kilometers to nearby TCN.

One farmer moved from the Tam Hiep area in 1966, preferring to farm vegetables in TCN and leave his Tam Hiep rice field fallow. A member of the household returned every day by bicycle to Tam Hiep to check the family's house and feed the remaining pigs. Meanwhile, the rest of the family (thirteen members) was occupied cultivating vegetables near their temporary house in TCN. The farmer left his home village for two reasons. First, the insecurity was so great that it allowed him "one work day every two to four to six days." Moreover, while living in Tam Hiep the family had to pay both rent (4,000 piasters for 2 hectares in 1966) to a landlord (who continued to live and collect rent in Tam Hiep despite the presence of the Viet Cong— a rare occurrence) and taxes to the Viet Cong of 1,000 to 3,000 piasters each year for 2 hectares.

The rapid rise in transportation costs beyond the point where free trade was disrupted by insecure conditions was a strong factor favoring the expansion of vegetable growing near daytime secure areas adjacent to major road routes and deprived the population residing in Viet Cong areas of major economic benefits.

Marketing

THE RICE MARKET

The fact that the French developed a highly efficient transportation network in the 1920–1935 period does not imply that these benefits were passed on to the farmer. On the contrary, a 1936 study by the Ministry of Colonies (see Table 4.2) showed that the producer got only one-quarter of the Saigon export (FOB) price. Similarly, in Table 4.2 (b) it is seen that only beginning in World War II did the Delta price move to within 80 percent of the Saigon wholesale price. By 1965, however, after the first rice imports, Saigon wholesale paddy prices were generally 10 to 15 percent lower than Delta paddy prices.[19]

In 1966–1967 not only was the Delta paddy price as high as or higher than the Saigon price but Delta farmers were, with the exception of the transport and labor handling costs, taking home most of that price. Merchants and middlemen were circumvented as most farmers sold their rice over the back fence to other rural or nearby Delta urban inhabitants. Following a trend noted by Hendry in 1958,[20] rice milling, previously controlled by the Chinese in Cholon, had become almost a village-level enterprise. There were rice mills in both villages studied, and two more mills were located within five kilometers of each village. Generally these mills operated on a small scale, milling for home or local use rather than for shipments from the village. A few mills made irregular (usually monthly from December to July) shipments to Saigon in hired trucks when the Saigon rice price rose. These shipments were of five to fifteen tons each.

---

[19] Average (weighted) lower Delta paddy prices per 100 kg were V$N 381 in 1964 and V$N 441 in 1965. The Saigon wholesale paddy price in 1964 averaged V$N 343 and in 1965, V$N 375 per 100 kg. See Republic of Vietnam, Ministry of Agriculture, Agricultural Economics and Statistics Service, *Agricultural Statistics Yearbook, 1965* (Saigon, 1966), pp. 108, 113.
[20] Hendry, *Small World of Khanh Hau*, pp. 143–144.

TABLE 4.2   Rice Marketing

(a) 1936 Share of Export Rice Price		(b) Delta Paddy Price as Percentage of Saigon Wholesale Paddy Price	
Recipient	Share (%)	Year	%
Producer	26.0	1898	67
Middleman	33.6	1915	68
Carriers	21.0	1925	59
Rice mills	5.0	1929–early 1930	57
Public treasury	14.4	1931	35
		1938	68
		1940–1943	80
		1958	81

Sources: (a) from Charles Robequain, *The Economic Development of French Indo-China*, trans. I. A. Wood (London and New York: Oxford University Press, 1944), p. 346; (b) from Table 2.3 and Appendix B.
Note: In comparing parts (a) and (b), note that the Delta paddy price was typically higher than the producer's sale price.

CROP SALES

In Table 4.3, data are presented showing the households' disposition of the rice crop. For both villages the results were similar; slightly over 40 percent of the crop was consumed at home, a third of the crop was sold, an eighth of the crop was paid to harvest laborers, and an eighth to a tenth was paid to landowners as in-kind rent. These statistics conceal wide variations. Some households consumed not only their entire crop but purchased additional supplies as well. Only 12 of the 97 households sold more than half their crops (none sold more than 65 percent), and 32 households had no surplus for sale.

TABLE 4.3   Disposition of 1966/67 Rice Crop (Sample, n = 97)

	MT	%
Total production	381.5	100
Consumed by producing households	163.1	43
Sold (including sales to pay rent)	123.8	32
In-kind payment to harvest labor	48.7	13
Seed	3.8	1
In-kind payment of rent (residual)	42.1	11

TRENDS IN EXPORTS

Farm wage and rent payments were usually consumed by other villagers. Using the basis of sample selection (80 percent of the households in the village were farm households, of which 25 percent were in the sample), it was calculated that of the total rice production in LBD, village consumption needs (at 0.24 metric tons of paddy per capita) took 53 percent of the crop. In TCN, where vegetable growing was common, village consumption needs amounted to 73 percent of the rice crop. Dinh Tuong Province, with an urban population of approximately 100,000 of a 520,000 total population, in the 1964–1967 period exported annually an average of 35,000 to 45,000 metric tons of paddy equivalent. This is a small surplus from an estimated total production of 250,000 metric tons and is further evidence that population growth, refugee movements into urban areas, and higher incomes among rural inhabitants had, compared with pre-1940 conditions, moved the rice market to the rice producer, eliminating the middleman.

Exports of the 1965/66 Delta crop amounted to 320,000 metric tons of rice; exports from the 1966/67 crop dropped to 270,000 metric tons. These exports were so low that in neither year was there a sufficient surplus in South Vietnam for export. In 1965, 129,593 metric tons of rice were imported into South Vietnam; in 1966, 434,194 metric tons;[21] and in 1967, about 860,000 metric tons. These results contrast with exports of 1,500,000 metric tons in 1935 and in 1936.[22] In South Vietnam's last good crop year (1962/63), 322,570 metric tons of rice were exported,[23] a figure representing the highest exports of the post-1945 period.

THE RICE MERCHANT AND THE WAR

The rice merchants were Vietnamese and usually natives of the village in which they worked. Two of the subjects interviewed in LBD were rice merchants as well as rice farmers. Their social and economic characteristics were suggestive of historical market conditions, contrasted with post–Viet Cong 1966–1967 conditions: They were the largest landowners in the sample, owning 10 and 18 hectares, respec-

21 USAID, ASB, 1966, p. 111.
22 Annuaire statistique de l'Indochine, 1936–1937, p. 100.
23 Agricultural Statistics Yearbook, 1965, p. 154.

tively. One was a 58-year-old widow of a former village chief killed by the Viet Minh in 1947. At that time her husband was a rice merchant, and the family owned 40 hectares of land. In 1966 this widow complained that her rice-trading activities were restrained because she was afraid to leave her house except to farm 5 hectares of rice land located nearby. Fear of the Viet Cong prevented her from collecting rent on land she owned in a nearby village. In contrast to her disfavor with the Viet Cong, she had a privileged relationship with the GVN. In both 1965 and 1966 she was the recipient of the largest (40,000 piasters) loan granted by the Vietnamese government to any farmer in the village.

The second rice merchant was the wife of the village administrative council chief. In 1966 she earned a profit of 60,000 piasters on her rice sales. Her husband had been the council chief since 1962 and in early 1967 was reappointed by the newly elected village popular council. His official salary was 4,130 piasters each month, and his daughter worked as a clerk in the village office, earning 3,500 piasters monthly. He received a 20,000-piaster government loan in 1966.

The council chief's rice trading with Saigon dealers had also been interrupted by the Viet Cong. He did not dare go to his nearby rice field to supervise the farming work done there by hired laborers; instead, his wife assumed this task. He was afraid to live at home at night and slept in the fortified village office. Although he owned 10 hectares of land, farmed by ten tenants in Cho Gao district 5 kilometers away, he had not seen this land since 1958. From 1960 to 1964 he collected his rent through the local village police chief, who took 30 percent of the amount collected. After 1964, such collections proved unfeasible (the insecurity was too great), and he accepted what rent his tenants wished to pay. As a result he collected only 10 percent of the crop in rent, compared with 25 percent before 1964.

Although it is impossible to assess precisely to what extent Viet Cong pressures against rice merchants and landowners were responsible for the improved rice-marketing system in effect in the Delta in 1966–1967, they were undoubtedly significant. In these activities the Viet Cong have provided evidence supporting the institutionalists' view of the obstacles to development. The benefits of transport and rice-marketing activities (but not of the money market transactions) can be rationed by a government (for example, by licensing); these benefits may accumulate to the few who receive special privileges. And if, as was true in Vietnam, the few do not bear the costs of developing roads or markets, but have merely acquired benefits because of their social or political status, then the mass of the population may have grounds for discontent or revolution.

Summary

In this chapter we have seen how, in the 1960s, the constraints on production in the traditional economy began to break down. Technological developments like new rice varieties and the use of new irrigation devices permitted diversification into vegetable growing and the cultivation of a second rice crop. Attention has been drawn to the complexities of the production processes, for example, the difficulties of raising fruit and fish, and to the scope for still further technological improvements, particularly those that can save labor in periods of peak demand and those that can save land. We have also noted the special economic status of the buffalo as a store of wealth and the pig as a savings device. For each production possibility, we have seen the important role played by low opportunity cost resources such as family labor.

In the study of transportation and marketing, it was found that by 1966 the traditional system, whereby the benefits of a low-cost transport system accrued to those few who controlled both the transport and the marketing of rice, had broken down. Multiproduct opportunities allowed farmers and transport services to operate independently of the rice merchant. The rice market moved into the Delta. The Viet Cong assisted in the destruction of the traditional system by forcing large merchants to withdraw from marketing activities.

5 Capital

Usury or a Reasonable Return?

The supply of capital necessary to exploit production opportunities—both new and old—came primarily from the retained earnings of the family farm enterprise, that is, revenues from the sale of farm products, and secondarily from credit sources. This chapter considers only the supply of credit to the farm household, whether for investment or consumption purposes; it examines the credit institutions accessible to the farmer and the characteristics of the various types of credit offered (interest rates, length of loan, and quantity of funds loaned).

The institutions and practices of Asian credit have not fallen easily within the framework of Western economic analysis. It has been common for Western observers in Asia, having encountered monthly rates of interest in excess of yearly rates in developed economies, to conclude that these observed rates, for example, 5 percent per month, were "usurious," implying that by Western standards they were excessive or unlawfully high. The belief is particularly strong among the institutionalists and structuralists[1] and widespread elsewhere that these high interest rates are the result of monopolistic capital markets that limit the free movement of funds from those with surplus cash balances to those with deficit cash balances. However, as Long observes,[2] after one

[1] See, for example, Dudley Seers, "A Theory of Inflation and Growth in Under-Developed Economies Based on the Experience of Latin America," Oxford Economic Papers, vol. ns. 14 (June 1962), pp. 173–195. Seers makes the assumption that the availability of credit to the rural sector is limited by "monopolistic capital markets."

[2] Millard Long, "Interest Rates and the Structure of Agricultural Credit Markets," ibid., vol. n.s. 20 (July 1968), pp. 275–288.

accounts for the higher rates of default, the greater costs of administering small-scale loans, and the seasonal demand for credit in the rural sector of developing economies, the comparision with similar loans in developed economies is not unfavorable. Further, interest rates on comparable loans in developed economies often run above 10 percent per year and consumer-credit finance rates average 24 percent per year.[3] Finally, the weakest link in the argument of those who emphasize capital market imperfections in rural economies is that they have offered no evidence that entry into the market as a creditor is not free.

Interest Rates and Indebtedness

PRE-1945 INTEREST RATES

Historically speaking, one must remain agnostic on the issue of usury in Cochinchina. The evidence available on pre-1945 credit conditions is not sufficient to test such issues as default and entry. Some observers found that the monthly (money) interest rate ranged from 2 to 25 percent per month,[4] although the more circumspect sources indicate that unsecured small loans cost 3 to 5 percent per month.[5]

To prominent Western observers like Goudal, Robequain, Thompson, and (later) Buttinger, high interest rates were accepted as proof of usury, which is an improper deduction. Moreover, these writers saw high interest rates as the cause rather than the effect of low productivity —the more probable conclusion. A more circumspect source wrote:

[3] Paul F. Smith, *Consumer Credit Costs, 1949–59* (Princeton, N.J.: Princeton University Press, 1964), p. 11.

[4] See Pierre Gourou, *The Peasants of the Tonkin Delta*, trans. Richard R. Miller (New Haven, Conn.: Human Relations Area Files, 1955), pp. 401, 652; Jean Goudal, *Labour Conditions in Indo-China* (Geneva: International Labour Office, 1938), p. 281; Virginia Thompson, *French Indo-China* (New York: Macmillan Co., 1937), p. 224; Charles Robequain, *The Economic Development of French Indo-China*, trans. I. A. Wood (London and New York: Oxford University Press, 1944), p. 148; and Joseph Buttinger, *Vietnam: A Dragon Embattled* (New York: Frederick A. Praeger; London: Pall Mall Press, 1967), p. 105.

[5] Pham Huy-Loc, "For the Suppression of Usury," *L'Annam Nouveau*, December 13, 1936. Over the 1913–1941 period, prices in Cochinchina were stable or declining. See *Annuaire statistique de l'Indochine, 1939–1940*, pp. 290–293, and Appendix B, "Historical Data and Statistical Notes," in this volume.

It should be emphasized that the Oriental method of lending has certain advantages for improvident borrowers. Usury has many advantages in that it demands a minimum of security and formalities. But since the borrower is always under threat of urgent necessity, he prefers the lender who responds forthwith to these needs. Usury is the price paid for the accommodation and the risks involved.[6]

Although interest rates were high, their level was probably not a reflection of credit-market control—for the debtor could go to any creditor and the creditor could enter new markets—but a reflection of the low return on the capital employed. To be sure, control was exerted over the poor by the rich; however, the basis for this control, as we have seen, was not control of the credit market, but control of land resources.[7]

1945–1965 INTEREST RATES

According to the available evidence, post–World War II credit conditions in Southeast Asia did not differ from prewar conditions. Hendry's 1958/59 findings, again in a period of relative monetary stability, showed that of the debts outstanding (65 percent of the village sample was indebted), 33.0 percent were interest free, 26.8 percent were at rates from 0.1 to 4.0 percent, 28.6 percent were at 5.0 percent, and 10.7 percent at monthly rates greater than 5.0 percent.[8]

1966–1967 INTEREST RATES

Real rates of interest in 1966–1967 were much below historical levels. These real rates are computed in Table 5.1 for the prevailing 5 percent

TABLE 5.1 Annual Real Interest Rates

Monthly Interest Rate	1966	1967
5% (unsecured loan)	9.0%	37.8%
3% (secured loan)	−29.2%	−0.4%

[6] M. Ganay, in *Bulletin du Comité de l'Indochine*, June 22, 1933, p. 20, as quoted in Robequain, *Economic Development of French Indo-China*, pp. 40–41.

[7] The same was true in China. According to Chen Han-seng, "As it is clear, in this land monopoly, it is rent and not capital that sways the entire economy." See Chen Han-seng, *Landlord and Peasant in China: A Study of the Agrarian Crisis in South China* (New York: International Publishers, 1936), p. x.

[8] James B. Hendry, *The Small World of Khanh Hau* (Chicago: Aldine Publishing Co., 1964), p. 231.

monthly rate of interest on short- and medium-term small unsecured loans and the 3 percent monthly rate on secured loans. Because of the 76.6 percent rate of inflation in 1966 and the 41.8 percent rate in 1967, the creditors for secured loans were receiving a negative real rate in both years. Without accounting for defaults, creditors on unsecured loans obtained a positive interest rate. Therefore, in the Delta in 1966–1967, credit conditions were highly favorable, with the prevailing rates often lower than those in developed economies. For the Vietnamese, in the words of a 66-year-old illiterate farmer, "the interest rate is now lower than in previous years. It is also easier to borrow money now than in the years before."

Table 5.2 compares the interest rates paid in 1966 on the debts held by the surveyed farmers and Hendry's 1958/59 findings from a nearby village. It is seen that over 85 percent of both the number and the

TABLE 5.2   Monthly Interest Rates

| | | Percent per Month | | | | | | | |
| | | 0 | | 0.1 to 1.0 | | 1.1 to 5.0 | | 5.1 to 10.0 | |
	Total	V$N	% of Total	V$N	% of Total	V$N	% of Total	V$N	% of Total
Sample, 1966/67									
V$N	59,200	33,500	56	20,500	35	4,200	7	1,000	2
Number	73	38	52	26	36	6	8	3	4
Hendry, 1958/59[a]									
Number	56	19	34	6	11	26	43	6	11

[a] See James B. Hendry, *The Small World of Khanh Hau* (Chicago: Aldine Publishing Co., 1964), p. 221.

value of the loans obtained in 1966 were at an interest rate of 1 percent per month or less. Compared with Hendry's 1958/59 finding that 45 percent of the loans cost 1 percent per month, the 88 percent obtained at this rate in 1966/67 is evidence of a dramatic improvement in credit conditions. It is clear that in 1966/67 the farmers were paying very low or negative real rates of interest for loans, and that the price of capital was much below historical levels.

1966–1967 INDEBTEDNESS

Comparing the sample with Hendry's data in Table 5.3, we find that the extent of indebtedness is slightly greater among the households

surveyed in 1966/67 than among those surveyed in 1958/59. Therefore, while the real interest rates paid in the 1966 sample fell well
below those paid in the earlier period, the use of credit did not decline
between the two periods, and it may have increased slightly.

TABLE 5.3 Indebtedness

| | Number of Loans per Household | | | |
	0	1	2	3
TCN, 1966/67				
(70 households)	24 (34%)	38 (54%)	8 (12%)	0 (0%)
LBD, 1966/67				
(50 households)	12 (24%)	21 (42%)	12 (24%)	5 (10%)
Sample total				
(120 households)	36 (30%)	59 (49%)	20 (17%)	5 (4%)
Hendry, 1958/59[a]				
(100 households)	35 (35%)	65 (65%)		

[a] James B. Hendry, *The Small World of Khanh Hau* (Chicago: Aldine Publishing
Co., 1964), p. 206.

Table 5.4 reports the responses to a question intended to explore
the farmers' use of the loaned funds. From the results it is clear that
indebtedness in 1966 was not a last-resort effort to obtain funds to meet

TABLE 5.4 Use of Loans

	Total Number	Investment	Consump-tion	Investment and Con-sumption	No Response
TCN	55	31 (56%)	5 (9%)	18 (33%)	1 (2%)
LBD	58	37 (64%)	9 (16%)	10 (17%)	2 (3%)
Sample total	113	68 (60%)	14 (12%)	28 (25%)	3 (3%)

the family's immediate consumption needs. Associated inquiries found
that the most common use of loans borrowed for investment was to
purchase fertilizer, whereas the most common use of consumption loans
was to purchase building materials—cement and tin or lightweight
aggregate roofing—for home-construction use.

Credit Institutions

The village credit institutions were of five basic types. First, and of historical importance, were those involving repayment in kind, for example, labor services or rice. Second, and of greatest importance in the sample as a whole, were loans obtained from relatives. These loans commonly carried no interest charges, were for short periods, and must be viewed within their social context. Third, were loans from money-lenders, merchants, friends, and landlords, which usually carried the interest rate that the villagers referred to when they spoke of the "monthly rate of interest." Fourth, the government loan program was a source of credit where, security conditions permitting, the government made such funds available—always at very low interest rates compared with those in the third category. Last, the *hui* was a common source of credit that, because it does not fall into any Western category of credit institution, will be discussed in detail in a later section.[9]

THE SA MAI LOAN

A *sa mai* loan is one made in money by the creditor to be repaid in kind at a later date by the debtor. Examples of three types of such loans were found: one involving repayment in harvest labor, another stipulating repayment by provision of buffalo plowing services, and a third calling for in-kind repayment of the crop grown, the latter known as a "green-crop" loan. The villagers' attitudes toward *sa mai* loans differed from those toward the more conventional forms of indebtedness; they considered the details of these loans a quasi-sensitive matter. One reason for this view was that the Viet Cong looked upon such loans with disfavor. Those interviewed said that the incidence of this type of indebtedness in earlier periods had been great but that in 1966–1967 *sa mai* loans were uncommon, no doubt largely as a result of the eased credit conditions.

An example will demonstrate the operation of a green-crop loan. One farmer had sold his December crop every year in the previous February to obtain cash for Tet consumption and dry-season family consumption.

[9] The *hui*, or variations thereof, is probably the most common non-Western credit institution in the world. It is found throughout Asia, Africa, and even in the Americas. See Clifford Geertz, "The Rotating Credit Association," *Economic Development and Cultural Change*, vol. X, no. 3 (April 1962), pp. 241–263, and Shirley Ardener, "Comparative Study of Rotating Credit Associations," *Journal of the Royal Anthropological Institute*, vol. 94 (1964), pt. 2, pp. 201–229.

In December 1966, the farmer harvested 1.7 metric tons of rice paddy. The previous February he had sold 1.2 metric tons to three nonfarmers for 60 piasters per *gia* when the prevailing price was 100 piasters per *gia*. When the in-kind repayment was made, the rice price was 180 piasters per *gia*. Therefore, he paid an interest rate of 300 percent for the loan for ten months.[10] Because his crop was too small to cover both the loan and his family's consumption needs, he had to purchase rice to meet the family's food needs after the harvest. Yet, despite these seemingly harsh conditions, the farmer appeared satisfied with the arrangement (his budget showed a considerable surplus in 1966—from his wife's income as a fish merchant and his salary as a member of the village militia), and he entered into a similar arrangement in February 1967.

For the creditor who found that his tenant could not repay a green-crop loan, the risks were high. When default was imminent, an adjustment was made that frequently involved additional interest as well as the creditor's right to receive a larger share of the succeeding year's crop. One should note that in earlier periods, when the rice price often fell at harvesttime, the creditor bore a price risk.

When made on the basis of labor services to be performed at a later date, the *sa mai* arrangement followed those just described. For example, if the expected price of the work to be provided was 12,000 piasters and the term of the loan was four to five months, the debtor would receive 10,000 piasters at the beginning of the period. Although a scarce supply of labor at the periods of peak demand probably placed the 1966 debtor in such an agreement in a strong bargaining position with his creditor, it is easy to see how, under the less satisfactory economic conditions of the past, the labor-service loan as well as the other *sa mai* loans discussed previously could have been the source of burdensome debts accepted by the poor to meet their immediate consumption needs of the dry season or planting season. Even in 1966–1967 the surveyed *sa mai* debtors were the poor and illiterate, and the creditors were the wealthy landowners and village officials.

---

[10] But this loan, with built-in price protection for the creditors, was outstanding over the most inflationary period in Vietnam since World War II—the period of the devaluation in June 1966.

MAJOR SOURCES AND CONDITIONS OF LOANS

Table 5.5 shows the relative importance of the various types of credit in the sample. We see that the supposed traditional sources of credit were

TABLE 5.5   Types of Credit by Number and Amount

	Number	V$N (00)
Relatives	40 (32%)	351 (41%)
Hui	52 (41%)	251 (29%)
Government	26 (20%)	199 (23%)
Moneylender	1 (1%)	4 (0%)
Merchant	3 (2%)	23 (3%)
Landlord	1 (1%)	12 (1%)
Friends	4 (3%)	17 (2%)
Total	127	857

of minor significance: the landlords, moneylenders, and merchants, who accounted for less than 5 percent of the number and value of the loans outstanding in 1966. The predominant sources of credit were relatives, the *hui*, and the government.

When the loans were grouped according to their duration and rate of interest, it was found that loans from relatives carried low interest rates and lasted a median period of six months; loans from friends were of short duration and carried little or no interest charges. Government loans usually terminated after a year, and they carried 0.8 to 1.0 percent monthly interest.

THE GOVERNMENT LOAN PROGRAM

The government loan program[11] had a twofold purpose. First, it offered loans to increase agricultural productivity. Two types of loans were available for this purpose, and both went only to those with collateral. One provided medium-term credit (less than one year) at 12 percent per year. The other offered long-term credit (more than a year) at 8 percent per year; these loans were available in sums from 5,000 to

[11] The administering institution was known as the National Agricultural Credit Organization (NACO) until May 1, 1967, when it became the Agricultural Development Bank.

20,000 piasters. The second purpose of the NACO program was to grant small loans of 1,000 to 5,000 piasters to "poor farmers" who had no collateral.[12] The interest rate on these loans was 10 percent per year.

The success of the NACO program in achieving its objectives can be fairly judged by its performance in Long Binh Dien, where the government had been in control since the Viet Cong General Uprising in 1960. In LBD, 22 farmers, or 44 percent of the sample, had NACO loans. (In TCN, where the Vietnamese government did not have control until December 1966, only 2.9 percent of the sample had government loans.)

Table 5.6 shows that 79.7 percent of the loaned funds went to 13 of the 27 landowners in the LBD sample. By contrast, of the 23 tenants in the sample, 9 received loans amounting to a fifth of the total funds

TABLE 5.6   Government Loans in LBD

	Loan Size			
	Landowners		Tenants	
	Less than V$N 5,000	More than V$N 5,000	Less than V$N 5,000	Total
Number of recipients	4	9	9	22
Total piasters	11,000	151,600	42,000	204,600
Percentage of GVN loans	5.4	74.3	20.3	100

available. In themselves these results are not surprising; it should be expected from the provisions of the loan program that those with collateral would receive the largest share of the funds.

DISTRIBUTIONAL EFFECTS OF THE GOVERNMENT LOAN PROGRAM

One can have reservations about the efficiency of aiding the poor in an underdeveloped economy with a loan program based primarily on collateral loans. If the problem is a shortage of capital for consumption in

---

[12] The procedure for obtaining a NACO loan was complex and invited favoritism. The prospective recipient had to be placed on a list made up by the hamlet or village chief and approved by the province chief and the NACO chief. This elaborate procedure was designed to ensure the "morality" of the recipient, that is, loosely defined, whether he was a Viet Cong or was, through relatives, associated with the Viet Cong.

the short run as opposed to a shortage of capital to meet available and profitable production opportunities (a condition that applied under the static technological conditions in existence from 1930 to 1955 in Vietnam), then a collateral loan program may exacerbate the existing unequal distribution of income. The mechanism by which these conditions can arise is best described in the words of the former Governor General of Indochina, Pierre Pasquire, in an address to the Grand Council of the Economic and Financial Interests of Indo-China on November 25, 1931:

> If only most of the loans had been granted directly to the needy *nhaque* or the poverty-stricken *ta-dien!* The depressing fact is that the credit facilities so far granted have had no psychological or economic effects. It has indeed proved almost impossible to bring these advances within the reach of the small farmer, the *ta-dien* or *nhaque*, except through the large or medium-scale landowners. These persons charge exorbitant rates of interest for their direct loans or for guaranteeing loans, so that the small farmers get no benefit from the advantageous rate of interest offered by the rural credit funds. All the efforts made by my administrative officers to improve the situation of these poor people are therefore brought to naught; any attempt to lower the cost of production of rice by reducing the interest on loans is doomed to failure in advance. The large and medium-scale landowners charge a tremendous commission, equal to the difference between the interest charged on loans by the rural funds and the rates at which they lend money directly or which they charge for standing security. Their maleficient influence prevents any direct contact between the authorities and the rural masses.[13]

In 1966 these static technological conditions did not exist, and the efficiency of the loan program in raising agricultural productivity through its promotion of greater fertilizer use per hectare seems unquestionable, whatever its distributional characteristics may have been. It is likely, moreover, that to the extent that these loans were directed to investment uses—over three-fourths were—they permitted greater employment for the nonrecipients. Yet from evidence presented in Chapter 9, particularly the significant positive regression coefficient between indebtedness and fertilizer use per hectare, combined with a significant negative coefficient between farm size and fertilizer use per hectare, one can conclude that, had the loans been granted to tenants instead of landowners, a larger

---

[13] As quoted by Goudal, *Labour Conditions in Indo-China*, p. 215.

share of these funds and the funds displaced from investment uses by the loans would have been spent on fertilizer. The benefits of this alternative policy would have to be weighed against the cost of a higher default rate, since the tenant who refused to repay his loan had no collateral to confiscate. But the cost of the existing GVN program, which gave the landowners who received loans a windfall profit easily gained by loaning out funds obtained at 1 percent or less per month to others at the going market rates of between 3 and 5 percent a month, would also have to be considered.[14]

The *Hui*

After loans from relatives, the most important source of credit in the villages studied was the *hui*, a credit institution with a social as well as economic role in community life. The *hui*, in various forms, is found throughout South Vietnam;[15] its similarity to the Chinese *ho-hui* suggests that its origins lie in that culture.[16] Because of its open basis for membership—anyone with a small cash surplus can join—and because its members have access to all the other sources of credit and opportunities for investment available in the rural economy, the *hui* is the appropriate subject of an analysis intended to determine the prevailing interest rate during the period under study.

The typical *hui* has ten to fifteen members and an organizational life of ten to fifteen months. The *hui*'s life is determined by the number of members and the time period on which its meetings are based; for example, a twelve-member monthly *hui* holding its first meeting on Jan-

[14] The recipient of one of the largest government loans was a major landowner and a large creditor in the *hui* (see the next section). Because such landowners had land to offer as collateral and were not fearful of being unable to repay a loan, they obtained government loan funds and used them to make private loans or to join the *hui* as creditors.

[15] The type of *hui* described here is known as the *hui thao* and is common in the Mekong Delta region of South Vietnam. It differs only slightly from the *hui hue hong* more common in Central Vietnam.

[16] Arthur H. Smith, in *Village Life in China* (New York: F. H. Revell Co., 1899), described (p. 154) a cooperative loan association that is identical to the Vietnamese *hui* except that bids were made on an auction basis instead of by secret ballot as is common in Vietnam. Lien-Shen Yang, in "Buddhist Monasteries and Four Money-Raising Institutions in Chinese History," *Harvard Journal of Asiatic Studies*, vol. 13 (June 1950), p. 180, traces the *ho-hui*'s existence in China back to the T'ang period (seventh–ninth centuries).

uary 1 would have its final meeting on December 1. Daily, weekly, and monthly *huis* are known to exist, but *huis* that meet once a month are the most common. (For example, the *hui* to be analyzed in detail in Table 5.7 had thirteen members who met once a month from February 2, 1966 until February 2, 1967.) The first meeting is convened by the organizer, who serves a meal or rice cake to the twelve people he has persuaded to participate. The share value is determined at this meeting, and each member other than the organizer deposits this sum with the organizer. (For the *hui* in Table 5.7, this value was 1,000 piasters; it may be 100, 200, 500, or as much as 20,000 piasters.) At the second meeting, a month later, the bidding process begins; each member other than the organizer submits a bid for the sum to be paid in by the organizer and every other *hui* member, excluding the person who submitted the winning bid. In any month the sum received by the winner is determined as follows: Every member, including the organizer, who has received funds from the *hui* pays the successful bidder an amount equal to the share value of the *hui*; added to this is a payment, from each member who has not yet submitted a winning bid, that is equal to the share value minus the value of the winning bid. In the example *hui* for the month of July 1966, member 6 submitted a winning bid of 195 piasters (last line, Table 5.7). This bid entitled him to receive a sum of 10,635 piasters—1,000 piasters each from members 1 through 5 and 1,000 piasters less 195, or 805, piasters from members 7 through 13. (Members in Table 5.7 are numbered according to the month in which they were successful bidders.) This same bidding procedure is followed at every meeting until the final month, when the member who has not yet won the monthly sum receives by default a full share payment from every other member.

TYPES OF MEMBERS
The *hui* offers different advantages to different types of members. Basically, members fall into three categories. First, there is the "saver," or member who joins the *hui* to achieve a return on his excess cash balances. The largest landowner in LBD village was such a member, belonging to five different *huis* simultaneously. Members from this category (for example, members 12 and 13 in Table 5.7) are not active bidders, although they are known to feign financial hardship as they

TABLE 5.7 *Hui* Data

Member Number	Feb. 2, 1966	Mar. 2, 1966	Apr. 2, 1966	May 2, 1966	June 2, 1966	July 2, 1966	Aug. 2, 1966	Sept. 2, 1966	Oct. 2, 1966
1	+12,000	−1,000	−1,000	−1,000	−1,000	−1,000	−1,000	−1,000	−1,000
2	−1,000	+9,360	−1,000	−1,000	−1,000	−1,000	−1,000	−1,000	−1,000
3	−1,000	−760	+10,250	−1,000	−1,000	−1,000	−1,000	−1,000	−1,000
4	−1,000	−760	−825	+10,605	−1,000	−1,000	−1,000	−1,000	−1,000
5	−1,000	−760	−825	−845	+10,400	−1,000	−1,000	−1,000	−1,000
6	−1,000	−760	−825	−845	−800	+10,635	−1,000	−1,000	−1,000
7	−1,000	−760	−825	−845	−800	−805	+10,950	−1,000	−1,000
8	−1,000	−760	−825	−845	−800	−805	−825	+11,075	−1,000
9	−1,000	−760	−825	−845	−800	−805	−825	−815	+11,200
10	−1,000	−760	−825	−845	−800	−805	−825	−815	−800
11	−1,000	−760	−825	−845	−800	−805	−825	−815	−800
12	−1,000	−760	−825	−845	−800	−805	−825	−815	−800
13	−1,000	−760	−825	−845	−800	−805	−825	−815	−800
Winning bid (V$N)	n.a.	240	175	155	200	195	175	185	200

TABLE 5.7 continued

Member Number	Nov. 2, 1966	Dec. 2, 1966	Jan. 2, 1966	Feb. 2, 1966	Net Cash Flow	% (r) Lending	Weighted Lending	% (r) Borrowing	Weighted Borrowing
1	− 1,000	− 1,000	− 1,000	− 1,000	0	n.a.	n.a.	0	n.a.
2	− 1,000	− 1,000	− 1,000	− 1,000	−2,640	0	1,000	4.9	8,360
3	− 1,000	− 1,000	− 1,000	− 1,000	−1,510	8.4	2,000	3.7	8,250
4	− 1,000	− 1,000	− 1,000	− 1,000	− 980	7.4	3,000	3.5	7,605
5	− 1,000	− 1,000	− 1,000	− 1,000	−1,030	6.1	4,000	5.2	6,400
6	− 1,000	− 1,000	− 1,000	− 1,000	− 595	5.5	5,000	5.7	5,635
7	− 1,000	− 1,000	− 1,000	− 1,000	− 85	4.9	6,000	5.8	4,950
8	− 1,000	− 1,000	− 1,000	− 1,000	+ 215	4.4	7,000	7.2	4,075
9	− 1,000	− 1,000	− 1,000	− 1,000	+ 525	3.9	8,000	9.6	3,200
10	+11,460	− 1,000	− 1,000	− 1,000	+ 985	3.6	9,000	10.6	2,460
11	− 820	+11,650	− 1,000	− 1,000	+1,355	3.3	10,000	13.8	1,650
12	− 820	− 825	+11,835	− 1,000	+1,715	3.1	11,000	19.8	835
13	− 820	− 825	− 835	+12,000	+2,045	2.8	12,000	0	n.a.
Winning bid (V$N)	180	175	165	n.a.					

Weighted average lending rate = 3.7%

Weighted average borrowing rate = 5.1% without organizer

Note: Signs indicate direction of cash flow. All data, except as otherwise noted, are in piasters (V$N).

arrive at the monthly meeting, hoping to frighten those who actually need the money into raising their bids.

Second, there is the "accumulator," like one *hui* member who viewed his participation not as a loan or credit but as a "savings device." (This attitude, similar to that discussed earlier regarding the purchase of a pig, demonstrates again the difficulty encountered by farmers living at a low level of income when they need to accumulate funds for a large investment.) *Hui* members in this category do not see themselves as debtors; they view their membership just as a Westerner would view his participation in a Christmas savings club. Members 5 through 11 in Table 5.7 fell in this second category.

The third category of participant is the debtor; for example, members 2 through 4 were debtors because they probably joined the *hui* to obtain an immediate loan to buy fertilizer, hire labor, begin vegetable farming, or even purchase a cyclo rig (a motor bicycle with tow cart)— all specific examples cited by *hui* debtors.

THE BIDDING PROCESS

The bidding process is not competitive as in an auction. Instead, each member who in the particular month in question has the right to bid submits his bid on a piece of paper. If the members are illiterate, they indicate their bids by placing a number of grains of rice or corn or similar item with a specified unit value in a small bowl or nontransparent cup. The bids are not determined on the basis of elaborate calculations but are said to be the result of "experience" and to depend on the peculiar needs of the bidders. Since such calculations would involve discounting a nonuniform geometric series, thus being beyond the capacity of one not aided by interest tables, a knowledge of intermediate mathematics, or access to a computer, the failure of *hui* members to use sophisticated bidding techniques is understandable. However, when bidding, members do reason that the higher their bid, the higher the interest rate they will be paying relative to that paid for a lower bid in the same month.

THE 1966–1967 HUI INTEREST RATE

If the calculated *hui* interest rate is representative of the credit situation in the village, it must be assumed that the opportunities for membership were open to people of varying economic status. If this was true, one would then expect that the observed bids reflected the alternative opportunities to borrow or lend in the village; that is, any member when bidding would have been expected to weigh his bid and the resulting sum he might receive against other financial opportunities. If he estimated that he could invest or become a creditor for a higher rate of return, he would raise his bid. Conversely, if he found that he had a cheaper source of credit than that available from the *hui*, he would join a *hui* with the intention of acting as a creditor or he would not bid to win.

Membership in the *hui* was open to rich and poor, landowner and nonlandowner, rice grower and vegetable grower alike. The farmer with surplus cash balances attempted to join a *hui* with others who had deficit cash balances. Otherwise, if he joined a *hui* of predominantly creditors, there would not have been competition among bidders, and his return as a creditor would have been low. Conversely, the prospective debtor preferred to join a *hui* with prospective creditors.

The organizer determined the membership of any particular *hui*.[17] Since he was responsible for contributing each member's monthly installment if that member was unable to make his payment,[18] the solvency of those to whom he offered an invitation was of vital concern.

A further factor tending to increase the representative nature of any particular *hui* with respect to village credit conditions was the fact that many farmers were members of two, three, and on occasion even five *huis* simultaneously. Some *hui* organizers operated several *huis* at the same time, but in the rural areas no one specialized in *hui* organizing per se.[19] Since the *hui* is a local institution with a membership selected from within one hamlet or village, it would not be expected to reflect credit

---

[17] In urban areas *hui* shares could be purchased at many local stores; the buyer checked every month on his position, paying and bidding as required. *Huis* are also known to operate by mail.

[18] This is true as a general rule. Of additional importance, however, was the social pressure exerted by every member of the *hui* on a member who appeared unwilling or unable to make his monthly contribution.

[19] This statement does not apply to urban *huis* where, for example, women *hui* organizers are known to be involved in as many as ten 10,000-piaster-share *huis* at one time. (Available evidence indicates that the *hui* is a major source of commercial credit among businessmen and women in urban areas of Saigon-Cholon and elsewhere.)

conditions outside that village or hamlet except to the extent that its members received loans from or made loans to relatives or friends outside the hamlet or, because they worked in urban areas, had opportunities to borrow or invest there. There was no formal institutional tie between the *hui* and money markets in urban areas.

To determine the rate of interest from the *hui*, we first divide the cash flow to and from each individual into debtor and creditor flows.[20] For example, taking member 5 (Table 5.7), we can consider him to have loaned funds to members 1 through 4 in the first four months and in the fifth month to have been repaid by those debtors. Therefore, his interest rate as a creditor is computed from the series in Equation 5.1:

$$-\frac{1,000}{1} - \frac{760}{(1+r)} - \frac{825}{(1+r)^2} - \frac{845}{(1+r)^3} + \frac{4,000}{(1+r)^4} = 0 \quad (5.1)$$
$$r_c = 6.1\%$$

Next, as a debtor, in the fifth month he received loans from members 6 through 13 and repaid these loans in months six through thirteen.

From Equation 5.2 we calculate his rate of interest r as a debtor, where n is the number of *hui* members and m is the number of the member whose rate of interest is being determined ($n - m = 8$):

$$\sum_{i=0}^{8} + \frac{1,000}{(1+r)^i} - \frac{(800)\,(8)}{1} = 0 \quad (5.2)$$
$$r_d = 5.2\%$$

Similar calculations can be made for every *hui* member. By taking a weighted (by amount and time period) average of these results one obtains a single creditor rate and a single debtor rate for each *hui*. For the *hui* in Table 5.7, these weighted averages are 3.7 percent for lenders

[20] An attempt to use the internal rate of return method (finding the interest rate that discounted each member's cash flow to zero present value) failed to yield useful results. This failure is attributable to two problems: First, to calculate an internal rate of return, one must assume that each individual lends and borrows at the same interest rate, an assumption that rarely applies in any economy; second, and related to the first problem, is the fact that the type of series involved—negative, positive, and then negative cash flows—often cannot be discounted at a single interest rate but may also be discounted either by two interest rates (both in a reasonable range) or, in some cases, by no real interest rate. I am indebted to T. A. Cotton of Nuffield College for an extensive discussion of this matter.

and 5.1 percent for borrowers. The debtor average does not include the organizer's sum, since his relationship with other members is fixed by the rules of the credit society.

In Table 5.8 a weighted average or *hui* interest rate is computed from the five *huis* on which data were collected. If the *hui* is representative of credit conditions, as has been argued, the 2.9 percent creditor and the

TABLE 5.8 Average *Hui* Interest Rate

Number	Weight	Creditor Rate (%)	Debtor Rate (%)
1	1,000	3.7	5.1
2	100	4.7	6.0
3	1,000	2.3	2.7
4	200	2.2	2.9
5	300	1.4	2.2
Weighted average		2.9	3.8

3.8 percent debtor rates obtained reflect credit conditions in the villages studied over the period of their life, from November–December 1965 until January–February 1967. These rates place the *hui* in a more preferred position than the moneylender as a source of credit and in a less preferred position than a relative. Not surprisingly, the 3 to 4 percent monthly rate is approximately that demanded by moneylenders on secured loans and by friends on unsecured loans.

COMPARATIVE INTEREST RATES

By comparing the weighted monthly *hui* interest rates with the monthly rate of inflation (Saigon working-class cost-of-living index without rent) and monthly paddy and gold price changes, it was found that a *hui* creditor rate of 3 percent yield per month (range 1.1 to 8.4 percent) was quite favorable for the period studied. Three percent compounded over fourteen months gives a 51.2 percent return. Over the period, the price index rose 91.0 percent, the paddy price 92.4 percent, and the gold price 36.6 percent. However, it is not possible to state categorically how the *hui* member's return compared with that of one who purchased gold or paddy; the result would depend on the particular months of purchase and sale. A farmer who, instead of joining a *hui*, purchased paddy with his monthly payment and sold at the termination of the period in order to purchase fertilizer would not, accounting for losses (often estimated at 10 percent) and storage costs, have been in a clearly superior position.

It is particularly inappropriate to judge ex ante *hui* decisions on ex post price data. At the time of joining, each member had no certain knowledge of the future prices of paddy or gold. In fact, some farmers, fearing a rapid deflation, were reluctant to acquire debts. The rice market was unstable during the period of study: The rice price doubled in 1966, but it was stable or declining throughout 1967. Accustomed to an environment of relative monetary stability until 1965, farmers were not inflation-oriented in a French or Brazilian sense; it was not their habit to purchase gold. With the steady decline in gold prices after September 1966, due to government gold sales, such a habit could have proved costly.

CONCLUSION

The doyen of French writers on Indochinese economic affairs, Charles Robequain, once wrote, describing the Vietnamese peasant: "Thrift is not one of his virtues; there is nothing corresponding to the French peasant's woolen stocking."[21] On the basis of the evidence presented here, it appears that the reverse of Robequain's conclusion is warranted: French peasants unfortunately never had access to the *hui*, an efficient credit institution open to anyone with a small surplus.

[21] Robequain, *Economic Development of French Indo-China*, p. 148.

6   Labor

Labor Supply, Labor Policies, and Wages

INTRODUCTION: THE FAMILY PRODUCTION UNIT

The objective of household farm operations—maximization of the net income of the members of the household or family farm enterprise—determined the allocation of the land and labor available to the family as well as the number of man-days of hired labor it employed. The family labor supply itself was an inconclusive quantity rarely combinable with hired labor to form a single labor factor; it was both a labor input and a management input. Families of identical size employing identical amounts of hired labor, land, and capital often received very different incomes. For this reason the problems of imputation defy solution; for example, the opportunity cost to the family of employing a 15-year-old boy at home varied widely from family to family. Each family chose from among the income opportunities available to it the group of activities most suited to its particular collective preference. More often than not, it would be incorrect to assume that the opportunity for the employment of all factors available to one family was available to another of similar physical characteritics. Friendship, house or field location, and preference often determined the opportunities pursued. Where conditions were similar and inputs and outputs well defined, for example, with rice farming, formal production analysis along Cobb-Douglas lines was feasible. But for the farm unit as a whole, faced with multiple-income earning opportunities of varying attractiveness and access, such a straightforward model was seldom useful.

From the supply side, a major reason for the prevailing labor shortage is seen in Figure 6.1. (This population pyramid was constructed from data obtained from the farm sample.) The sharp narrowing of the pyramid in the 19- to 34-year age-group, a narrowing more marked on the male than the female side, is evidence of the severe shortage of labor in this, the primary working group. It appears that some women in this age-group also left the village—either with their husbands or, if single, to seek employment in Saigon or elsewhere. However, without the war, a portion

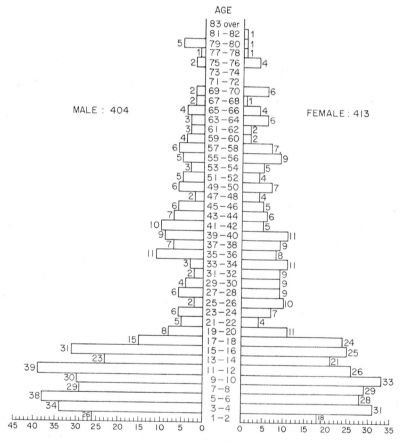

FIGURE 6.1 Sample (LBD and TCN) Population Pyramid

of the age-group, both males and females, would be expected to have left the village, at least temporarily, to seek other opportunities.

Males from 20 to 33 were subject to the draft.[1] Draftees remained in the service for varying periods; prior to the general mobilization of 1968, they remained in the service for approximately five years. Therefore, the absence of a larger number of males in this draft-eligible group reflects those working as civilians in urban areas; those who, having completed their service, did not return to the village; those with the Viet Cong; and those who had been killed fighting on either side.

A closer view of the effect of the draft was obtained from the results of a question designed to assess movements from households between 1964 and 1966.[2] Of the sample of 120 households, 47 (39 percent) reported having members away, 10 (8 percent) had two members away, and 37 (31 percent) had one member away. Of the 57 household members who had left their households after 1964, 50 were said to be employed by the Vietnamese government in either civilian or military roles, the majority being draftees.[3] The remaining 7 were employed in civilian occupations (including 2 janitors, 1 taxi driver, and 1 Tri-Lambretta driver). This group of absent household members included 4 household heads.

STRUCTURAL CHANGES IN THE LABOR MARKET

In his 1958 survey, Hendry found that 20 to 25 percent of the household heads regarded laboring as their primary activity.[4] But for the villages surveyed in 1967, only 5 to 10 percent of the household heads were in this category. There are two reasons for this sudden change—a change that caused farmers in 1966 to speak of a "severe labor shortage" and "the unavailability of hired labor." One reason was economic, that is, the demand resulting from new opportunities for employment in the urban sector, in vegetable farming, or in the transportation industry, coupled with withdrawals from the labor supply to meet the demands of war.

[1] On October 26, 1967, the draft eligibility age was lowered from 20 to 18 years.
[2] See Appendix A, interview question 4–2a.
[3] Of a population of 16,500,000 in South Vietnam in 1966, approximately 650,000 were employed by the South Vietnamese armed forces, 330,000 by the Vietnamese government as civilians, and 142,000 by the U.S. sector (USAID, ASB, 1966, p. 10).
[4] James B. Hendry, *The Small World of Khanh Hau* (Chicago: Aldine Publishing Co., 1964), p. 129.

The other reason for the absence of an agricultural laboring class in 1967 was political. In the words of one farmer:[5]

In the last ten years, even in relatively secure areas, the liberators [colloquial for Viet Cong] have intimidated village residents to prevent them from cultivating more than one hectare for small families and two hectares for large families. They also encourage people not to work as hired laborers for those who operate on more than the "permitted" amount or plan to do so. For this reason it is only rarely that one finds an operator on more than four hectares, and it partly explains the shortage of labor.

For these economic and political reasons, the labor market conditions of the late 1950s had been completely changed by 1966. In 1958/59, Hendry found that a laborer worked only 150 days in the year.[6] Of conditions in the labor market at that time, Hendry wrote:

The most important type of formal organization used in agriculture is a labor contracting service. . . . These labor groups stem from a need to have several workers . . . at one time for certain farm activities, e.g., the transplanting of young rice shoots and the harvesting of the crop. Each labor contractor has from 40 to 60 people, both men and women, working under his direction. The laborers approach a contractor of their choice at the beginning of the year, and once having agreed to work under him they may not change to another during that same year.[7]

By 1966 a laborer could work 250 days a year,[8] and it was seldom possible to gather more than fifteen workers in one field at one time. Labor organizers were uncommon and served only to organize and supervise female labor for planting seedlings.[9] For all other tasks, including seedling pickup and harvesting, male labor was recruited on an ad hoc basis by those in need of it.

[5] A 59-year-old small-scale farmer who rented 0.7 ha of rice land acquired from a friend in early 1965; this farmer was a laborer until 1966.
[6] Hendry, Small World of Khanh Hau, p. 136, found that over half of the laborers had four months' work or less in any year.
[7] Ibid., pp. 133–134.
[8] This is the estimate generally given by the laborers interviewed. For rice work alone one worker gave the following breakdown, which adds up to approximately 210 days or 30 weeks: plowman for first crop, 4 weeks; transplanting first crop, 2–3 weeks; harvesting first crop, 3–4 weeks; plowman for second (primary) crop, 8 weeks; transplanting second crop, 3–4 weeks; harvesting second crop, 4–5 weeks; and miscellaneous weeding and dike cleaning for both crops, 4 weeks.
[9] Known as replanting bosses or "dike sitters" (ngoi ba), these organizers were paid 1/30 of the wages paid to the female replanters.

So profound were these changes that the laborer's position in 1966 was in some ways better than that of the small-plot rice farmer, a condition unheard of in the past, when every laborer aspired to rent his own plot, however small. One laborer and his wife who in 1966 worked as laborers told how the 2,000 kilograms of paddy and 25,000 piasters they earned from these activities were "much better than a rice grower could do." A farmer who until 1966 was a laborer stated that his economic welfare had deteriorated after he became a rice grower on 0.7 hectare.

WAGE RATES

Figure 6.2 shows that, compared with the Saigon working-class cost-of-living index, the rural unskilled daily wage for males older than 18 years actually deteriorated over the 1959–1966 period; however, because the number of workdays per worker had increased from 150 to 250 days, the rural worker's net income position improved greatly.

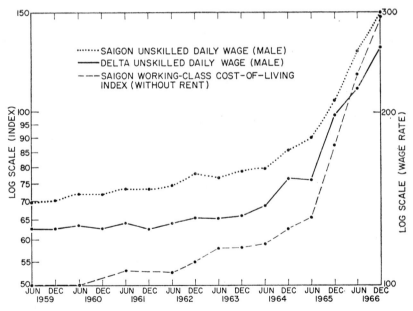

FIGURE 6.2 Wages Sources: Wages from National Institute of Statistics, *Yearbook, 1966* and succeeding monthly reports; cost-of-living index from USAID, *ASB, 1965*, p. 21, and ibid., *1966*, p. 23.

It is surprising, however, to find from the wage trends in Figure 6.2 that after the arrival of large numbers of U.S. troops in the summer of 1965 rural wages rose more rapidly than urban wages, despite the fact that the U.S. troops drew on labor resources in the urban areas. The explanation is that steady employment in secure areas was preferred to high wages and irregular employment in insecure areas.[10]

WORKING CONDITIONS

The effects of the war on working conditions differed slightly between the villages studied. In LBD, the more secure area, there was a curfew until 7:00 A.M., but laborers stated that "as a matter of practice" people were free to work in the fields from 5:30 A.M. to 6:00 P.M. For most the workday began at 7:00 A.M. and ended at 6.00 P.M., with an 11:00 A.M. to 2:00 P.M. noon break. In 1966 in TCN, because of less secure conditions, the workday began at 8:00 A.M. and ended at 5:00 P.M. In noting these conditions, the farmers spoke of their desire not to get involved with either side in the war, or, as they put it, "not to get caught in the cross fire of the war"—a phrase used in both the narrow and the broad sense.

Wartime working conditions put a particular strain on work performed during the transplanting and harvesting seasons. Even in peacetime these tasks were conducted on an "emergency" basis. For example, after being uprooted, a seedling could not be transplanted after more than one day; accordingly, within the short period of eight to ten hours available for work, arrangements had to be made for a male labor force to uproot the seedlings from the seedbed, a transportation group to move them to the field, and a group of women to replant the seedlings. In peacetime these operations often continued into the night. At harvesttime, for example, workers arrived in the fields in early morning, worked all day cutting rice stalks, remained through the coolness of the night under moonlight to thresh or "beat the grains," and returned to their homes with the harvested paddy the following morning. Insecurity, therefore,

[10] In the rural areas between Hué and Phu Bai on July 15, 1967, the writer found that the rural unskilled wage rate was V$N 120 a day (150 a day for difficult labor operating a waterwheel) compared with the then prevailing Hué unskilled wage of V$N 75–90 a day. (In 1967, Hué was considered a secure place of employment.)

severely restrained these "bottleneck" activities. Insecurity also eliminated nighttime fishing, an important off-season activity for many and the major source of income for a few.

GVN AND VIET CONG LABOR POLICIES

The opposing organizations—the Vietnamese government and the Viet Cong—played a direct role in the economic life of the laborers. Of the 50 households surveyed in LBD, 19 had household members engaged as full-time or part-time government employees (3 households with two members each, the remaining 16 with one each). Of these 22 employees, 11 were in the village or district militia, a job considered as half-time work. The other 11 employees were civilians, including the village chief, 1 hamlet chief, 1 agricultural service extension agent, 6 village and district office workers, and 2 public works employees. In 7 of these 22 cases, or 14 percent of the LBD sample, the government employee was the head of the household; in the remaining 15 households (30 percent) the employees were draft-age sons or relatives residing in the household. In the more recently Viet Cong–controlled TCN, among the 70 families in the sample, 8 households had a member holding an official job; 3 of these were heads of households.

Those in the official employ of the Vietnamese government usually worked only part-time. Members of the militia often worked at night standing guard. In the daytime they changed to native dress and worked in the fields as farmers. Only the village chief complained that his official status hampered his economic activities. His worries were probably a result of his status as a large landowner and rice merchant rather than as the village chief.

The Corvée Despite official denials to the contrary—often voiced at the national level—the corvée was a reality for the village inhabitants. However, no uniform corvée policy existed; there was no rotating list or prearranged work schedule. In the survey responses, farmers voiced two major objections to the corvée. First, some farmers were exempt while others were forced to work regularly. Second, the corvée was an ever-present threat to the conduct of farming operations. Farmers said that they were frequently drafted when their vegetable crops were near harvest; often they were suddenly taken away for work on short notice before other arrangements could be made for the care of their fields.

Although no specific question was designed to examine the conditions of the corvée, from the unsolicited responses of 17 farmers on the subject, an adequate view of its operation can be constructed. Most of the corvée work was on local military fortifications—digging ditches, setting up wire defense barriers, and so forth. No pay was received nor, except in rare cases, was food provided. Often the families of the drafted worker traveled to the place of work and provided food for the working member; in a few instances, nearby residents provided the food. Recruitment for the corvée took place, without warning, on the morning the work was required. This threat prompted some farmers to wait until late morning before starting their work. Those drafted had worked an average of about twenty days in 1966—usually they worked three to four days a month for six months in the year, although one farmer said he had worked forty days in 1966.

The farmers, when describing the corvée, juxtaposed its burden with that on farmers living in Viet Cong areas who were drafted for work at night and frequently worked under conditions of great insecurity. One 51-year-old farmer who had worked ten days at corvée labor in 1966 said, "The corvée is not very harmful to farming operations; moreover, it is a price one must pay for the present circumstances of war." But his was not the common view. Most farmers looked upon it as an unjustified imposition by the GVN, and the poorer and less privileged villagers were acutely conscious of its arbitrary impact on their class.

The Viet Cong Labor Exchange The labor policy of the Viet Cong was designed to improve the position of the laborers and small-scale tenant farmers. Slogans such as that embodied in the "Sharing One's Food and Clothing Campaign" were often used, but no specific program carried the collective principle of the ideology as far as that of the "work-exchange team" or the "labor-exchange association." These "teams" were designed to encourage farmers to work together on projects such as ditch cleaning, instead of working as individuals hiring labor from one another. Partly because of the labor shortage conditions of 1965, Viet Cong political cadres urged farmers to employ work-exchange teams to save scarce labor. Their success was limited because laborers were reluctant to work in large groups; they feared being treated as a Viet Cong unit by overflying aircraft. By 1966 the labor shortage had become so severe in Viet Cong areas that local guerrillas were ordered to join exchange teams and assist in farm work.

In Hoi Cu village in 1958–1959 the labor-exchange association took on a major political role.[11] It was used by the Viet Cong to organize and commit the "very poor farmers" (laborers), "poor farmers" (small-scale tenants), and "middle farmers" to the Viet Cong program and to isolate and pressure the "rich farmers" and "landlords" into either leaving the village or joining the Viet Cong.

Under the rules of the association, if a member wished to pay another member for labor services performed instead of returning the obligation in kind, he could do so by paying wages at a rate set by the association. In this exchange, landlords and rich farmers were discriminated against in three ways. First, to join the association, one had to be willing to work; that is, one could never pay for all of the labor he received and return none of it in kind. Second, those admitted from the rich farmer and landlord classes were required to pay for labor at a rate 60 percent above that paid by the very poor, poor, or middle farmers. Third, if a landlord or rich farmer did succeed in gaining admission to the association by agreeing to accept these rules, the Viet Cong who controlled it and allocated work tasks and requests ensured that those members were asked to perform only the most undesirable types of work, for example, cleaning irrigation ditches. Using this organization, the Viet Cong in Hoi Cu village denied the labor resources of the village to those they found unacceptable and forced them to leave the village, eventually acquiring complete political control.

THE LABOR SHORTAGE AND REAL WAGE RATES

There is no better example of how the confluence of economic, political, and military developments of the 1960–1966 period affected the economic welfare of the rural inhabitant, particularly the welfare of certain economic and social classes, than that of the harvest wage.

The harvest wage was paid in kind to the laborer. It was the most important single source of income for the rural laborer and was fixed as

[11] I am indebted to Mr. David Elliott of the RAND Corporation for this information, which he obtained from interviews with Viet Cong prisoners and defectors.

a share of the crop harvested by the worker. In the 1950s this share was one-eleventh to one-twelfth of the crop,[12] meaning in the latter case that for every 24 gia of paddy harvested, the worker took home 2 gia, or 40 kilograms. By 1966, however, the average wage had risen to one-sixth, and large-scale rice farmers were paying up to 20 percent of their crops as an in-kind harvest wage.[13]

This wage change took place despite the fact that the price of paddy had moved close to parity with other rural prices over the period. It is noteworthy that the change in the harvest wage rate took place in 1960 and 1961 before the general inflation and labor shortage of the post-1964 period. There could be no economic justification for this sudden increase, but a political explanation was forthcoming.

Farmers and laborers recalled that in 1960 the Viet Cong began to encourage workers to seek higher wages and pressured those hiring workers accordingly. In 1960 in Long An village, south of TCN, only a small portion of which was under GVN control, the Viet Cong instituted the one-sixth harvest wage rate, which appears to have come into effect in TCN and LBD at that time or soon thereafter.

By 1966 the economic changes already discussed had almost validated this wage increase. It took approximately 22 man-days to harvest one hectare of land yielding a total of 2,000 kilograms, or 91 kilograms per man-day. In 1966 prices (10 piasters per kilogram of paddy) the money wage equivalent at the one-sixth rate was 152 piasters per man-day. A task of comparable difficulty was that of cleaning drainage ditches, for which in late 1966 workers received 130 piasters a day. This wage rate was identical with the one-seventh harvest wage rate received by the harvester for a good crop on a nearby field.[14] We conclude, therefore, that the Viet Cong in the early 1960s, employing the political technique of a minimum wage, had done what the Vietnamese government accomplished by 1966 with the help of massive American economic assistance.

[12] The farmers cited the 1/11 and 1/12 rates for the 1950s. Hendry's 1958/59 finding was 1/11 (see *Small World of Khanh Hau*, p. 76).
[13] The following harvest wage rates were in effect in 1966: for a poor crop (difficult to harvest) on a distant (3–5 km) field (transportation to farmer's home plot was provided by the laborer), 1/4 to 1/5; for a normal crop at an average distance (1–2 km), 1/5.5; for a good crop on a distant field, 1/6; and for a good crop on a nearby field, 1/7.
[14] See previous footnote.

Labor Supply, Labor Policies, and Wages

For the sample, rice farming provided 36 percent of the income earned, vegetables 35 percent, and nonfarm wages (mostly from part-time government civilian and military employment) 10 percent. Alternative occupations to farming were agricultural labor, urban unskilled work in nearby towns, work in the local transportation industry, and selling vegetables or fish. Entry into these occupations, including vegetable farming, was relatively free, with the exception of rice farming, for which land was not readily available.

In Table 6.1, Part (a), comparisons are made among a list of income opportunities. (For rice and vegetable farming, the results are from the sample data; information on nonfarm incomes was obtained from separate inquiries.) The method of computation assumes that only the household head and his wife can earn off-farm income. For example, a male agricultural laborer in 1966 could work 250 days and a female 120 days at the indicated wage rates. A rice farmer on 2 hectares earned a net income of 25,000 piasters from rice cultivation and had the opportunity to earn an additional 22,600 piasters from his own and 9,600 piasters from his wife's labor at outside employment.

Table 6.1 demonstrates that the aspirations of most villagers to become rice farmers had an economic justification. However, note the high income of agricultural laborers, a reflection of the labor market conditions already described. Those occupations for which laborers had ready access, such as vegetable farming and urban unskilled work, show a not unexpected similarity in income levels. In fact, most vegetable farmers came from the laboring class or were refugees having only that alternative.

The real income level represented by these incomes can be readily calculated by using the 1966 paddy price average of 10 piasters per kilo. For example, the family supported by a farm laborer had a real income of 3,460 kilograms of paddy, which represents 450 kilograms per capita for a family of average household size (7.7 members). Considering that the subsistence minimum per capita is around 240–300 kilograms, these results reflect the relatively high level of 1966 incomes.

In Part (b) of Table 6.1 the calculations are tabulated on the basis of pre-1960 conditions of employment and rent. These figures reflect the higher rents paid in the earlier period and the conditions of labor abundance before 1965, when a laborer worked only 150 days a year compared

TABLE 6.1 Family Earnings, by Occupation

Category	Income from Primary Source (V$N)	Income as Hired Laborer						Total Earnings (V$N)[a]
		Male			Female			
		Days	Wage (V$N)	Total (V$N)	Days	Wage (V$N)	Total (V$N)	
Part (a): 1966								
Agricultural laborer	n.a.	250	100	25,000	120	80	9,600	34,600
Rice farmer (1 ha)[b]	13,000 per yr	229	100	22,900	120	80	9,600	45,600
Rice farmer (2 ha)[b]	25,000 per yr	226	100	22,600	120	80	9,600	57,200
Vegetable farmer (0.2 ha)	24,000 per yr	80	100	8,000				32,000
Urban worker	n.a.	300	110	33,000				33,000
Cyclo-driver	3,000 per mo for 10 mo							30,000
Fish merchant	4,000 per mo for 10 mo							40,000
Mason (My Tho)	5,000 per mo for 10 mo							50,000
Mechanic (rural)	53,000 per yr							53,000
Village militia	2,200 per mo							26,400
Public works employee	3,200 per mo							38,400
Village official	3,500 per mo							42,000
Village chief	4,000 per mo							48,000
Part (b): At 1966 Prices and Wages under pre-1960 Conditions[c]								
Agricultural laborer	n.a.	150	100	15,000	10	80	800	15,800
Rice farmer (1 ha)[d]	10,000 per yr	129	100	12,900	8	80	640	23,540
Rice farmer (2 ha)[d]	19,000 per yr	126	100	12,600				31,600

a For conversion to real terms use paddy price of V$N 10 per kg. c Work available: 150 man-days per year.
b At 10% rent. d At 25% rent.

with 250 days in 1966. These adjustments drop the real per capita income (at 1966 wages and prices) for the 1958 average family size to 2,870 piasters, which represents 287 kilograms of paddy, or an income in the subsistence range. Therefore, we see again that pre-1960 economic conditions were much worse than those prevailing in 1966.

Disguised Unemployment

Few issues have dominated recent literature on economic development as has the debate over disguised unemployment; the largest portion of the literature on this subject examines the intersectoral implications of its existence or nonexistence. From the early contributions of W. Arthur Lewis and Ragnar Nurkse to later ones by Enke, Ranis and Fei, and Jorgenson, much theoretical effort has been devoted to the economic implications of an abundant labor supply available to the industrial sector at a low and often constant wage.[15] Typically these studies have rested on as yet empirically meaningless assumptions—for example, the "dualistic landlord" or the tautological assumption that there is little scope for increasing agricultural productivity in the rural sector—that in turn have on occasion been accepted at face value and used as the justification for import substitution policies and export taxes on agricultural commodities in countries like Argentina.

Unfortunately, the major portion of the empirical work available gives little direct attention either to the landlord-organizational question or to the question of agricultural opportunities for technology. Theoretically, the former question has been constructively approached by Mathur, the latter by Eckaus, and both by Eckaus again.[16] Yet empirically, except for

[15] W. Arthur Lewis, "Economic Development with Unlimited Supplies of Labour," *Manchester School*, vol. n.s. XXII (May 1954), pp. 139–191; Ragnar Nurkse, *Problems of Capital Formation in Underdeveloped Countries* (London: Oxford University Press, 1963); S. Enke, "Economic Development with Unlimited and Limited Supplies of Labour," *Oxford Economic Papers*, vol. n.s. 14 (June 1962), pp. 158–172; John C. H. Fei and Gustav Ranis, *Development of the Labor Surplus Economy: Theory and Policy* (New Haven, Conn.: Yale University Press, 1964); and Dale W. Jorgenson, "Surplus Agricultural Labor and the Development of a Dual Economy," *Oxford Economic Papers*, vol. n.s. 19 (November 1967), pp. 288–312.

[16] Ashok Mathur, "The Anatomy of Disguised Unemployment," *Oxford Economic Papers*, vol. n.s. 16 (July 1964), pp. 161–193; R. S. Eckaus, "The Factor Proportions Problem in Underdeveloped Areas," *American Economic Review*, vol. XLV, no. 4 (September 1955), pp. 539–565; and idem, "Notes on Invention and Innovation in Less Developed Countries," ibid., vol. LVI, no. 3 (May 1966), pp. 98–109.

the recent closely reasoned contribution by Paglin, only the sector-wide manpower supply and demand studies of Rosenstein-Rodan for Southern Italy, Cho for Korea, and Pepelasis and Yotopoulos for Greece, with their necessarily inconclusive dynamic and microeconomic implications, are available.[17]

THE CETERIS PARIBUS CLAUSE

We have examined the withdrawal of a large portion of the working population from the rural economy over the 1965–1966 period, a withdrawal resulting from population movements to urban areas to gain more advantageous employment, and from the drafting of large numbers of workers from the rural labor force for both local and nonlocal military use.[18]

Because of the sudden yet orderly nature of this change, Vietnamese conditions are particularly suited for an examination of the *ceteris paribus* clause commonly associated with the disguised unemployment issue. That is, if disguised unemployment exists, to prove its existence those who support the null-hypothesis (that disguised unemployment does not exist) insist it be shown that a withdrawal of a portion of the labor supply can take place without a fall in agricultural production. Most demand a strict formulation of the hypothesis, a formulation requiring that the withdrawal take place unaccompanied by technological change. Organizational changes are permitted, but the strict formulation is commonly seen to prohibit the introduction of capital-intensive, labor-saving devices, for example, tractors, into the rural sector.

The *ceteris paribus* clause is instructive in the usually accepted sense because it is intended to focus attention on the cost of maintaining

[17] Morton Paglin, " 'Surplus' Agricultural Labor and Development: Facts and Theories," ibid., vol. LV, no. 4 (September 1965), pp. 815–833; P. N. Rosenstein-Rodan, "Disguised Unemployment and Underemployment in Agriculture," *Monthly Bulletin of Agricultural Economics and Statistics*, vol. VI, July/August 1957, pp. 1–7; Yong Sam Cho, *"Disguised Unemployment" in Underdeveloped Areas* (Berkeley and Los Angeles: University of California Press, 1963); and Adam A. Pepelasis and Pan A Yotopoulos, *Surplus Labour in Greek Agriculture, 1953–1960* (Athens, 1962).

[18] The movements in two of the major exogenous determinants of this change are seen in the following statistics. In 1961 the Vietnamese army numbered 170,000; in 1963, 210,000; in late 1964, 250,000; and in late 1966, 650,000. U.S. forces in December 1964 numbered 23,000; in December 1966 they numbered 350,000. Viet Cong force levels probably increased in proportion to these changes in GVN and U.S. force levels.

production at old levels with new, more capital-intensive techniques, a cost that presumably must be weighed against the benefit of employing the withdrawn labor force outside the rural sector. If, however, this strict formulation of the hypothesis is intended to imply that no organizational or relatively costless technique or technological changes can take place, then it has hardly any useful theoretical or policy implications. For the basic issue is how quickly and at what cost the resources available in the rural sector, after a withdrawal of a portion of the labor force, can be reallocated to obtain a new level of production comparable with that before withdrawal.

The resolution of the foregoing issues involves three basic considerations. First, what changes in the organization of the labor force will take place to reallocate the tasks presumably performed before withdrawal on a shared basis between the residual and withdrawn workers? Involved here are changes in techniques that may conflict with long-established habits and customs and might be opposed by social inertia. Also relevant are considerations related to the potential emergence of a backward-sloping supply curve of effort. If, before withdrawal, the withdrawn workers had pushed techniques far out to the more labor-intensive portion of the production function, obtaining a diminishing but still positive marginal return because they were motivated by a desire to meet basic subsistence needs, the absence of this motivation among the residual labor force would lead to the application of a lesser amount of labor, reflecting the diminishing marginal utility of additional income at above subsistence levels. This condition would give a lower total product for the rural sector after withdrawal.

Second, the institutions of tenancy are important in that they must adapt to the changing economic conditions; evidence of nonadaptability would contribute to landlord dualism arguments because landlords are generally seen to oppose—for often unclear albeit presumably noneconomic reasons—the most "economical" allocation of the rural sector's resources.

Third, what changes in technique or technology will emerge from within the rural sector in a short period (one or two years), and will they permit production to reestablish itself at prewithdrawal levels? This is potentially the key issue, one often neglected in the debate. It must be assumed that the marketing system is not poised to deliver new tools and machines borrowed from outside sources (for example, Japan), which can replace the departed labor. Further, if a native technology is to emerge, it can be seen only as the product of the prewithdrawal store of knowledge or the immediate response of native thinking to the new conditions, unaided by elaborate research and extension facilities.

THE EVIDENCE

The Seasonal Demand for Labor The outstanding characteristic of prewithdrawal (before 1965) conditions in the labor market in the Mekong Delta was the seasonality of the demand for labor (see Figure 6.3). Pre-1965 conditions show clearly delineated peaks in the demand for labor during the transplanting and harvesting periods. Under post-1964 conditions, the peaks in demand were spread over a longer period. If the null-hypothesis is to be rejected and we are to conclude that disguised unemployment does exist, then it must be shown that, within the *ceteris paribus* conditions just described, the postwithdrawal rural labor force of L_1 produced as much as or more than the prewithdrawal labor force of L_2.

After 1964 the available labor force was fully employed at L_1. If it can be shown that the pre-1965 labor force was at level L_2 and that production in the postwithdrawal period did not decline, then the hypothesis that disguised unemployment did exist in the earlier period can be

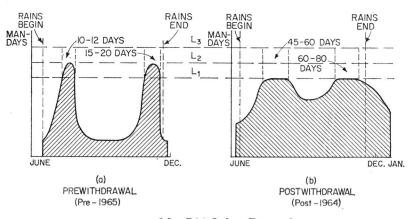

(a)
PREWITHDRAWAL
(Pre-1965)

(b)
POSTWITHDRAWAL
(Post-1964)

FIGURE 6.3 Rice-Labor Demand

accepted. (Labor force level L_3 is not directly relevant to the discussion to follow, although it may describe pre-1965 conditions—if open unemployment existed even at periods of peak demand.)

The preceding schedules apply to the rural rice sector and not to an individual household plot. The area under the curves represents mandays of labor employed in rice production. Both before and after 1965, other work was available during the unoccupied periods, although under pre-1965 conditions such other work consisted of collecting wood for sale, fishing, and cultivating low-yielding root crops. Many farmers did nothing during the off-season. The income accruing to these enterprises or the disutility of a day's work was only marginally below that paid to a daily-wage worker before 1965. That is, the daily wage at peak rice-labor demand was the same as that at nonpeak periods and was only that necessary to draw the needed laborers from alternative employment opportunities. Farmers recalled that even at the peak periods an unlimited supply of labor was available at a constant wage rate; therefore, the prewithdrawal force level was probably L_3.

There were three reasons for the peaked demand cycle for rice labor. First, for the large-scale operators common under pre-1960 conditions, it was profitable to limit the recruitment and supervision costs associated with rice cultivation using hired labor. If such labor was performed in a short period by many workers using mass working techniques, the management task was simplified as opposed to the piecemeal performance of these operations. Second, the availability of water constrained labor demand within certain periods: Planting could not begin before the monsoon arrived, and harvesting took place as the monsoon ended. Third, there were economies of scale, not only in the organization of labor but also in the application of capital-intensive techniques, such as buffalo transport for rice seedlings. The cultivation of a small area required transportation services on a scale that would not fully occupy a buffalo, and even at the low pre-1965 wages the buffalo was a cheaper means of transport than the available supply of human labor.

Hired Labor and Family Labor: The Labor Mix   Table 6.2 contains data on the labor requirements on various-sized plots of rice land. Labor costs are divided into two categories: hired, and hired or family. Hired labor costs are those incurred in the form of a constant cash outlay per

TABLE 6.2 Labor Requirements[a]

Task	Date	Plot Size (ha)													
		0.5		1.0		1.5		2.0		3.0		4.0		5.0	
		Family	Total	Family	Total	Family	Total	Family	Total	Family	Total	Family	Total	Family	Total
Hired labor only															
1. Plowing seedbed (man-days)	June		½		1		1		2		3		4		5
2. Plowing rice field (man-days)	July		4½		9		13½		18		27		36		45
Hired or family labor															
3. Seedbed preparation (man-days)	June	1	1	2	2	3	3	4	4	4	6	5	8	6	10
4. Rice field preparation (man-days)	July	1	1	2	2	3	3	4	4	5	6	6	8	7	10
5. Seedling pickup (man-days)	Aug.	2	4	2	8	2	12	2	16	2	24	2	32	2	40
6. Seedling transplant (woman-days)	Aug.	2	5½	2	13	2	18½	2	26	2	39	2	52	2	65
7. Weeding, thinning, drying of harvested crop (woman-days)	Aug.–Dec.	3	3	6	6	9	9	12	12	18	18	22	22	26	26
8. Fertilizer application (man- or woman-days)	Sept.–Nov.	1	1	2	2	3	3	4	4	6	6	7	7	8	8

TABLE 6.2 continued

| | | Plot Size (ha) | | | | | | | | | | | | |
| | | 0.5 | | 1.0 | | 1.5 | | 2.0 | | 3.0 | | 4.0 | | 5.0 | |
Task	Date	Family	Total	Family	Total	Family	Total	Family	Total	Family	Total	Family	Total	Family	Total
9. Reaping (man- or woman-days)	Dec.	2	5	2	10	2	15	2	20	2	30	2	40	2	50
10. Threshing (man-days)	Dec.	2	5	2	10	2	15	2	20	2	30	2	40	2	50
11. Transportation (man-days)	Dec.	1	1	1	2	1	3	1	4	1	6	1	8	1	10
Total (days)		15	26.5	21	55	27	81.5	33	110	42	165	49	217	56	269
Percent family (or hired) labor		58	(42)	38	(62)	33	(67)	30	(70)	26	(74)	22	(78)	20	(80)

a For plots farmed in a single crop on a single cycle.

141

hectare and for which family labor cannot be substituted. For the case at hand these include the plowing and harrowing requirement of ten days per hectare. The table is based on data from a subsample of 40 farmers of average household size (3.0–4.5 manpower)[19] operating on various-sized farm plots. The final row of the table shows that while the total labor requirement increases linearly with the size of the plot farmed, the family contribution declines rapidly at first, then diminishes less rapidly as the size of the plot increases. This decline in the family's contribution as well as its inability to perform all the work on even a small plot is the result of the seasonality in the rice production requirements for labor. The two peak activities (tasks 5, 6, 9, 10, 11) of transplanting and harvesting are responsible for the sector-wide peaks in labor demand seen in Figure 6.3).

All farmers contributed family labor to rice-growing activities. Any owner not wishing to participate in farming activities rented his land, becoming a landlord. Tenants considered it unprofitable to rely entirely on hired labor.

The Declining Efficiency of the Large Plot The effect of the labor shortage on the financial returns to family farm operations on various-sized plots is seen by contrasting the pre- and postwithdrawal diagrams of Figure 6.4. Each diagram represents the financial results obtainable by a family of average size. (The curves represent costs and revenues, not real inputs and responses.) The outstanding difference between these two periods—the different costs of labor—is reflected in the shapes of the variable labor cost (VLC) functions, which in turn, because of the similar fixed cost (FC) curves, determine the different total cost (TC) curves.[20]

We see from Figure 6.4 that changed labor costs were responsible for the different sizes of the optimum plots in the two periods. In the

[19] Manpower of 3.0–4.5, determined on the basis of the following weights: males 16–20 years old, 1.0; females 10–70, 0.5; and males 10–15 and above 60, 0.5. Family members employed outside the household were given a weight according to their availability for family work, for example, a village guard, 0.5, and a fish merchant or village office employee, 0.

[20] The indicated costs are those paid by the household, usually in cash, for non-household sources of capital and labor. It is for this reason that the TC curve for the farmer is identical to the FC curve until the plot size reaches the size at which labor is first hired.

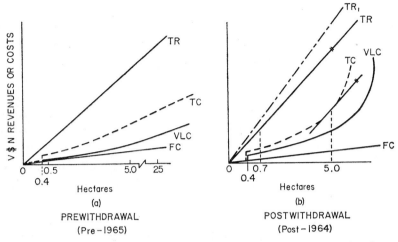

FIGURE 6.4 The Effect of the Labor Shortage on Efficient Plot Size

earlier period, profits continued to increase as the size of the plot farmed increased; there was no optimum-size plot, only the nonoptimum 0.4 to 0.5 hectare plot dictated by economic conditions. (In Figure 6.4, the optimum plot size is determined by the point at which a straight line tangent to the total cost TC curve is parallel to the total revenue TR curve.) During this period, as we have seen, demographic and landownership conditions determined the size of the plot cultivated. In the postwithdrawal period, there was an economic optimum of limited size and a wider nonoptimum range for the small holder (0.4 to 0.7 hectare).[21] No farmholdings outside the optimum range were found in 1966–1967. Moreover, there was evidence that farmers were aware of the unprofitability of large holdings. For example, one farmer who hired 180 man-days of labor in 1966 on his 3.8 hectares of one-crop land said he did not want any more land because "more hired labor would make the cultivation of more land unprofitable."

[21] Problems of recruitment and supervision explain the discontinuity of the VLC and TC curves in the 0.4-hectare range. In this range the average family first began to rely on hired labor; the precise point varied with the family's exact size. As Figure 6.4 shows, it also varied between the pre-1965 and post-1964 periods; the higher recruitment costs in the later period account for the more marked discontinuity and greater nonoptimum range (0.4 to 0.5 ha versus 0.4 to 0.7 ha) under postwithdrawal conditions.

A brief recapitulation may help clarify how the labor shortage produced these divergent results. Before withdrawal, the farmer on a large plot had no problem obtaining the necessary labor to meet peak-season demand, even if he needed 50 man-days each for a period of only two days at transplanting time and harvesttime. He contacted a labor contractor who, having been approached by workers seeking employment, provided the necessary supply of labor at a constant wage.

After withdrawal, even small-scale farmers complained of the non-availability of labor. One remarked that "the labor shortage is severe; even with money I cannot hire labor." Another said, "hired labor makes the exploitation of land unprofitable." In short, hired labor was not available in large quantities because it was otherwise employed and could be obtained only by *increasing the wage offered* to draw larger numbers of workers from other attractive and often steady employment opportunities. (Not only did an increasing wage have to be paid to hire larger quantities of labor but those hiring labor had to bear recruitment costs and supervision burdens less advantageous than in the period when workers were anxious for work and reluctant to risk the displeasure of a labor contractor or hiring farmer.)

Additional Evidence Conditions of labor shortage prompted two adjustments on the part of those employing hired labor. First, there was an incentive to attempt to adjust cultivation dates and varieties used so that the periods of peak demand on a field coincided with off-peak conditions for the sector as a whole. Off-peak wages rose less rapidly from lower levels than peak wages as additional man-days were hired. Second, farmers who could make the necessary irrigation adjustments and plant the appropriate varieties began farming their fields piecemeal, cultivating a single crop on the entire field but farming it in two portions, one with an early-maturing variety and the other with a late-maturing variety. They began to explore the margins of cultivation for their fields, seeking new rice varieties and means of irrigation, with the result that for the rural sector as a whole the seasonal peaks of labor demand were lowered and broadened.

For example, in 1967 one farmer, an owner of 2.4 hectares of one-crop land, planted her land in two stages, using an early-maturing variety on 1.4 hectares and a late-maturing one on 1 hectare. She explained her decision by saying, "This mixture of varieties is intended to avoid failure in getting enough labor on the rush days of the harvesting season." Such a decision involved greater managerial effort, higher labor recruitment costs, and more supervisory effort than were necessary under prewithdrawal conditions, when the entire holding of 2.4 hectares was farmed as a single operation in a single crop. This example suggests that important dynamic inducements to production innovations may come from changed labor conditions; these inducements would have some bearing on the disguised unemployment debate.

It is also evident from the preceding example that the rice farmer was concerned with two types of labor: labor for the management of all resources applied to the plot, and labor to provide additional man-days of labor input. In his article on this issue, Morton Paglin, using Indian data, has examined the possibility that low opportunity cost family labor is responsible for his finding that farmers of smaller plots obtained higher yields.[22] Paglin concludes that the importance of family labor arises from the fact that it leads to a more generous application of labor per land area on small family-farmed plots than on large farms that use hired labor.

Although Paglin's results are similar to those arrived at here, there are important differences. His information was based on surveys made in the 1950s, when the conditions of the Indian economy were similar to pre-1964 Mekong Delta conditions, particularly with respect to the price and availability of labor. Also, Paglin found a much greater variation in the size of farmed holdings (holdings of over 4 hectares were common) than was found in Vietnam.

Paglin's findings show that cultivators on smaller holdings used larger quantities of labor and capital inputs per hectare than farmers on larger holdings, who frequently used only hired labor. He suggests that large farmers prefer "the low-effort, low-risk, low-output package to the higher-risk, higher-profit, higher-output combination."[23] He

---

[22] See Paglin, " 'Surplus' Agricultural Labor and Development"; also "Comment" and "Reply" in American Economic Review, vol. LVII, no. 2 (March 1967), pp. 194–207 and 202–209, respectively. John W. Mellor has made the same point in "The Use and Productivity of Farm Family Labor in the Early Stages of Agricultural Development," Journal of Farm Economics, vol. 45 (August 1963), pp. 517–533.
[23] Paglin, " 'Surplus' Agricultural Labor and Development," p. 828.

maintains that, due to the cash risks of crop failure, large owners are reluctant to borrow funds to purchase hired inputs; being at higher income levels, they do not value additional income increments as highly as small farmers near the subsistence level; and they do not have available to them the low opportunity cost supplies of family labor available to small holders.

In an economy offering alternative employment like the 1966–1967 Delta economy, Paglin's first explanation does not apply, since the farmer on the small plot weighed the same risks of crop failure in contemplating an additional day of work on his own land as opposed to hiring himself out for that day. The second explanation, relying on differing marginal utilities of income, is plausible and consistent with results obtained in this study and will be discussed in the next section. More convincing is his argument that the farmer on the smaller plot has labor available on which he can rely at a low opportunity cost; that is, even under labor-shortage conditions, such labor may not have outside employment opportunities. But here Paglin's results need more careful interpretation.

In his article Paglin fits a linear regression relating inputs per acre and outputs per acre and finds that those farmers using more inputs per acre were operating in a profitable range (above the 45-degree line).[24] He then breaks down the data on inputs by size of farmholding and finds that the small farms use more inputs per acre than large farms: hence the conclusions just discussed. Unfortunately, Paglin's method is misleading because, in a rice economy, production analysis based on inputs per hectare of land *area farmed* (which he uses) as opposed to inputs per hectare of *area cultivated* can lead to ambiguous conclusions. Paglin's results do not provide any basis for concluding, as he does, that smaller farmers were farther out on the production function using low opportunity cost inputs; they may have been on a different production function using different techniques. This conclusion would follow if small cultivators were employing different techniques of production that allowed them to multiple-crop their smaller land area. If the latter conclusion is tenable, then it must be determined why such techniques were not employed on large farms,

[24] Ibid., p. 820.

a determination that may have some relevance to the findings on the Mekong Delta economy.

AN ALTERNATIVE EXPLANATION: THE DUAL ROLE
OF FAMILY LABOR—AS A MANAGEMENT AND AS A LABOR INPUT

An alternative explanation for Paglin's results as well as for the decline in the efficiency of the large holding in Vietnam after 1964 derives from the fact that the family is an efficiently organized and managed economic unit operating at a small scale (at a larger scale it may become inefficient). In Vietnam and in India the productivity gains obtained by the large-scale farmer hiring labor piecemeal would have been lower than the productivity of the same labor working in the family unit. That is, to hire and apply the same number of labor-input hours per hectare as a small farmer applied using family labor, the large-scale farmer had to anticipate a higher product return per man-hour because these hours would be less efficiently applied and supervised than the equivalent hours on a family-managed small plot. This follows because the large-plot farmers could not hire labor in the less than single-day units in which it was used on small plots; they had to bear recruitment costs not relevant to family-applied labor; and they could not direct the hired labor as efficiently as self-directing family labor was directed, because, for example, the child obeys its parents and the family is familiar with its plot, tools, and tasks.[25]

In short, the large-scale farmer failed to employ more labor per hectare not because of the risks of crop failure, nor (possibly) because the additional income held less utility for him, but because he did not have the *low-cost, high-yield* option of applying labor that was available to the family-plot farmer. Moreover, this higher efficiency of the small plot arose not solely from its utilization of labor but primarily from its use of all resources, including irrigation opportunities and varietal options in a more efficient "package" than the large-scale operator could employ over a wider area.

Two examples may help to clarify this finding. One large-scale

[25] Mellor arrived at conclusions similar to these, saying, "In the case of hiring additional labor, the problems of supervision of a hired labor force provide a disutility in themselves as well as lessening the returns through inefficiencies in the labor force" (see "Use and Productivity of Farm Family Labor," p. 521).

farmer—a widow cultivating 5 hectares of two-crop land—before 1962 farmed only one crop despite the fact that water was available for two crops. After 1962, when her children had grown to an age (sons 19 and 13) at which they could assist in the supervision of additional hired labor, double-cropping began on the larger area to which the family's management resources were suited. At the other extreme of this life cycle, a 56-year-old farmer, who in 1966 farmed 1.5 hectares as a first crop and 4 hectares as a second crop, employing 80 man-days of hired labor, farmed only 4 hectares in a single crop in 1967 because "no home labor is available for the supervision of the additional hired labor necessary to farm two crops; my wife and I are old, and 4 hectares is enough to keep us busy [as managers] all year." This important role for managerial labor is implicit in one farmer's representative view of hired labor: "Hired labor needs more supervision, lacks initiative, and cannot solve its own problems."

OTHER FACTORS

The influence of rents, fertilizer use, plowing costs, and irrigation costs on the optimum-size plot can be seen by returning again to Figure 6.4. Any increase in the fixed costs per hectare, for example, plowing, irrigation, or fertilizer price increases, lowered the optimum plot size by raising the FC curve. But the use of fertilizer as opposed to its nonuse would raise the optimum through its effect on the TR curve, moving it to TR_1. Lower rents can be seen as either raising the TR curve or lowering the FC curve, either of which would raise the optimum plot size. Conversely, higher rents per hectare would decrease the optimum plot size.

Conclusions

In 1960 the Viet Cong began to chip away at the advantages of large-scale tenant cultivation by, for example, persuading workers not to work for large-scale farmers. More importantly, the Viet Cong prohibited large-scale farming and reallocated plots accordingly. That the war-caused labor shortage conditions of early 1965 dictated the same small-plot solution was merely coincidental but also of great potential political importance (see Chapter 12). From this probably unprecedented set of developments, we gain valuable insights into the issues of the disguised unemployment debate and into the broader structuralist controversy.

These results lead us to accept the disguised unemployment hypothesis; for in fact, a withdrawal of the labor force was not followed by a decline in rural production. The prewithdrawal labor force is most appropriately seen as that indicated by level L_2 in Figure 6.3, although the results are not inconsistent with its being at level L_3. Assuming that it was at L_2 before 1964, there was marked seasonal unemployment in the rural sector, whereas after 1964 there was little seasonal unemployment. On the basis of the accompanying adjustments in techniques and management, the *ceteris paribus* clause was not violated by injections of nonnative technology. Native skills kept production at prewithdrawal levels because yields were at or above 2.0 metric tons per hectare cultivated, placing them above prewithdrawal levels; because improved plot management allowed more land to be *cultivated* (there was more double-cropping); and because in the areas studied no land was removed from production. On the basis of these results, the disguised unemployment hypothesis is accepted. (In Chapter 8 a major, though still indigenous, technological development is discussed, which allowed *further* increases in production, often 20 to 30 percent above those discussed here.)

The wider implications of the acceptance of the disguised unemployment hypothesis must be stated with caution. This is evident in the lower Delta, where the reallocation of land prompted by the same political and economic changes evident in the upper Delta produced altogether different results. In the lower Delta higher labor costs on all the land in cultivation before 1965 could not be offset by a reorganization of the rural population on smaller plots. As labor withdrew, production declined. The explanation for this different response is that irrigation and varietal—in short, technological—conditions in the lower Delta were not conducive to expanded production on smaller family-operated plots. The lower Delta experience suggests that a useful application of the *ceteris paribus* clause to the disguised unemployment hypothesis will lead those who wish to argue the production (as opposed to the distribution) merits of withdrawal for any particular economy to look closely at the prevailing *technological* conditions in the rural sector.[26] It also suggests that there is no general case for either position in the disguised unemployment debate.

In these political and economic events and their economic results we find evidence to support both the institutional and market views of development. No doubt in any traditional Asian economy the withdrawal of a portion of the rural work force will raise the income of the residual population. And if technological and physical conditions are permissive, as they were in the upper Delta, production may even increase. The market solution *does* work. But it will not have wide application unless nonrural jobs can be created on a massive scale, and this seems unlikely. Therefore, the benefits of organizational change stressed by the institutionalists acquire significance not only because the available rural product is redistributed but also because these changes broaden the range of opportunities for increased production, providing dynamic inducements to further innovation, and utilize the productivity of the well-managed family production unit. The succeeding three chapters discuss the remarkable multiplied production benefits of these structural reforms.

[26] Prewithdrawal *institutional* conditions are not relevant to the argument at this point. This conclusion follows from the fact that the economic conditions arising from the higher price of labor in effect validated some of the economic effects of the political and social reforms of the Viet Cong. Without these Viet Cong efforts, similar but less substantial economic results would have followed had the labor been withdrawn. For a specific example of similar results without the preceding unrest, see Margaret Haswell's study of Gangaikondan village in India, where she found that new opportunities for urban employment for village residents caused rents and land values to decline (M. R. Haswell, *The Economics of Development in Village India* [London: Routledge & Kegan Paul, 1967], chap. 6), but since immediate technological conditions were not conducive to higher yields on smaller plots, her findings are similar to those found in the lower Delta in South Vietnam between 1964 and 1967; that is, production did not increase, yet rural wages rose.

7 Irrigation

Introduction

In the preceding chapters the following disequilibrating economic developments were noted: (1) the post–World War II development of new rice varieties that, combined with an increased use of fertilizers in the 1950s, allowed double-cropping on fields previously only single-cropped; (2) the development of garden vegetable cultivation as a major economic activity; (3) the availability of abundant supplies of capital at low interest rates; (4) the eclipse of traditional conditions of abundant labor by those of labor shortage; (5) the farmers' recently gained access to more proximate markets and low-cost transport; and (6) a changed institutional environment resulting in lower rents and a diminished presence of landlords, but nonetheless characterized by a limited mobility of land among both owners and tenants and a still short supply of land.

Not surprisingly, these conditions precipitated major economic changes in the villages studied. In any rice economy there are three primary means by which rural output can be increased: organizational changes that utilize the available factors more efficiently, improved irrigation of the land (in effect increasing the supply of land), and increasing yields by additional applications of fertilizer (in effect substituting capital for land). We have already studied the organizational changes precipitated by the Viet Cong. This and the following chapter will examine the irrigation developments in the villages studied.

Before 1960 and dating from the arrival of the French, the major water problem in the Delta was drainage, not irrigation. We saw in Chapter 2 how canals dredged by the French drained off excess monsoon rains into the Mekong River and the nearby South China Sea and allowed one-crop rice cultivation throughout the Delta. But in recognition of the limited irrigation function of the resulting canal system, Robequain wrote in the late 1930s, "Actually these water level changes [the tides] as yet benefit only a small number of rice plantations located along the main canals." He concluded, "Most of the rice plantations in Cochin China are not really irrigated."[1]

There was, however, a great potential in the Delta for the development of irrigation systems. The crop season was limited by the monsoon period—in effect from July to December—but there was no physical reason why the growing season could not be lengthened from six months of the year to eleven or twelve months. This was a possibility because the Mekong River is a year-round source of fresh water. The Mekong's mean water level—determined by tidal pressures from the South China Sea—is one or two meters below ground level, and at high tide throughout the year these waters are raised an additional 1.0 to 1.5 meters, to within a meter of most upper Delta fields.[2] In short, the water problem was not one of water availability but of water movement. First, irrigation canals had to be excavated so that the tide could move the Mekong's waters into a position adjacent to and usually within a meter's elevation of the upper Delta fields. Second, the water had to be raised the final one-half to one meter to the field, where it would be available for rice or vegetable cultivation. Before 1962, man-powered (by foot pedal) waterwheels were used in the fields but only as a means of water level adjustment between fields. For the accomplishment of the crucial second task, these devices proved inadequate: They did not permit water to be raised more than one-half meter, thus limiting their use to the lowest fields.

---

[1] Charles Robequain, *The Economic Development of French Indo-China*, trans. I. A. Wood (London and New York: Oxford University Press, 1944), p. 221.

[2] These favorable conditions applied to approximately 100,000 ha in Dinh Tuong Province and an additional 400,000 ha in the upper Delta region. Saltwater intrusion was a problem in provinces bordering the South China Sea, like Go Cong (see map, Figure 1.2), but was not a problem in provinces with conditions similar to those in Dinh Tuong. In the lower Delta, natural water conditions were less advantageous because the area was not traversed by the Mekong River or its tributaries.

A Framework for the Analysis

This chapter analyzes the developments of the 1962–1966 period that led to a solution of the two problems outlined. The changes involved were of a social, economic, and technological nature and are best examined in the following framework. For each change there is first the question of motivation. In nearly every case, the precipitating event was a drought. A shortage of water would threaten the near-subsistence existence of the small owners and tenant farmers and cause them collectively to seek a remedy. So threatened, they had to enlist the support of those who were capable of bringing about social and economic change. They approached the large owners still residing in the village and expected them to assist in solving their problems and in soliciting government support. These landowners had to accede to their demands or be subject to majority and possibly Viet Cong–imposed sanctions. In this manner the farmers obtained organizational assistance from local large farmers and material assistance from the government and also were able to overcome the obstructionist activities of some of the remaining landowners and the larger landowners who had left the village.

To clarify this process of irrigation systems development, two propositions are helpful. First, it is argued that the subsistence motivation is stronger than the profit motivation. The effect of a drought on the profits of a large tenant or owner is seen as temporary, not demanding an immediate remedy, whereas to the small tenant or owner whose survival is threatened, an immediate remedy is of paramount importance. The small farmer has a greater incentive to act.

The second proposition arises from broader considerations. Recognizing that the threat of drought to the subsistence incomes of the farmer had been relevant before 1960, why was a remedy forthcoming after that date and not before? In reply, technological considerations can be put aside in the first case—canal construction—because the labor-intensive techniques employed were those used before 1900 in the construction of drainage ditches, that is, manual labor. Nor were recently improved economic conditions relevant to the absence of earlier changes; we have seen that in the 1960s the real price of rice actually declined slightly from historical levels and that factor prices rose.

Therefore, the second proposition is that the major changes between the two periods were social and political, not economic or technological. These changes can be outlined briefly. First, the reallocation of land to smaller owners and tenants in both villages placed the control of the villages' resources in different hands than in previous years. Before 1960 the threat of drought *did* bring starvation, but only to the laboring and small tenant class who were in no social or political position to seek a remedy. Second, before 1960 the wealth and power of the village lay in the hands of those whose positions were not based on considerations of social service, who were unresponsive to subsistence considerations, and who, being landowners, frequently opposed canal construction with the argument that it encroached on their lands. After 1960, there were major changes in the social environment, the basis of social prestige, and the government's role.

Yet, despite the social and political impetus provided them by the Viet Cong from 1960–1967, farmers occupying lower social and economic positions were still *afraid* to approach the government directly. Instead, they took their grievances to the larger owners remaining in the village, whom they saw as those most able to solve their problems. This confidence was pragmatically placed, for the government also saw these same farmers, the remnants of the landed elite, as its contacts within the village—the ones on whom it relied for assistance in village affairs.

Caught in the middle, the landowners recognized and took advantage of the new basis for social prestige in the village: community service. Their story is undoubtedly a central piece in the structure of the economics of insurgency. They were the primary focus of the pressures of the war. They sought neutrality but found they were denied it by both the poorer farmers and the Vietnamese government. The Viet Cong correctly identified and attacked them as those potentially responsible for the development of a new relationship between the Vietnamese government and the peasant farmer and worker.

Irrigation Developments in LBD and TCN

In TCN and LBD the irrigation problems were similar. It was necessary to tie the fields of each village to the fresh-water source—the Mekong River—by digging irrigation canals and connecting them with the nearest stream or natural waterway, which, eventually meeting the Mekong, would be inundated at high tides with the needed fresh water.

THE IRRIGATION SYSTEM IN LONG BINH DIEN

As a rule of thumb, the individual efforts of a single farmer were sufficient to get water to fields within 100 meters of a canal; therefore, on fields more than 100 meters from the canals shown in Figures 1.4 and 1.5, farmers grew just one rice crop. The only major canal in LBD before 1961 was the Tien Canal (see *DF* on map, Figure 1.5) built before 1917 by the canton chief at that time, O Tong Tien, a large landowner. Tien's tenants had asked him to build the canal, arguing that more stable yields would improve their ability to pay rent, and Tien provided the funds for the 2,500-meter canal.

In March 1961 the threat of a drought prompted some LBD farmers, who, recalling the success of the Tien Canal,[3] approached the village officials and asked them to approve and organize the construction of a canal from *E* to *K* (see Figure 1.5). District and provincial approval was obtained, and the work was organized on the basis of 5 linear meters of labor per nonfarm village household and 10 meters per farm household. The canal was to be 2.0 meters wide and 1.5 meters deep. The village officials had to ensure that everyone participated or that those who did not participate paid a sum sufficient to hire labor to excavate their portion. There was some difficulty in convincing the nonfarmers— laborers, merchants, and so on—to participate. They argued that they obtained no benefits yet were forced to forgo immediate work and earnings. Eventually, the village officials, with the assistance of some village elders, persuaded the reluctant nonfarmers to perform the as- signed work. The obvious benefits brought by this canal to all village

[3] In this and other cases cited here, an example served to show those desiring change what the possibilities were. It is argued that these examples were merely fortuitous or coincidental events whose significance was not in their happening but in their being seen by those who could profit from the example. That is, the multiple examples cited by the different parties demonstrated that, had the specific examples not been proximate, another example would have been available. This conclusion relieves us of the need to explain the source of these examples, a com- forting conclusion since in each case the examples cited were products of very diverse events seemingly without common cause.

residents limited further opposition from nonfarming groups to similar post-1961 projects.

One expected obstacle to the construction of canal *EK* did not materialize. In the past, landlords had often been against canal construction because it took portions of their land and led tenants to seek lower rents; but in this case the village council encountered no opposition when it adjusted the rents paid by the affected tenants. One farmer commented that "there was no opposition from the landlords because most of them had left the village and their land was in the effective control of their tenants." Village officials recalled that deputations sent as far as Saigon to get landlord approval of the canal encountered attitudes of powerless acquiescence.[4]

The construction of other canals in the village followed a similar pattern. In March 1962, 200 participants dug canal *KL* (2.0 meters wide and 1.2 meters deep) with work allocated on the basis of 7 meters per household. Opposition was encountered from a small owner who stood to lose a portion of her orchard to the canal. She threatened to kill anyone who dug on her land; only after she was visited by the village and district chiefs and a deputation of village elders, who attempted to persuade her of the resulting community benefits, did she allow the canal work to continue. Prompted by the success of the 1961 project and by the threat of another drought in 1962, the village built two other canals in 1962.

The events surrounding the construction of these canals demonstrate that post-1960 conditions, aided by a drought, were conducive to the construction of an extensive canal system. The effort was entirely a community one. External finance was limited to the provision of some concrete pipes and culverts by the government. By implication, the obstacles to such developments before 1960 were largely organizational and often related to the landlord problem. That such obstacles were not yet fully removed is evident in the opposition to a canal proposed for construction in 1967. Village officials reported such a plan but said, without giving a reason, that it had been postponed. However, a very

[4] As the example canal *DF* demonstrates, it would be incorrect to conclude that all landlords opposed all canals. Also, opposition was encountered from *both* tenants and landlords who stood to suffer while others benefited. However, in the past, objecting landlords, not objecting tenants, held veto power.

poor 66-year-old farmer renting one hectare of land had another view of the cancellation, namely, that several absentee landlords opposed it. When asked for specifics he pleaded, "We are poor, we are afraid of everyone. We are very afraid of these people, and should I disclose their names, they will kill me."

That the construction of irrigation works was in the last analysis an organizational problem complicated by social differences was again evident in the responses to general questions about irrigation works. One former village chief recalled, in pointing up the conflicts of interest involved, that in one case a dispute over rights to use a drainage ditch led to a pick-and-hoe battle between two residents; one farmer was seriously injured and his assailant was jailed by the government. Whereas in their comments about the past, farmers frequently mentioned landlord opposition to irrigation projects, in 1966 they usually saw these obstacles in personal terms, such as a lack of money or labor, and in community terms because, according to one farmer, "cooperation is very low here; few people are willing to pool their efforts for community work."

THE CASE OF THAN CUU NGHIA

In TCN the development of irrigation facilities in the 1960s was equally impressive and, in light of the greater obstacles confronted, more worthy of study. TCN is located more than 10 kilometers from the Mekong River. There were no instances of irrigation before 1954, and the prospects for community effort and government support were less promising than in LBD because of the greater insecurity of the village.

However, a possible conclusion from the LBD example is that the more complete the breakdown of the old social order, with its associated landlord control, the greater the chances for community-based development success. The LBD case also demonstrated that necessity or hardship (for example, a drought) is often the impetus for innovation. We will see that both of these conclusions receive further support from the experience of TCN.

The task facing the TCN farmers who wanted to irrigate their land was to build canals between their fields and the three fresh-water sources —the Bao Dinh, Hao, and Tha La streams (see map, Figure 1.4). Predating the community irrigation projects in TCN were three private projects that served as examples. In 1954, Bay The, an owner of 7 hectares in the village, built canal *PQ* to provide water for his orchard and home plot (Bay The was later selected by the farmers to represent them with the government and to have the major responsibility for the organization of work designed to develop the village's irrigation system).[5] In the same year Thay Hai, a bus company owner in My Tho, built canal *HI* to provide water for an orchard he developed as a "hobby."[6] This canal was 1,000 meters long (1.5 meters wide and 1.0 meter deep) and cost 105,000 piasters to excavate. It was promptly extended from *I* to *B* by adjoining farmers. As early as 1956, prompted by the 1955/56 drought, farmers had begun to discuss lengthening it to serve other areas.

[5] Bay The's family purchased 78 ha of land in Kien Tuong Province (Plain of Reeds) in the 1920s. Bay The had not seen this land nor collected rent from it since 1945. Against his will, he was appointed chief, by the district chief, of the newly formed GVN Farmers' Association in 1960. As a result of his holding this official post he was forced to move from house to house, sleeping in a different place every night, to avoid encounters with the Viet Cong. He resigned this honorary (nonpaying) post in 1964; thereafter, he slept at home. Bay The farmed 1.5 ha in rice and 0.5 ha in vegetables. He rented out 0.2 ha in fruit, from which he took enough rent to pay his land tax. He rented 4.0 ha of rice land to four tenants, a portion of which had been converted to vegetables by tenants who paid no conversion fee nor a higher rent. He had paid Viet Cong taxes since 1962, paying V$N 6,000 in 1967. He stated that a higher rent on his land would not benefit him because the Viet Cong would demand more taxes. Bay The was the largest landowner found still to be living in any of the rural villages studied. His view of the social climate in the village was simply that "the wealthy people are afraid of the poor people."

[6] Hai in 1967 owned 41 buses and had a "monopoly" on the Saigon–My Tho–Bien Hoa route. (A new bus was valued at V$N 1.3 million in 1967.) He earned profits of V$N 30 million in 1966, reinvesting 10 million, spending 10 million on his house, and saving 10 million (used to finance imports through a nonbank channel, obtaining 2% per month). A former civil servant who resigned his post (as a nurse) in 1939 to join his brother in a bus company, he was in 1966 the largest bus owner in Vietnam. He purchased 5.5 ha of land in TCN in 1946 from a friend for V$N 10,000 per hectare. He had never seen the land, knowing only its location from a map—the Viet Minh controlled TCN at that time. The Viet Minh redistributed the land from its single tenant to five tenants who paid no rent from 1946 until 1953. In 1954, after the armistice, several tenants attempted to pay one-half of their 1953 rent, which Hai refused to accept. In 1954 he evicted the tenants. He said he encountered no opposition because the government had established a guardpost nearby. He (correctly) maintained that the law allowed an owner to repossess his land for his own use. However, Hai hired a farmer to develop his orchard. Asked if it pleased him that the particular canal link he provided eventually allowed several hundred TCN merchants to obtain water, he replied: "I am not proud of being a benefactor as an occidental would be; I did it as a hobby."

In 1967 Hai was looking for new investment opportunities. In particular he was interested in agro-based industries, which he felt would thrive in the postwar environment. Asked why he did not buy land, he replied, "To buy land would be to buy trouble."

Canal XY, constructed in 1959, served as a third example. It was built by a doctor and his wife who, having moved from an insecure area in the 1946–1954 war and from the refuge of Tan Hiep in 1955, wanted to develop an orchard. The canal project encountered immediate opposition from four landowners through whose land it had to pass.

An appeal was made to the village council, which intervened and eliminated the opposition of three of the owners; the fourth, who used a brother on the council to represent his views (according to the retired former village chief), continued to oppose the project. An appeal was made to the district chief, who refused to intervene, arguing that the matter should be settled at the village level, where the objecting owner eventually withdrew his opposition. The construction of the 500-meter canal followed, benefiting not only its builder but several nearby tenants.

COMMUNITY EFFORTS

In 1961 these three examples moved several of the smaller tenants and owners to approach Bay The, the Farmers' Association chief, and suggest that a canal be built between points *B* and *J*. Government approval was obtained, but a request for financial assistance was denied because of a lack of funds. Under The's direction, twenty families were organized, and in early 1962 they completed the project, each excavating 30 to 50 meters (2.0 meters wide and 1.2 meters deep). By 1962 and 1963 the canal permitted many farmers to grow a second rice crop and vegetables.

In the following years new projects came in rapid order. In early 1964, canal *BJ* was widened to 3 meters, deepened, and extended to *F* by another community work effort organized by The. It involved 109 participants. A government plan to provide 40,000 piasters for this project did not materialize, although culverts were provided. The government also donated 6,000 piasters for "refreshments," but the sum was used instead to hire laborers to replace those who refused to participate.

Several farmers argued that if the government did not assist, they would not participate. One small owner held up the project by objecting to the loss of a portion of his land. Efforts by government officials and village residents to convince him of the community benefits of the project failed. Finally he was taken to the district chief, who said, "If you will not contribute your land, I will take it or buy it." The farmer withdrew his opposition.[7] The project was initiated on May 1, 1964 and terminated on June 12, 1964; it benefited 180 hectares.

In September–October of 1964 a contractor, hired by the government for 470,905 piasters, dug canal *DB* as requested by local farmers. By this time the demands on the original canal *HB* were too great. In December 1965 the government paid a contractor 300,000 piasters to widen the 1,700-meter canal.

THE WAR

In November 1966 the Viet Cong exploded a mine in the culvert at *F*, destroying a Vietnamese army jeep passing above and killing an army major and a district official. The district office directed that the culvert be filled in, arguing that a wire screen would not prevent its use by the Viet Cong and that the TCN residents, knowing the mine was placed there, had failed to warn government officials. The farmers replied that they were hiding in their homes obeying the nightly curfew and had no knowledge of the mine. (Because culverts were an ideal location for mines designed to destroy roads, the Viet Cong's use of them had destroyed irrigation works in other areas in the Delta and had led to similar confrontations between the Vietnamese government and local farmers.)

Conclusions

The major achievements in irrigation developments outlined in this chapter demonstrate the considerable "costless" gains an economy can obtain if its labor resources are mobilized on a community basis. Yet just as strikingly, these results show the scarcity of the critical factor: organization.

Organization was not simply a problem of gathering idle laborers and putting them to the task. Anterior to the problem of organization in the traditional Vietnamese society were the larger issues of community

---

[7] According to the then district chief (in 1966–1967 the Dinh Tuong Province chief), this was a bluff. Asked what his next move would have been, assuming the owner refused, he replied that the farmer would have been taken to the province chief and the entire process repeated. Failing this, the province had a contingency fund available from which money could be drawn to buy land or relocate displaced farmers on new plots elsewhere.

motivation on the part of the potential participants and a recognition of social responsibility on the part of the potential organizers.

Comparing the pre- and post-1960 periods, the social climate before 1960 was not conducive to the accomplishment of those tasks completed in the later years. If a single reason can be given for this change, it must be that the landlords no longer determined village attitudes and controlled village activities. Nevertheless, although the old system had been largely demolished, a new system capable of organizing village resources had not been developed. Old inhibitions remained. Consider the following statement from a tenant farmer on one hectare, speaking of a proposed canal project:

> People want to do it, but so far no one will initiate the community work project. No one is willing to contact the district officials to get authorization or assistance. Even the hamlet chief is reluctant to approach them, so we are waiting to be asked about our problems and be organized for the work.

Buffeted from side to side since 1946, the village government was ineffective. Effective power lay in the district government. The channel to that power was an informal one, through the larger landowners still residing in the village. But these owners, in whom resided the ability and often a recently acquired willingness to play an organizing role, could not take an official government post without risking assassination by the Viet Cong. Semiofficial positions like that of chief of the Farmers' Association offered an alternative—but not without risk.[8] More likely,

---

[8] When Bay The resigned from this post in 1964, his replacement resided in Tan Hiep, a location that effectively eliminated him from an active role in village development. In 1966–1967 the major development role in the village was assumed by another farmer, Huynh van Hoi, an owner of 4 ha. Hoi, 44 years old, was appointed chief of the "4-T group," an organization of local farmers who received special government assistance in trying new rice varieties, experimenting with new methods of cultivation, and using new tools in return for their keeping records on the results obtained. He acquired a reputation as an innovator in the village, and his activities were closely watched by other farmers, who imitated the successes. It was common knowledge in the village that Hoi had been beaten at least twice by the Viet Cong. His own attitude toward his role was one of pride resulting from the fact that, "when the farmers' fields are dry they come to me and I take their problems to the government." He added: "Anyone who wants to have prestige must sacrifice for others so that they know about it. He must do this soon after his speech so that people will immediately see the good results." Yet because of the pressures of the conflict, Hoi tried to resign his post in both 1966 and 1967, but no replacement could be found. Hoi was also from the landlord class; his father was TCN's largest landowner in

informal channels and ad hoc organizations would continue to serve a vital function until either side achieved complete control of the village. Therefore, *while complete security was not a prerequisite for economic development, it was a prerequisite for political development, and its absence prevented the organization of development-minded political institutions.*

To stress the role of local organization is not necessarily to stress the role of government, particularly government above the village level. Indeed, with respect to its role in assisting in the irrigation developments in the villages studied, it is difficult to fault the Vietnamese government. In most cases, had the government acted, its efforts would merely have replaced otherwise forthcoming local contributions. Outright reliance on a contractor was necessary or desirable only for large projects.

The strength of the government's role was in *responding* to local initiative and in clearing the path for local action by mediating disputes and obtaining the necessary permissions from absentee landlords. Moreover, a government that moves in too quickly and assumes too great a burden can be counterproductive. For example, in early 1966 in a village near LBD work was completed on a large GVN-USAID irrigation project costing over one million piasters (it included a concrete-walled canal approximately 2,000 meters in length). Yet by early 1967, few farmers were using the new canal for irrigation, a fact that prompted a high-level Dinh Tuong USAID official to label them "lazy." A short investigation produced the following explanation. On one side of the canal was a road, constructed at the same time as the canal, which blocked water movement to land on that side of the canal (there were no culverts under it). On the other side a large portion of the adjacent land was farmed by two old women who said they did not want to farm a second crop. However, one farmer had succeeded in subleasing a part of their land for off-season vegetable cultivation. A tenant farmer questioned in another area argued that if he dug a connecting canal to bring water to his land his landlord would repossess the land and farm it himself in two crops. Finally, in most places the walls of the canal were too high, preventing the use of the inexpensive motor pump as a lifting device.

---

the 1920s. His maternal grandfather, a tenant farmer on 27 ha in the late 1940s, lost most of his land in the Viet Minh expropriation.

Conclusions

It is likely that had the government's effort been directed to respond to local initiative, this canal would have been constructed to local specifications and would have found ready users. Instead, the government, acting independently of local needs and local organizations, wasted money and effort that could have been put to other productive uses.

8 The Motor Pump: A Subsistence Innovation

Introduction

The recognition of the potential returns from irrigation development in the early 1960s served to point up one of the most constraining bottlenecks in the rural economy: the waterwheel, a wooden device powered by a two-man team operating foot pedals, which under most conditions could lift water no more than 0.5 meter. Whereas irrigation in combination with the waterwheel could increase the area cultivated by only about 10 percent and prevent single-crop losses from drought on an additional 20 percent, irrigation in combination with a lifting device that could raise water up to 1.5 meters had the potential of increasing the area in cultivation by an additional 40 percent or even more, depending on how rapidly the canal systems were extended.

In 1962 a mechanical pump was invented by a Delta farmer to solve the problem of lifting water to field level. By any standard, the result was economic revolution in the upper Delta area, with production increasing as much as 40 percent within three years.[1] In the benefits it brought to

---

[1] From 1963 to 1967, USAID estimated that 75,000 small engines were imported into South Vietnam for irrigation use; 50,000 of these were used in the upper Mekong Delta region. On the (pessimistic) assumption that each pump irrigated an additional 2 ha of rice land, an additional 100,000 ha came into cultivation. These gains, however, were largely offset by the fact that in insecure areas many hectares were removed from cultivation. Nonetheless, Dinh Tuong Province exported 52,526 MT of rice in 1966/67 compared with 24,379 MT in 1965/66, a year affected by both drought and war. The 1966/67 export level was the highest achieved by the province since 1962/63, a bumper-crop year when 74,000 MT were exported. The figure is best compared with the nondrought, nonwar (in general, hostilities did not disrupt production until 1965) years of 1961/62, when 62,000 MT were exported, or 1963/64, when 46,000 MT were exported.

the Delta economy, the motor pump reminds one of the tube well's role in Pakistan. The evidence offered here not only supplements that from the tube well study but provides knowledge not available from that example.[2] An important aspect of the motor pump invention (which was not true of the tube well) is that it was the product of an intermediate technology. The motor pump provides a clear example of the value, within underdeveloped economies, of innovative activities that are designed to modify imported technologies to meet local conditions to which foreign goods are not (for economic and technical reasons) precisely suited.

The Innovation

By the late 1950s another water-moving device, besides the waterwheel, was in use in the rural areas. It was a large, 10- to 20-horsepower diesel-powered centrifugal pump costing 30,000 to 35,000 piasters and usually of German or Japanese origin. This pump was not widely used; only one or two were available in each village, and these were owned by the larger landowners who had use for its labor-saving characteristics, not for economic reasons but simply because they wished neither to work physically nor to be dependent on hired labor.[3] The diesel pump was technically and economically inferior to the waterwheel when operating at a 0.5-meter lift. The flow rate through its 10-centimeter hose was less than that of the waterwheel and its rental cost was above that necessary to hire labor to operate a waterwheel for an equivalent period.[4] At lifts higher than 0.5 meter, it was technically superior to the waterwheel, but it did not represent a profitable investment. The purchase price was six

[2] In a study of this major breakthrough for the Pakistani economy, the writer concluded that several gaps in the relevant knowledge remained, among which were the role of economic incentives in the diffusion process and information on: "Who are the individuals who were the first to install a well? What is their status or caste? Their education? Their financing?" See C. H. Gotsch, "Technological Change and Private Investment in Agriculture: A Case Study of the Pakistan Punjab" (Ph.D. dissertation, Harvard University, 1966), pp. 150–151. In the similar case of the motor pump, these questions can be answered.

[3] In 1957 one of these pumps was purchased by an owner of four hectares of land in TCN. Hendry reported one such pump in Khanh Hau in 1958. See James B. Hendry, *The Small World of Khanh Hau* (Chicago: Aldine Publishing Co., 1964), p. 70.

[4] Ibid., p. 72.

times the gross revenue from one rice crop on one hectare of land. Because the pump was immobile (it took at least four men to lift it), it could not easily be rented to others.

A SUBSISTENCE INNOVATION

As we have seen in Chapter 7, the serious drought in 1962 prompted Delta farmers to undertake major canal works to save their crops. One owner of 4 hectares of land in LBD even purchased a diesel pump for 32,000 piasters. Most farmers, however, could not afford this expensive item. Mr. Van Nam of Song Binh village near LBD was such a farmer. Nam, who rented one hectare of rice land, was also a part-time mechanic, servicing motor-bicycle engines in his village area. In 1936, at the age of seventeen, he had trained at a French vocational school in Saigon and, before returning to his home village in 1955, had worked for twelve years as a mechanic for a French dredging company in Saigon.

In 1962 Nam invented[5] the motor pump (see Figure 8.1). While

FIGURE 8.1   The Motor Pump

searching for an alternative method to obtain fresh water, he recalled that the French dredges he repaired in Saigon operated on an impeller principle, using a propeller to inject water and river-bed sediment into a large pipe, and he sought to devise a new type of pump based on this principle.

When he began his experiments in March 1962 he faced three basic problems. First, he had to find an adequate source of power; second, he had to apply the operating principle of the French dredge to a work-

[5] The term "invented" is used loosely. The same or similar device may have been available in other countries prior to 1962. But such a device was not, until Nam invented it, available in the Delta of South Vietnam.

able tin sleeve arrangement enclosing the shaft and impeller of the pump and allowing water pushed by the impeller to traverse this sleeve; and third, he had to design an impeller, since the existing sampan propellers, even when reversed, would not impel water.

He began with a Mobylette engine from a French-built motorbicycle; it was available in his workshop and inexpensive. His first impeller was a modification of a copper propeller, which involved trimming the blades at their extremities, cutting them at their base, changing their pitch, and rewelding them to the base at the new angle. Since this impeller was 10 centimeters in diameter, he enclosed the shaft and impeller with a sleeve of approximately the same diameter, fitting it at its upper end (see Figure 8.1) with a boxlike chamber through which the water was expelled. This exit chamber was a direct imitation of the French dredge; in later models it proved unnecessary and was dropped.

Nam's first model failed; the Mobylette engine was too weak to transport an appreciable quantity of water through the sleeve. After two months of unsuccessful testing, he purchased a Bridgestone (Japanese-made) 4.0 horsepower engine for 2,000 piasters and used it to build a second model. On this model he began with the standard 25-centimeter diameter propeller, changing the pitch but not trimming the blades. This impeller proved too large for the engine, and its blades were progressively trimmed in several steps from 25 to 20 centimeters and ultimately to 18 centimeters on the final model. After nearly four months of testing at a cost of 6,000 piasters, Nam was successful. On the basis of his success he was able to borrow 4,300 piasters from a relative to purchase a 4.5-horsepower (U.S.) Clinton engine that, running at a higher speed (revolutions per minute), proved an ideal source of power for the motor pump. By September 1962 he was renting the pump to neighboring LBD village residents for 40 piasters per hour.

Nam's invention received the immediate attention of other nearby residents, and the innovation spread rapidly as motor dealers, acting on descriptions from farmers, built similar models. However, since there was no patent system to guarantee the rights of the inventor nor any formal system to spread knowledge rapidly, fifteen months after the original invention the motor pump was "invented again," by Pham Van Thanh, a small-engine merchant in My Tho who had no knowledge of Nam's product. Thanh's experience deserves equal attention because it illustrates the importance of the common problem and the commonality of the relevant ideas and skills.

Thanh was twenty-three years old in October 1963 when he accompanied a friend—an engineer and officer in the Vietnamese army—to view a dredging operation under the latter's supervision on the Binh Duc Canal near My Tho. There Thanh, who had graduated from secondary school in My Tho in 1956, watched the operations of a French-built dredge like the one that Nam had worked on in Saigon.

Thanh recognized that neither the American centrifugal pumps nor the large German and Japanese diesel pumps were efficient water-moving devices under local conditions. As he stated, "the diesel pump was too expensive for most farmers to purchase. Also it was heavy; it could not be moved from field to field, so the wealthier buyers were unable to rent it to others." Most of Thanh's engine sales were the small (4.5-horsepower) Clintons and Kohlers used to power sampans.

Thanh realized that merely reversing the propeller on a Clinton or Kohler engine would not produce an impeller. But he also recognized that the shaft of the Sach's engine (German-made), which he sold in small quantities, turned clockwise—viewed from the shaft end—while the Clinton and Kohler engine shafts turned counterclockwise. Taking a Sach's propeller and placing it on a Clinton engine, he solved the impeller problem. Finally, he ordered a tin sleeve from a local merchant, determining that its diameter should be 2 centimeters larger than the 20-centimeter Sach's propeller and its length the same as that of the available propeller shaft (2.5 meters) used on sampans.

Thanh's first model was tested on a friend's farm near My Tho in December 1963 and proved successful; the farmer purchased it on the spot. Thanh's invention brought him immediate profit. By mid-1964 he had sold 600 of the new pumps. Between then and mid-1967 he sold an average of 200 pumps per month. In early 1967 Thanh owned three imported cars and a new house, was building a hotel in My Tho at a cost of fourteen million piasters, and was considered one of the town's wealthiest men, all at the age of twenty-eight. He had established himself as an entrepreneur in the best Schumpeterian tradition.

Diffusion of the Innovation

PROFITABILITY

In his book *Diffusion of Innovations*, E. M. Rogers has noted that "economists have claimed that the rate of adoption of innovations can be explained by such economic variables as profitability, while sociologists claim rate of adoption can be explained by sociological variables such as compatibility."[6] The motor pump was not compatible with any technique or factor of production employed by Vietnamese farmers before its adoption (no machine was employed at any farm task), yet by mid-1966, less than four years after its invention, 43 percent of the farmers in TCN and 38 percent of those in LBD owned one. It completely replaced the waterwheel as a water-moving device. Farmers who did not own a pump rented one from those who did. Whereas before 1962 the waterwheel was an item of capital equipment in almost every upper Delta household, in 1966 none were in use and several could be seen discarded at the side of the road. One farmer, when asked about his waterwheel, replied, "I burned it."

Perhaps the reason for the rapid acceptance of the innovation lay in its profitability. One farmer explained his purchase of a pump as follows: "The waterwheel costs too much hired labor; I expect to get more water with less labor, to save time. A pump can do in two hours the work of six to eight men toiling all day." Another farmer, asked why he had not purchased a pump before 1964, replied, "There was no suitable engine before 1964. The type available in previous years was too expensive."

A test conducted by USAID engineers on a motor pump moving water a height of 1.1 meters showed that it moved 95–100 cubic meters per hour. Although no comparable test was possible on the waterwheel, the farmers agreed that one hour of work by the motor pump equaled four to five hours' work by the waterwheel, meaning that the waterwheel moved approximately 22.2 cubic meters per hour. Assuming that the motor pump moves 100 cubic meters per hour a height of 0.5 meter, it is possible to determine, using present value at 1966 prices, whether the motor pump, if purchased simply to replace the waterwheel and do nothing else, was a worthwhile investment in 1966.

[6] Everett M. Rogers, *Diffusion of Innovations* (New York: The Free Press, 1962), p. 138.

Before making the calculations, we set out the pertinent data. The price of a motor pump was 8,000 piasters,[7] and gasoline cost 10 piasters per hour. Because pedaling a waterwheel was among the most arduous rural tasks the work of a two-man team in 1966 was valued at 260 piasters per day. An interest rate of 60 percent per year, or about 5 percent per month, is assumed.[8] Research results showed that the life of the pump was rarely less than four years, and in 1967 no farmer had employed one for a longer period. However, users in 1966/67 were operating pumps fifty and sixty hours a year, farming a second rice crop, growing vegetables, and renting pumps to other farmers. Since the first calculations (in Equation 8.1) are based on the assumption that a pump replaces only the waterwheel's efforts, such replacement on 2 hectares of one-crop rice land[9] would entail, according to the farmers' requirements, 16 two-man (eight-hour) days of work by the waterwheel. Using the 4 to 1 ratio the equivalent motor pump time is four days or thirty-two hours. Because this usage is below the fifty to sixty hours common in TCN, we will assume an engine life of six years for this task alone. It is assumed that an operator is paid 100 piasters per eight-hour day to oversee the engine. An additional 200 piasters a year are added for miscellaneous repairs, and a scrap value of zero is assumed.

$$\text{present value} = -\text{initial cost} + \sum_{i=1}^{n} \frac{\text{labor costs saved} - \text{operating costs}}{(1+r)^i}$$

$$= -8,000 + \sum_{i=1}^{6} \frac{4,160 - 920}{(1+r)^i} \tag{8.1}$$

$$= -2,910$$

[$r = 0.60, n = 6$;
labor costs saved $= (16 \text{ days}) (260 \text{ per day})$;
operating costs $= 320 \text{ (gas)} + 400 \text{ (labor)} + 200 \text{ (maintenance)}$]

[7] From 1962 to 1965 the pumps sold for V$N 4,000–5,000; in 1967 for V$N 9,500, a price increase due to inflation. Rental rates were V$N 40 per hour in 1962 and only V$N 50 per hour in 1967, reflecting more widespread pump ownership in the later period.

[8] Although above the 2 to 3% of 1966, this is probably the best representation of credit conditions in 1964, when the first pumps were purchased (see chap. 5).

[9] Of the 50 farmers interviewed in LBD, the average size of farmholding was 1.97 ha (1.62 in rice); for those rice farmers who purchased pumps, the average holding was 2.50 ha (2.24 in rice).

The present value is calculated using Equation 8.1, and the results are negative: The motor pump would not have been profitable. In fact, this is fortunate, for had the investment been profitable without also creating additional employment by enabling farmers to grow a second rice crop and vegetables, its adoption would have involved the replacement of otherwise unemployable labor, causing more disguised unemployment.

Because the pump could move water to higher levels and irrigate more land, to compare it by task with the waterwheel clearly understates its profitability. A better comparison (because it was a typical situation) is to assume that the purchaser grew one rice crop on 2 hectares of land before buying the pump, and afterward two crops on 1 hectare and one crop on 1 hectare. From the sample, it was found that the average net profit on 1 hectare of single-crop rice was 15,000 piasters and on 2 hectares, 29,000 piasters. These profits were obtained under the rent conditions prevailing in 1966; that is, farmers paid 15 percent on one crop but no additional rent on a second crop. The return on a motor pump investment would then include the labor costs saved by replacing the waterwheel on 2 hectares in one crop (4,160 piasters), plus the net profit obtainable from another crop on 1 hectare (14,000 piasters), less the additional operating costs on the second crop (920 piasters). It is assumed that the pump was used for the same period (thirty-two hours) to farm a second crop on 1 hectare as to farm one crop on 2 hectares; therefore, the gasoline and operating costs are simply doubled. The pump's life is reduced to four years because it is operating more hours per year. The calculations are seen in Equation 8.2.

$$\text{present value} = -8,000 + \sum_{i=1}^{4} \frac{18,160 - 1,840}{(1 + r)^i} \tag{8.2}$$

$$= 15,070$$

$$[r = 0.60, n = 4]$$

The results (Equation 8.2) demonstrate not only that such an investment was profitable in 1966 but that, after purchase, the pump paid for itself in the first year, yielding 10,200 piasters.[10]

---

[10] Similar calculations under the more stringent rent conditions of 25% on both crops (Hendry's 1958 finding) also gave favorable results; or, at that time, had the innovation been available, it would have been a profitable investment (see Hendry, *Small World of Khanh Hau*).

The Motor Pump

One attraction of the motor pump was that the monetary outlay was not large by rural standards. It was roughly equivalent to the price of a pig. In fact, several farmers raised a pig, feeding it table scraps and rice bran purchased with "small change," and marketed it after five to six months to buy a motor pump.

COMMUNICATIONS

Despite these advantages, one might have expected a slow diffusion of this "incompatible" item in an environment without radio or printed dissemination of the news of such developments. Information spread by word of mouth and personal observation. For example, one farmer from LBD told his relative from another village about the pump at a family gathering; another farmer passing on the road saw the pump in operation and stopped to examine it. Before purchasing a pump, each farmer personally viewed one in operation. Trips of ten to twenty miles were often taken for this purpose. For example, at a family gathering in Nhi Qui village in June 1963, a farmer heard a distant relative from TCN describe a motor pump he had recently seen in operation in his home village. A month later this farmer made the fifteen-mile trip to TCN to see the pump in operation. In December 1963 he became the first farmer in his village to own a motor pump. By 1966 over half of the farm operators in Nhi Qui village owned motor pumps. Before the pump, the farmers of Nhi Qui grew one crop of rice; after the pump became available, a second crop was grown on over 80 percent of the village's fields, almost doubling farm incomes.

A farmer in LBD, when asked where he got the idea to purchase a pump, replied, "I was excited by the results obtained by the pioneer users in TCN." Although TCN was not the home of the pump's inventors, it acquired a reputation as the home of its pioneer users. There appear to be two reasons for this reputation. First, TCN is strategically located on the most important transportation route in the province. Whatever goes on in this village soon becomes common knowledge in the province as friends, children, and soldiers passing on the road from Saigon inevitably see and report on developments there. Second, because TCN farmers had less water initially and had extended their irrigation system to grow vegetables and rice, the changes brought by the pump to TCN's economy were greater than those brought to most other villages in the province.

The pump came to TCN in 1963. Early that year it was rumored in the village that a new type of pump was being used in Kien Phong Province, adjacent to Dinh Tuong. This machine was operating in a Viet Cong–controlled area, and rumor described it as a Viet Cong machine. Because it was an insecure area, most farmers were afraid to travel to Kien Phong, a distance of 100 kilometers, to see the pump in operation. However, one TCN farmer, who was described as being "fearless," made the trip, convinced himself of the pump's value, and, after instructing an engine merchant on its assembly, purchased the first one he produced.

The process by which the pump's attributes became known was an imperfect one. Due largely to the curiosity of the farmers and to their willingness to experiment with potentially profitable new techniques, however, the pump was quickly assimilated into the economic environment.

The argument that profitability was the major determinant of the rate of diffusion is further supported by a comparison of the characteristics of those in the sample who by 1966 had purchased a pump and those who had not. The average age and family size did not differ significantly between buyer and nonbuyer.[11] Results relating literacy and pump ownership were inconclusive.[12] There was no significant difference in the level of indebtedness between the two groups: 73 percent of the nonpurchasers had debts averaging 10,300 piasters per household compared with 68 percent of the purchasers, who owed an average of 10,000 piasters.[13] As noted, the only significant difference between purchasers and nonpurchasers was the size of holding farmed (2.5 hectares versus

[11] The average age of the 46 purchasers was 49.5 years compared with the sample average of 49.0 years.

[12] The pump was purchased by 3 of the 11 (27.2%) illiterate and 43 of the 109 (39.4%) literate farmers. However, the small size of the illiterate sample precludes any statistical conclusion from these results.

[13] Rose K. Goldsen and Max Ralis, in their study "Factors Related to Acceptance of Innovations in Bang Chan, Thailand," mimeographed, Cornell Thailand Project, Interim Reports Series, no. 3 (Ithaca, N.Y., June 1967), p. 29, found that 79% of those with debts owned or used a motor in farm operations (primarily irrigation) while only 60% of those without debts owned or used an engine.

1.2 hectares).[14] This result would be expected if profitability was the major consideration separating buyer and nonbuyer.

INSTITUTIONAL RESISTANCE

A curious aspect of the diffusion process was the negative attitude of the Vietnamese government, the Viet Cong, and USAID advisory officials. The Vietnamese government feared that the pump engines would eventually fall into Viet Cong hands and be used to power sampans for military use. In 1965 the government instituted a strict licensing system that required any prospective pump buyer to receive clearance from village, district, and province-level officials. In the process he usually had to pay 300–500 piasters in assorted "fees and taxes" and convince the officials that he did not live in a Viet Cong area, was not a Viet Cong, and had no "friends" in the Viet Cong. About 20–30 percent of the applications were rejected.[15]

In fact, however, the Viet Cong conducted an intensive propaganda campaign to persuade farmers not to use the motor pump. They argued that every purchase of a pump assisted the Americans in waging war, and backed their claim by elaborate calculations built on an estimate of the pumps sold, the price of each, and even the gasoline consumption per engine. This opposition was probably motivated in part by the fact that each small engine, its foreign exchange cost financed by the U.S. Commodity Import Program, carried an AID symbol.

Nor was the attitude of USAID particularly helpful. In July 1965, USAID's Delta agricultural representative saw the pump in operation near My Tho and suggested to the U.S. Information Agency that it publicize this new product. This was done on a small scale by publishing articles in the Vietnamese press. But AID's technical experts in Saigon were not easily convinced.

The Irrigation and Rural Engineering Branch of AID in Saigon was responsible for technical advice on irrigation matters. The following is a

---

[14] Significant at the .01 level.

[15] In addition to inviting favoritism and corruption, the licensing system denied economic benefits to many non–Viet Cong farmers in both contested and Viet Cong areas. These were precisely the population the government sought to appeal to and pacify. Moreover, the system had a practical defect. At night in the Delta the Viet Cong had access to almost every rice field—even those in government-held villages. Since farmers usually left their pumps in the fields overnight, the Viet Cong had no difficulty in obtaining pump motors if they so chose.

conversation the writer had with the branch chief and two of his assistants:[16]

WRITER: I am an economist doing research in the Delta, where I have encountered a recent innovation of some importance: the motor pump. Do you know anything about its origin or use?[17]

AID OFFICIAL: Yes, we have heard about it. The pump you are talking about has been the source of some unfortunate propaganda put out by the Public Affairs people, saying we [USAID] invented it. Actually we didn't have anything to do with its invention. We are engineers: We couldn't recommend an inefficient piece of equipment like that.

WRITER: What do you mean by inefficient?

AID OFFICIAL: We tested the pump and proved it was inefficient. We found that it was only five to forty percent efficient and that we could not recommend it. What would happen if you came back to Vietnam twenty years from now and found that they were still using that thing?

WRITER: What about efficiency in matters like this; how does one compare the waterwheel with, say, the motor pump?

AID OFFICIAL: Well, that is hard to say; it is difficult to compare manpower and horsepower.[18] You might begin by computing the calories consumed by a two-man team on a waterwheel and compare that energy with the horsepower of the motor pump.

WRITER: But the farmers tell me that one hour with the pump is equivalent to approximately five hours' work with the waterwheel. What about this type of comparison?

AID OFFICIAL: Oh, that's just a rule of thumb. It has no factual basis. Listen, you have to realize that this motor pump was thrown together in some guy's backyard; they know nothing about its efficiency.

WRITER: Well, don't you think it might be helpful to make a cost comparison on the alternative means of moving water, for example, comparing the labor costs on the waterwheel with the rental cost on the motor pump?

AID OFFICIAL: Oh no! That's economics; we don't know anything about that.

---

[16] The interview took place on July 10, 1967. All three of those questioned were engineers, one with over a year's experience in the Delta as a field engineer.

[17] At this stage I had not determined the inventor. Several Americans and Vietnamese had told me that the pump was invented by the Americans.

[18] The Food and Agriculture Organization publication, *Equipment for Rice Production*, by B. A. Stout (Rome, 1966), states that "man is not a very powerful machine. For short periods he may be able to develop 0.4 hp but for continuous work his capacity is about 0.1 hp" (p. 21).

Conclusions

1. By the early 1960s a set of circumstances existed that provided the motivation for the invention of the motor pump. Upper Delta farmers were attempting to irrigate their land as opposed to merely draining it. An extensive canal system had already been developed in TCN before the invention of the pump. One crucial piece of knowledge—the example of the French dredge—was available as early as 1920, but the relevant skills and experience were the result of the use of the small engine for sampan propulsion in the late 1950s. The labor shortage can be excluded as a causal element because it did not occur until late 1964, although it certainly hastened the diffusion process in 1965–1966. The drought, although not a new phenomenon, seems to have been the immediate impetus for the invention.

2. The diffusion process was rapid despite the lack of a formal communications system and government support. Profitability was the primary cause of the pump's immediate success and helped to overcome any obstacles of noncompatibility.

3. It does not appear that the example of the motor pump adds substantially to the meager body of knowledge on invention and innovation or technological change.[19] However, these findings do support conclusions found elsewhere in the literature on the application of technology to the problems of economic development. The invention of the motor pump represented an addition to existing technological knowledge in Vietnam, and the innovation caused a shift in the production function for the rural sector. It was not an example of a labor-saving technological change; in fact, on such grounds alone, the innovation would not have been profitable. By doing more than merely replacing labor, the motor pump allowed additional land to be double-cropped (substituting capital for land). For the rural sector as a whole (and for the individual farm), adoption of the pump raised the ratios of labor to land and capital to land. Its most profound effect, however, was in eliminating widespread seasonal unemployment. One farmer commented, "In the past we gambled and drank four or five months of the

---

[19] For example, the work of John Jewkes, David Sawers, and Richard Stillerman, *The Sources of Invention* (New York: St. Martin's Press, 1958), and M. Blaug, "A Survey of the Theory of Process-Innovations," *Economica*, vol. n.s. 30 (February 1963), pp. 13–32, do not appear relevant to the case at hand.

year; now we have steady employment and steady incomes even in the dry season."

4. In origin, the motor pump was a product of what Nelson has called a "demand theory of invention"[20] or, as Eckaus terms it, a "necessity is the mother of invention theory."[21] It met a social need, indeed a subsistence or survival need in the case of the drought, and provided an opportunity for private profit. Eckaus has juxtaposed this demand theory with a "supply theory" explanation, which views inventions as a product of a "step-by-step refinement of the known 'state of the art,' " arrived at independently of social or economic conditions.[22] The policy implications of this dichotomy are not altogether clear. In the motor pump case, if one accepts the demand theory explanation, is he then bound to depreciate the value of independent research and development work in underdeveloped countries and encourage them to draw on the already developed body of knowledge in advanced countries? No such conclusion is justified, although it is true that the basic inventive knowledge employed—the engine and the impeller method—was imported from American and French sources.

If nothing in the motor pump example points to the need for vast research and development complexes in less-developed countries, it does demonstrate the value to the rural sector of three types of policies. First, the rapid diffusion of the innovation was probably facilitated by the level of literacy and the general awareness (mobility) of the Vietnamese farmers—products of a basic elementary education program and an efficient transportation system. Second, the invention itself was the immediate result of the mechanical skills the first inventor acquired at a technical training school in Saigon. Above these levels of basic and technical education, the pump offers little evidence to support those who advocate mass education at the university level or high levels of basic research expenditures for less-developed countries. Third, if less-developed countries are to draw on the body of knowledge developed in other countries, they should select their sources with care. Had it not been available to them at zero cost, it would probably have been a

[20] Richard R. Nelson, "The Economics of Invention: A Survey of the Literature," *Journal of Business*, vol. XXXII (April 1959), p. 103.
[21] Richard S. Eckaus, "Notes on Invention and Innovation in Less Developed Countries," *American Economic Review*, vol. LVI, no. 3 (May 1966), p. 107.
[22] Ibid.

poor use of Vietnamese funds to import advice on agricultural techniques from the United States, assuming they could have drawn on the more relevant techniques of rice production already developed in Japan, Taiwan, and the Philippines. The vast differences in initial factor endowments and the resulting high labor productivity techniques in the United States, as opposed to the comparatively low productivity techniques employed in Asian rice economies, limit the benefits from exchanges of technical advice between the two.[23]

5. Economists often question whether an intermediate technology is an illusion or a fact in developing economies. The pessimists can usually find a product produced in an advanced country that is both technically and economically superior to an intermediate product. But such a counterargument misses the basic point, the one overlooked by the USAID engineers who maintained that "what Vietnam really needs is an advanced impeller-type pump like those now available in the United States"; these pumps were not available in South Vietnam in 1962, nor were they available in 1967. The gap between invented products in developed countries and available ones in underdeveloped countries is one of the most difficult an underdeveloped economy must bridge. The obstacles are primarily communicative and distributional. But they can also be economic in that the most efficient product in the developed economy may be too expensive for sale in the underdeveloped economy. Not one but four types of intermediate technologies are possible: One is intermediate in an economic sense, meaning that the best technology may be too expensive to warrant its adoption; one is intermediate in the distributive sense because the best technology is simply not available or familiar to the developing economy; a third is intermediate in a technical sense because no task in the developed economy is similar to that faced in the developing economy; and finally, a foreign exchange

---

[23] In this respect Robert Solo has recently drawn a broader conclusion, also supported in the Vietnamese case: "This [the high-low productivity gap] may account for the seemingly paradoxical emphasis on industrial development by predominantly agricultural low-productivity societies; since the ineradicable differences in the natural parameters of agriculture (and also the very deep differences in the social circumstances of agriculture) in low-productivity vis-à-vis high-productivity societies probably makes it more difficult to adapt advanced agricultural technologies than to adapt advanced industrial technologies for assimilation." Robert Solo, "The Capacity to Assimilate an Advanced Technology," *American Economic Review*, vol. LVI, no. 2 (May 1966), p. 94.

bottleneck might dictate an intermediate technology to save foreign exchange. This last factor, however, was not a problem in Vietnam, although with the motor pump the economic, distributive, and technical factors were important.

6. Because the invention of the motor pump provided a greater impetus to the development of the upper Delta in the 1965–1967 period than the rising product prices and the cheaper capital characteristic of the war economy, it supports Professor Schultz's generalization about increases in agricultural production in recent decades:

> The opportunities in general have not come from the opening up of new farm land for settlement nor have they originated primarily from a rise in the relative price of farm products. They have come predominantly from more productive agricultural factors.[24]

7. The motor pump invention provides evidence supporting the market view of development, which stresses the productivity benefits of such technologies. However, the origin of the invention—the subsistence efforts of a farmer attempting to overcome the effect of a drought—indicates that such production benefits may be more likely to arise from strongly motivated subsistence efforts than from market-oriented attempts to increase profits. This argument is stated with caution, and it implies that other considerations relevant to innovation (for example, education) should be more evenly distributed in underdeveloped economies. The merchant's invention of the same product was, of course, a market-type activity. But an institutionalist might argue that such a merchant, serving only landlords or large-scale farmers (as opposed to small-scale farmers), would have seen his innovative possibilities in some other area.

---

[24] Theodore W. Schultz, *Transforming Traditional Agriculture* (New Haven, Conn.: Yale University Press, 1964), p. 105.

9 Fertilizer: A Subsistence Investment

Introduction

Asian rice statistics show two major differences between the extensive rice economies of Thailand, India, and Pakistan, on the one hand, and the intensive rice economies of Taiwan, South Korea, and Japan, on the other: In the former, rice yields average less than 2.0 metric tons per hectare at fertilizer nutrient-use levels of less than 30 kilograms per hectare; in the latter, rice yields often average over 4.0 metric tons per hectare at nutrient-use levels of over 150 kilograms per hectare. In Japan yields have risen three times since the early twentieth century.[1] More recently yields in Taiwan have increased from predepression levels of 2.4 metric tons per hectare to over 4.0 metric tons per hectare in the early 1960s.[2] It has often been thought that the task of raising yields in the low-yield countries to Japanese or Taiwanese levels is largely one of increasing the level of fertilizer application.

In South Vietnam in the 1950s, fertilizer use averaged 30 kilograms per hectare; in the early 1960s this figure rose to 55 kilograms per hectare.[3] At the same time, yields that had been stable or declining in the 1.2–1.4 metric tons per hectare range from the 1920s until the early 1950s rose to 2.0 metric tons per hectare in the 1955–1965 period.[4]

[1] Yuzuru Kato, "Factors Contributing to the Recent Increase of Productivity in Japanese Agriculture," *Journal of Development Studies*, vol. 2, no. 1 (October 1965), p. 47.

[2] International Rice Research Institute, *Annual Report, 1966* (Los Banos, the Philippines, 1966), Table 1.

[3] Republic of Vietnam, Ministry of Agriculture, Agricultural Economics and Statistics Service, *Agricultural Statistics Yearbook, 1963* (Saigon, 1964), pp. 24, 197.

[4] USAID, *ASB, 1965*, p. 89.

Introduction

Most of this yield improvement was probably due to increased fertilizer use, since other techniques remained unchanged, although marginal varietal improvements were made. Drawing on this experience, Vietnamese and American development officials as well as Vietnamese farmers concluded that additional fertilizer applications would bring additional yield results similar to those obtained at low-use levels.

Through 1965 a major aspect of the USAID program for the rural areas was designed to encourage fertilizer use and raise yields. The value of fertilizer imports averaged over ten million dollars a year between 1961 and 1965.[5] To promote fertilizer use, in November 1964 a subsidy exchange rate of 35 percent of CIF cost was granted to fertilizer importers.[6] In 1966 it was a primary assumption of this USAID program that, as in the previous ten years, the marginal returns to additional fertilizer applications would continue to be significant; officially it was assumed that each additional kilogram of fertilizer would increase rice yields by 6 kilograms.[7]

Using 1966 planting-time prices for Vietnam and 1964/65 prices in selected countries, the results of this fertilizer program are seen in Table 9.1, which compares the ratios of nitrogen prices to paddy prices in eight countries with the ratio in Vietnam. The price ratio in Vietnam is the lowest in the table. Not surprisingly the level of nutrient use in the villages studied is among the highest reported; it is above the South Korean level but below that of Japan and of Taiwan.

Research at the International Rice Research Institute (IRRI) and elsewhere has demonstrated that the yield response to fertilizer use can vary widely from country to country and with the variety of rice planted. Between countries the yield response may vary because improved production techniques, such as those employed in Japan, are often prerequisites to achieving higher yields at high levels of fertilizer use. These techniques may not be easily acquired, since they are often the outcome of years of research and extension work, making productive fertilizer ap-

[5] Ibid., p. 69.
[6] Ibid., p. 65.
[7] The origin of this relationship appears to be a report on fertilizer experiments in cultivator fields in South Vietnam made during 1958/59 by Bui Huu Tri, Chief, Soil Fertility Section of the Ministry of Agriculture, and F. R. Moorman, FAO soil expert. As reported in the Food and Agriculture Organization study, *Statistics of Crop Responses to Fertilizers* (Rome, 1966), these tests were conducted at use levels in the 30 kg per ha range and not at higher use levels (p. 82).

TABLE 9.1 Fertilizer-Paddy Price Ratios and Nutrient Fertilizer Use in Selected Countries, 1964/65

Country	Price Ratio: (Kg Nitrogen)/ (Kg Paddy)	Kg Nutrient (N, P₂O₅, K₂O) Consumption per Ha
Ceylon	2.1	35.5
India	4.6	4.4
Japan	1.4	304.4
Pakistan	1.6	3.7
Philippines	4.3	8.1
South Korea	2.3	167.5
South Vietnam[a]	1.16	199.2 (LBD) / 164.4 (TCN)
Taiwan	4.4	237.0
Thailand	5.9	3.2

Source: International Rice Research Institute, *Statistics for Rice Research* (Los Banos, the Philippines, 1966), pp. 1–15, and sample data.
[a] 1966/67 Mekong Delta data. The small supply of organic fertilizer available in the villages was sold to vegetable growers, who paid a higher price than rice cultivators. The Mekong Delta price per kg of nutrient nitrogen was V$N 11.6; per kg of phosphorous, V$N 6.3; and per kg of paddy, V$N 10.0.

plication the result not of a movement along the production function but of a movement to a new production function. A study by Herdt and Mellor[8] stresses these technical aspects of fertilizer use as opposed to differences that might arise between varieties or result from differing physical conditions (for example, soil, water, or climate).

The data analyzed here are different from those used in the Herdt-Mellor study. First, the information acquired from the sample of 120 farmers in LBD and TCN was not the result of a controlled experiment as were the Herdt-Mellor data, taken from experimental station tests.[9] Therefore, the results are more instructive with respect to the motivational implications of investment decisions to employ fertilizer than the results obtained from a technical experiment. Moreover, by

[8] See Robert W. Herdt and John W. Mellor, "The Contrasting Response of Rice to Nitrogen: India and the United States," *Journal of Farm Economics*, vol. 46 (February 1964), pp. 150–160.
[9] "In general, the farm data did not include high enough applications of nitrogen to reveal the area of declining response; there were not enough farm data available to give a reliable estimate of the response functions; and, the available data covered only a very few years" (ibid., p. 155).

comparing data from two villages less than 30 kilometers apart as opposed to comparing data from different countries, the technical conditions stressed by Herdt and Mellor become of secondary importance, and differences in immediate economic conditions become more relevant.

The Yield Response

The yield responses of the surveyed farmers are plotted by village and observation number on two scatter diagrams, Figures 9.1 and 9.2. The LBD results show that approximately 20 percent of the users were experiencing negative returns at use levels above 234 kilograms, while in TCN, where the average level of fertilizer use was 164 kilograms (as opposed to an average dosage of 199 kilograms in LBD), very few farmers were in the negative-return range.[10]

Regressions on experimental data have shown that the quadratic curve, which admits data showing yield declines at high-use levels, gives a good fit.[11] A quadratic equation was fitted successfully to the LBD data, whereas nonsignificant coefficients were obtained using TCN data. To obtain satisfactory TCN results, two linear fits were made, one with only those observations using less than 250 kilograms and the other using all observations. These results showed a very high yield response at low-usage levels: The responses ranged from between 3 and 4 kilograms of paddy per kilogram of fertilizer, in the case of the TCN coefficient, to as high as 10 kilograms of paddy per kilogram of fertilizer on the basis of the quadratic LBD fit. At higher-use levels the returns to additional kilograms of fertilizer began to decline on the basis of the

[10] The fitted curve must be viewed as an average response curve. Because of the special characteristics of their plots, for example, special soil conditions, some of the LBD farmers observed in the diminishing-returns range were probably not experiencing decreasing returns. But the existence of a large number of observations beyond the fitted optimum, in combination with the recent highly permissive economic restraints on fertilizer investment (for example, the very low interest rates prevailing after 1965), and direct responses reporting negative returns, all point to the conclusion that different farmers were at different points on the fertilizer-response learning curves and that some were experiencing negative returns. Others, farther out on their learning curve, had already experienced negative returns and had moved back to the positive-return portion of the production function.

[11] FAO, *Statistics of Crop Responses to Fertilizers*, Appendix C, particularly pp. 89–90.

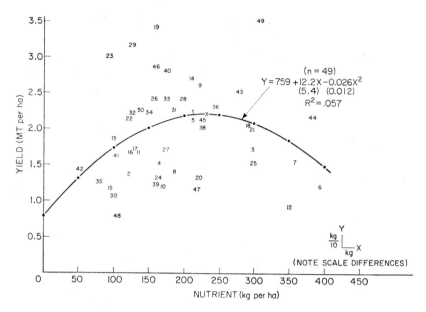

FIGURE 9.1   Long Binh Dien Yield Response to Fertilizer

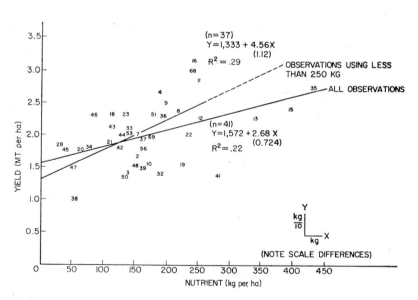

FIGURE 9.2   Than Cuu Nghia Yield Response to Fertilizer

quadratic equation, but even at the 150-kilogram level an additional kilogram of fertilizer yielded 4.4 kilograms of paddy. From these results it appears that as a rule of thumb the 6:1 response ratio was a realistic statement of the prevailing response relationship for usage levels below 150 kilograms. Above this level, a 6:1 response was seldom obtainable.

POSSIBLE HYPOTHESES

Before examining the question of profitability, several hypotheses were studied in an effort to clarify the yield-response relationships.

1. It was possible that the labor shortage caused farmers to substitute abundant capital for scarce labor, which might explain the wide range of yield-response results obtained. Farmers short on labor may have by-passed weeding, dike preparation, and similar activities, choosing to apply generous doses of fertilizer instead. This was a possibility despite the fact that the secular trend in Japan, for example, has shown that labor and capital are complementary factors in rice production.

To test this hypothesis, a variable representing the supply of labor available for rice cultivation was constructed on the following basis: The household manpower supply was weighted by a factor of 60 days for families farming one rice crop and 90 days for those farming two crops; to this result were added the man-days of labor reported hired by the family for rice cultivation. (Harvest labor was excluded, since its use was more a result of production decisions than a factor in these decisions—both because the harvester's share was constant at one-sixth and because the harvest wage was paid in kind rather than in cash.) The resulting available-labor-per-hectare-cultivated variable (including land double-cropped) was correlated with the nutrient use per hectare variable for both villages. A correlation coefficient of .178 was obtained for LBD and a coefficient of .244 for TCN. Both are positive and statistically nonsignificant at the .05 level. On the basis of these results, the factor-substitution hypothesis, which would require a significant negative coefficient, was rejected.

2. Next it was hypothesized that variations in insecticide use among the farmers might explain the variations in yield response. Insects were a serious problem for rice growers, but generally efforts to combat them with available insecticides had failed. Interview responses indicated that

the farmers applied small amounts of insecticides; then, if insect damage was detected, much larger quantities were applied.

In LBD 80 percent of the farmers used insecticides on their rice crops, spending an average of 199 piasters per hectare. The 7 farmers who used no insecticides obtained slightly higher yields (2.07 metric tons) than those who did (1.98 metric tons), indicating that insecticides were employed as a cure rather than as a preventive. A scatter diagram relating yield and insecticide use per hectare showed no conclusive relationship.

Two types of insects were common. One was a winged insect (con ray) against which available insecticides were judged effective; the other was a borer (con bo) that lived in the stem of the rice plant and against which no available product was effective. According to the farmers the con bo had not been a serious problem until the mid-1950's, yet in the 1960s it threatened the traditional confidence that farmers had in expected rice yields. An LBD farmer stated that "rice cultivation is now a risk-taking enterprise because of the con bo. One time, some ten years ago, it was not; then there could be some insurance that good results would be obtained; this was known beforehand, before the growing season."

Seven of the 120 farmers interviewed attributed the arrival of the con bo to the use of fertilizer. Hendry reported a similar speculation in 1958.[12] This association originates with the fact that the first years of marked damage from the con bo coincided in the late 1950s and early 1960s with the initial heavy use of fertilizer. But this did not necessarily imply causation, and most of the farmers knew it. Only in the case of urea might there have been some connection between the additional foliage produced and the ability of a field to support the con bo; yet the best evidence that the farmers rejected direct causation is that they used heavy quantities of fertilizer.

A more likely cause of increased incidence of the stem borer was the increased cultivation of a second rice crop. In the lower Delta, where irrigation obstacles limited farmers to one yearly crop, leaving the fields idle for six months, the stem borer was not a problem because, lacking foliage, the borers could not breed over the dry season. Only in the

[12] James B. Hendry, *The Small World of Khanh Hau* (Chicago: Aldine Publishing Co., 1964), p. 74.

upper Delta had the developments outlined earlier allowed 40 percent of the farmers to grow two crops. In this case, structural and technical changes had produced a disequilibrium that was not followed closely enough by further technological developments to meet changed conditions: No insecticide was available to combat the stem borer.

Therefore, the yield-nutrient results obtained for LBD cannot be explained by variations in insecticide use. This follows because those who used more insecticides did not obtain higher yields and because there was no evident relationship between fertilizer use and insecticide use. Also, we know that the influence of a random variable—insect incidence —on the expected relationship between two other variables—fertilizer use and yields—although it may increase the dispersion of the scatter, should do so with similar effects from low to high levels of fertilizer use.

3. Next it was thought that the difference in yield response between LBD and TCN might be due to differing soil or varietal conditions; that is, a higher yield response was obtained in TCN because the rice varieties employed were more responsive to fertilizer use or because the soils in TCN were more deficient in the chemicals provided. To accept this hypothesis, one would have to postulate further that the farmers in LBD were copying the usage habits of farmers in TCN or that they were irrational, in order to explain their use of fertilizers.

Farmers in both villages applied the two nutrients available (nitrogen and phosphorus) in ratios ranging from 1:3 to 1:4 nitrogen to phosphorus, implying that to the farmers at least the soil deficiencies were similar in the two villages. A soil study of Vietnam[13] describes the soils in both villages as undifferentiated alluvial soils. This similarity is also supported by the fact that the most common rice variety in both villages was *nang tra.* (The primary factors in the selection of the variety grown were the plot's soil and water conditions.) Because, of the ten rice varieties grown in the villages in 1966, 62 percent of the farmers in LBD and 70 percent in TCN selected *nang tra,* it is likely that soil and water conditions were similar.

To inquire further, the fertilizer-yield responses for the 52 *nang tra* growers in both villages (26 in LBD, 26 in TCN) were plotted on a scatter diagram. The results showed that the *nang tra* users in TCN ex-

13 F. R. Moorman, *The Soils of Vietnam* (Saigon: Ministry of Agriculture, 1961).

perienced a well-grouped result with increasing yields resulting from increased fertilizer use, while the observations from LBD were scattered around the TCN trend, generally displaying no association. Not only does this result support the rejection of the soil-varietal hypothesis, but it is further evidence that the fertilizer results obtained in the two villages were, for some not immediately evident reason, different. Moreover, the argument applied in rejecting hypothesis (2) applies *mutatis mutandis* to the influence of soil variations on the expected relationship if soil variation can be assumed to be a random variable.

A SUBSISTENCE HYPOTHESIS

Despite the historical and geographical similarity of the two villages, factors that led us to anticipate similar farmer behavior, important economic differences had emerged since 1962. In TCN, farmers had begun to grow vegetables for cash markets in Saigon, whereas LBD farmers did not grow vegetables on a large scale; LBD farmers were rice growers as they had been for decades. It is possible, therefore, that farmers in LBD applied fertilizer to meet a subsistence need, whereas TCN farmers were motivated by rate-of-return considerations. An alternative formulation of this hypothesis would be that cash and subsistence motives were evident in both villages, but the cash motive was stronger in TCN and the subsistence motive predominant in LBD. We turn now to a discussion of these possibilities.

The Determinants of Fertilizer Use: Profitability versus the Subsistence Need

PROFITABILITY

Differentiating the following equation[14] (fitted from the data in Figure 9.1),

$$Y = 759 + 12.2X - 0.026X^2, \qquad (9.1)$$

[14] For the purpose of the following analysis, it will be assumed that the quadratic equation represents the best general relationship for both sets of data. This assumption follows from the belief that had TCN farmers approached the fertilizer usage levels of LBD farmers, they would also have encountered negative returns as in fact three or four TCN farmers apparently did; the assumption does not obscure the reasons either for greater fertilizer application in LBD or for the greater dispersion of results obtained with the *nang tra* variety.

where Y and X are, respectively, kilograms of paddy and fertilizer, and setting the resulting equation equal to zero, we find that negative technical returns to additional fertilizer use occur at the 234-kilogram level (see Figure 9.1). This relationship becomes a total revenue function if it is multiplied by ten piasters, the prevailing paddy price.

The total cost function is constructed in the following manner: Because the only costs associated with fertilizer applications vary with the dosage applied, the form of the function is $Y = aX$, where a is the cost of application per kilogram of fertilizer. By weighting the nutrient cost of nitrogen by 1 and that of phosphorus by 4, the price per kilogram of fertilizer nutrient is 7.4 piasters for the 1966 period. Adding the cost of transportation and handling, 0.4 piaster per kilo, the cost of fertilizer application is 7.8 piasters per kilogram. From Chapter 5 it is assumed that the prevailing borrowing rate is 3 percent per month, or about 18 percent over the six-month period ($r = 0.18$). Substituting

$$TC = 7.8(1 + r)X \qquad (9.2)$$

into the total cost function, one obtains $TC = 8.5X$.

By plotting these two functions (see Figure 9.3), it is seen that the most profitable application is 220 kilograms of fertilizer per hectare.[15] LBD farmers were near this optimum (at 199 kilograms), while TCN farmers were short of it (at 164 kilograms).

From Figure 9.3 it is evident that the farmers were obtaining high profits from the use of fertilizer. The reason for these profits, apart from the yield response obtained, was the low cost of fertilizer. Doubling the price of fertilizer drops the most profitable level of application to

---

[15] At the most profitable dose, $P_P \Delta Y = P_F \Delta X$ or $\dfrac{\Delta Y}{\Delta X} = \dfrac{P_F}{P_P} = \dfrac{dY}{dX}$. From

Equation 9.1, $\dfrac{dY}{dX} = b - 2cX$ or $\dfrac{P_F}{P_P} = b - 2cX$. Substituting c, the relevant

prices and coefficients into $X = \dfrac{b - P_F/P_P}{2c}$, the result is:

$$X = \frac{12.2 - \dfrac{8.5}{10}}{(2)\ (0.026)}$$

or

$$X = 220 \text{ kg.}$$

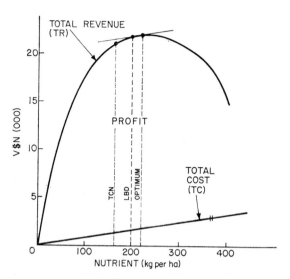

FIGURE 9.3   Returns to Fertilizer Use

only 202 kilograms; raising it three times lowers this level to 186 kilo-grams.[16] Put another way, doubling the price of fertilizer in 1966 would have had little effect on the amounts applied, absorbing twice the amount of piasters of inflationary pressure actually absorbed by fertilizer import purchases, and in the process would have saved the United States approximately seven million dollars in piaster costs (without any direct savings in foreign exchange costs).[17]

High profits certainly help explain the high levels of fertilizer use in the villages. The historical background is also revealing. Over the 1964–1966 period the price of fertilizer did not change, yet the price of paddy rose from 4 piasters in 1964 to 5 piasters in 1965 and jumped to 10 piasters in 1966, with most of the increase coming before August 1966 when these fertilizer decisions were made. Meanwhile the money rate of interest had fallen from 5 to 3 percent per month. These conditions suggest that farmers in 1965 and 1966 were confronted with vastly dif-

[16] Using equation in preceding footnote.
[17] Fertilizer imports in 1965 were valued at U.S. $11,021,000 (USAID, ASB, 1966, p. 81), approximately the 1961–1966 average. The United States in 1965 received approximately V$N 40 per dollar for these imports. Assuming the import price was doubled with the market price, the additional piasters valued at the then-prevailing exchange rate of V$N 60 to 1 had a value of U.S. $7,347,333.

ferent economic conditions from those prevailing before 1964. Interview results found that many farmers were still moving along their production functions seeking a new optimum. One farmer who had exceeded the optimum in 1965, using 219 kilograms, said, "A heavy application of fertilizer gives weak rice plants and a lower yield; it is both expensive and inefficient." Another said, "I tried to increase the amount of fertilizer used but failed to get any product in return."

Nonetheless, the profit explanation does not explain the differences in fertilizer use between the two villages, particularly why 20 percent of the LBD users applied fertilizer in the range of negative returns.

A SUBSISTENCE NEED

To explain the differences in the level of application between farmers and between villages, a subsistence explanation for fertilizer use was considered. Such an explanation followed from the fact that TCN farmers, who had an alternative use for fertilizer on vegetables at a higher return, were more "cash"-oriented and approached the fertilizer optimum in rice cultivation more cautiously than LBD farmers, who had no such alternative. An independent variable was constructed to test the possibility that the farmers were buying fertilizer in an effort to increase the likelihood that the subsistence rice requirements of each family would be met from its own field (substituting capital for land).

According to this possibility, one would anticipate that as the natural yield (the yield unaided by fertilizer) of the family's farmholding (size assumed to be institutionally determined and unchangeable) fell short of the subsistence food needs of the family—a function of household size—the use of fertilizer per hectare would increase, with secondary regard being given to profitability considerations.

Weighting the members of each family by 1.0 for males fifteen or above, 0.7 for females fifteen or above, and 0.4 for children—weights relating the consumption requirements of the last two groups to the standard adult male consumption unit—the resulting per family sum was divided into the rice area cultivated by the family to arrive at a land per male-consumption-unit variable. In Figure 9.4 this variable is plotted against the nutrient use per hectare of each family. The results were first plotted by village and fitted with reciprocal and log-reciprocal functions. (A correlation coefficient of r = .394 was obtained for LBD and a $r = .366$ for TCN, both significant at the .05 level.) But the fits were not good, nor were the fits on the pooled observations acceptable. There is in fact no reason to expect that the indicated economic relationship should be describable by a single function, like a hyperbola, throughout the range of the independent variable.

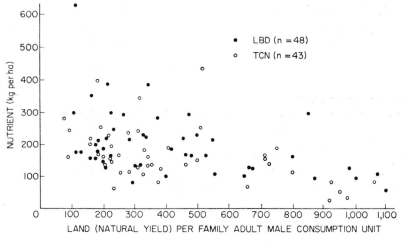

FIGURE 9.4   The Subsistence Response

Looking at the scatter diagram in thirds across the horizontal axis, we see that in the middle third there is a large variation in nutrient-use values, whereas for the leftmost third there is a tendency for Y to take on higher values. Even more clearly, in the rightmost third, Y takes on very low values. These results are compatible with nutrient use being a monotonically decreasing function of the land available per consumption unit. We would expect that, as the land available per consumption unit (CU) became very small and the diminishing returns to fertilizer use were recognized, the farmers would give more weight to profitability considerations, and that these would constrain the subsistence response. Conversely, as the land available per CU approached high values, the high rates of return to small quantities of fertilizer were not ignored and fertilizer use did not decline to zero.

This relationship between fertilizer use and the land available per family consumption unit is termed the "subsistence motivation" for fertilizer use. Besides the rate-of-return constraints on the relationship, there are other factors that would weaken it. Different families might have different attitudes toward risk. Or, in the case of crop failure, some families might be more able to rely on friends or relatives for assistance than others. Further, some farmers in both villages had other sources of cash income: 18 of the farmers in LBD and 8 in TCN received salaries as part-time government employees. These families had a fallback source of income in case of low yields. For these reasons one would expect some variation in the subsistence relationship.

Nevertheless, reasons for the subsistence concern on the part of farmers are not difficult to find. Very low levels of income had been common in the past, particularly on the part of former laborers. Even in 1966, 6.7 percent of the farm sample had incomes below the subsistence range and an additional 20.8 percent of the households were within the subsistence range. Every farmer sought to have an adequate supply of rice to meet the subsistence needs of his family and to provide the seed necessary for planting the next year's crop. The strength of this attitude is evident in the failure of both the Vietnamese government and Viet Cong programs to persuade each farmer to store rice in its designated "secure" area. Instead, the family's rice supply was always stored in the most protected corner of the house. Historically, at planting time farmers acquired debts at 5–10 percent per month to meet the basic expenses necessary to plant their rice crops. Otherwise they faced possible starvation as members of a laboring class subject to the economic success or failure of other farmers. Crop success implied freedom from starvation and a temporary escape from indebtedness until the next planting season.

This subsistence tendency lingered on in both LBD and TCN. As the newly available cash-crop alternatives prove themselves, it will quite likely become a consideration of less importance. Meanwhile, the uncertainties of war gave it added weight. In switching from a subsistence crop to a cash crop, the farmer is faced with a dilemma. If he grows a subsistence crop and is successful, his family's subsistence needs will be met regardless of the crop's market price. However, if he chooses to grow vegetables, the cash crop, he may fail to provide adequate food for his family (assuming a successful crop) either because vegetable prices decline or because rice prices rise unexpectedly.[18]

[18] See Walter P. Falcon, "Farmer Response to Price in a Subsistence Economy: The Case of West Pakistan," *American Economic Review*, vol. LV, no. 3 (May

Multiple Regression Analysis

The foregoing results point to two determinants of fertilizer use: the profit motive and the subsistence motive. On the assumption that rural capital markets are perfect, one would not anticipate, except as a result of different levels of experience or different subsistence requirements, that fertilizer use would vary between families. However, it is unlikely that all families had equal access to capital. Some families had high incomes, others obtained loans from relatives, and others had special advantages (for example, land) in obtaining government loans. Tenant farmers at low-income levels with small amounts of land per CU might not be expected to use as much fertilizer as higher-income landowners who had received government loans but had the same land per CU.

The following regression equations (9.3 and 9.4) were obtained, relating nonrice income (X_I), debt (X_D), and land per consumption unit (X_L) to the nutrient use (Y) per hectare cultivated:

$$\text{LBD} \qquad Y = 253.8 + 0.416X_D - 0.078X_I - 0.126X_L$$
$$\phantom{\text{LBD} \qquad Y = 253.8 +} (0.147) \quad\ (0.044) \quad\ (0.034) \qquad (9.3)$$
$$\phantom{\text{LBD} \qquad Y = 253.8} R^2 = .242$$

$$\text{TCN} \qquad Y = 211.2 + 0.212X_D + 0.093X_I - 0.161X_L$$
$$\phantom{\text{TCN} \qquad Y = 211.2 +} (0.140) \quad\ (0.075) \quad\ (0.043) \qquad (9.4)$$
$$\phantom{\text{TCN} \qquad Y = 211.2} R^2 = .220$$

The parenthetical figures with the equations are the standard errors for the regression coefficients. In LBD and TCN the income variable was nonsignificant at the .05 level. In LBD, where the income coefficient comes closest to significance at the .05 level, it has a negative sign indicating, if anything, that higher nonrice incomes are related to lower levels of fertilizer use. The debt coefficient in LBD is positive and significant at the .05 level, but debt and fertilizer use in TCN are not significantly related. This result follows from the presence of a government loan program in LBD that provided funds at 12 percent per year. In TCN there was no government loan program. In both villages the land per

---

1964), pp. 582–583. Falcon found that the supply response to sugarcane price increases was dampened because, to grow sugarcane, farmers had to forgo growing wheat, the subsistence crop. The price response coefficients between cash crops were larger than those between subsistence and cash crops.

CU or subsistence coefficients were significant at the .01 level and had negative signs, supporting the relationship discussed earlier.

Among these variables, 24 percent ($R^2 = .242$; the multiple correlation coefficient is adjusted for the degrees of freedom used up in the estimated parameters) of the variation in fertilizer use is explained by Equation 9.3 for LBD and 22 percent by Equation 9.4 for TCN. In an effort to improve the amount of variation explained, several other variables were introduced. Because results showed that those who raised a second crop used less fertilizer per hectare cultivated, a variable was introduced, which assumed a value equal to the amount of land double-cropped by the household (for example, for one-crop land it assumed a value of zero, for two-cropped land, 1.0, and for land half double-cropped, 0.5, and so forth). The correlation coefficients between second-cropping and fertilizer use were $-.327$ in TCN and $-.402$ in LBD. Both coefficients, significant at the .05 level, justify the inclusion of this variable in the regression analysis. In the following equations (9.5 and 9.6) this variable is X_C.

It was also thought that the level of rent paid might affect the use of fertilizer. This could happen in two ways. First, if, as assumed earlier, rents were a fixed amount per hectare, then farmers who had little land per CU would deduct from their crop the amount of rent they expected to pay before determining the amount of fertilizer to be employed in substituting capital for land. Alternatively, if rents were variable with yield, as they might have been in more secure LBD for farmers whose owners lived nearby, then a negative coefficient might be expected between rents and fertilizer use.

Two rent variables were used. One was the percentage of the crop paid in rent; the other adjusted this result using a dummy variable: For rents of zero (owners) the household received a 0, for rents of 0–10 percent, 1; 10–20 percent, 2; 20–30 percent, 5; and above 30 percent, 7. This adjustment was made on the likely supposition that the percentage of the crop paid in rent represented the strength of the owner's position vis-à-vis his tenant. In the absence of any time series data relating yields and rents paid, this variable would be an excellent proxy for the landlord's ability to raise rents if crop yields increased from fertilizer use. Compared with the first rent variable, the second was intended to demonstrate that an owner collecting 40 percent in rents was more than twice as "intolerant" as one collecting 20 percent in rent. Because this latter variable (X_R) gave better regression coefficients and higher correlation coefficients, it appears in Equations 9.5 and 9.6:

LBD $\quad Y = 250.4 + 0.253X_D - 0.097X_L - 0.785X_R - 68.0X_C$

$\qquad\qquad (0.129)\quad (0.036)\quad (1.00)\quad (33.6)\quad (9.5)$

$\qquad\qquad\qquad R^2 = .250$

TCN $\qquad\quad Y = 203 - 0.127X_L + 11.4X_R - 24.0X_C$

$\qquad\qquad\quad (0.043)\quad (4.86)\quad (24.5)\qquad\qquad (9.6)$

$\qquad\qquad\qquad R^2 = .280$

Notice in Equations 9.5 and 9.6 that nonrice income has been dropped from both equations, and debt from the TCN equation. The results obtained from the inclusion of the new variables $(X_R$ and $X_C)$ raise the proportion of variation explained by the TCN equation by 6 percent while having little effect on the LBD value of R^2. In both cases the coefficient of the X_C—second-cropping—variable has the expected negative sign, but only in LBD is the X_C coefficient statistically significant at the .05 level. It appears that only at the higher levels of fertilizer use common in LBD was the proportion of the field double-cropped an important determinant of fertilizer use.

The rent variable produced very interesting results. For more secure LBD, the coefficient is negative although nonsignificant. In TCN it is positive and statistically significant at the .02 level. This difference can probably be explained by the fact that, in LBD, a fear that landlords would take higher rents if more fertilizer was applied was sufficient to suppress the subsistence motivation as it related to rents. In contrast, in more insecure TCN, where landlords had less leverage with tenants, the subsistence considerations arising from rent payments could be given weight; that is, the TCN farmer could treat his rent payment as a fixed cost. For LBD farmers, rents had a variable cost component. Similar results were obtained from the simple correlation coefficients. In TCN, r for Y and Y_R was .35 (significant at the .05 level) whereas in LBD a nonsignificant r of $-.11$ was obtained.

In Equations 9.5 and 9.6 the statistical significance of the X_L variable, in every case at the .01 level, remained unchanged. Recalling that fertilizer use and the available labor supply variable were positively correlated in TCN, the labor supply variable was introduced into the regression analysis to determine if, in fact, the X_L variable was merely serving as a proxy for the labor supply per hectare. Because of the expected high intercorrelation between the labor variable and the amount of land per CU ($r = .56$), its inclusion lowered the significance of X_L to the .05 level, although the labor supply variable itself was nonsignificant and its inclusion did not raise the multiple correlation coefficient. A separate regression in which the labor variable replaced the X_L variable showed that, although the labor coefficient became significant (at the .05 level), the equation itself explained only 7.4 percent of the total variation in fertilizer use. These results indicate that X_L is the superior independent variable and is not merely serving as a proxy for the labor supply.

Conclusions

The findings of this chapter support those of studies in India and Pakistan and point again to the danger of an indiscriminate application of rate-of-return criteria to farming decisions in an underdeveloped economy. In particular, these findings support the earlier results obtained by Falcon and by Herdt and Mellor, which demonstrated that the effect of subsistence motivations on investment decisions may, if they are not recognized, give the appearance of irrationality.[19]

These results break new ground in two areas. First, they provide nonexperimental evidence that there are technical limits on the returns to fertilizer use in rice economies where high-yielding varieties and techniques have not been perfected. Second, the finding that the investment response varied with subsistence considerations even among farmers raising only the subsistence crop, as contrasted with Falcon's finding that the supply response varied between cash and subsistence crops,[20] is additional evidence that subsistence variables can provide valuable insights into the behavior of farmers in a traditional economy.

[19] Falcon, "Farmer Response to Price," and Herdt and Mellor, "Contrasting Response of Rice to Nitrogen."
[20] Falcon, "Farmer Response to Price."

10 Income
   and
   Investment

The chapter examines the aggregates of income and investment, how these variables were related to each other, and how they were affected by the attitudes of the Vietnamese.

Income

The net income of the family is the gross annual income derived from all sources (rice, vegetables, wages, salaries, trade revenues, animal sales, and so on) less the value of all investment expenditures (for example, fertilizer, hired and harvest labor, rent, and interest) made by the family.

The variable, gross income (Y_G), that is employed in this chapter includes the total rice crop produced valued at ten piasters per kilogram, thus imputing a value to all in-kind consumption of rice. Other items such as vegetable sales, salaries, rural wages, fruit and animal sales, remittances, rent and interest payments to the household, and revenues obtained from plowing, from merchandising, and from miscellaneous household industries are also included in Y_G. Additionally, each family was asked to estimate the value of in-kind consumption of vegetables—a major item in the Vietnamese diet; this figure is also included in Y_G.

Investment per household (I) includes money reported to have been spent for fertilizer, insecticides, hired labor (man-days $\times$ 100 piasters); in-kind harvest labor (at 10 piasters per kilogram harvested); rent paid for those renting rice land; interest at 1.0 percent per month on loans outstanding; depreciation of 2,000 piasters each year on a motor pump and a buffalo team, and 500 piasters on a sprayer; an estimated 3,000 piasters capital cost per *cong* of vegetable land cultivated; and 2,000 piasters per *cong* imputed rent on all vegetable land farmed.

No rent is imputed to owned rice land because to owners such land was used at zero opportunity cost; most rice-land owners would not rent out land under the prevailing Viet Cong pressures and lack of GVN legal control because there was no guarantee that the land could be repossessed when needed by grown-up children or if the supply of family labor expanded to justify its cultivation. However, an imputed rental value is given to all vegetable land because land was rented for vegetable use (since vegetable land eventually losts its fertility, its reversion to the owner or original tenant after three years was almost guaranteed). For reasons outlined previously (namely, the difficulty of assessing the nonfamily opportunities for the employment of family labor), no value is imputed to the household labor supply. This practice is consistent with the household's view of its objective in farm decision making, that is, to maximize the net income available for household consumption. Moreover, to impute a value to the transferable labor (for example, all males 16 to 60) in the household would involve the assumption that after removing the household head at this wage rate the family could continue to earn the residual income without his assistance and managerial talents. Since in some cases this would be true while in others it would not, a comparison of family performances after such a deduction is not possible. Instead, it is assumed that each farmer has weighed these opportunity costs as well as other considerations, such as the desirability of having land to farm because of the long-run stability of land-derived income compared with the uncertainties of the labor market.

By subtracting I from Y_G, one obtains the net annual income per household (Y_N). Figure 10.1 shows the results of this procedure. In the diagram, the approximate per household subsistence level of income range (240 kilograms per capita[1] or about 1,850 kilograms for the family of average size) is indicated. Only 8 (6.7 percent) of the sample's households had net incomes below the subsistence range; 7 of these were in TCN. By contrast, there were 12 "rich" farmers, evenly divided between the two villages. Otherwise, it is seen that 87 of the 120 house-

---

[1] See chap. 2, footnote 22. Using the sample's average household size of 7.7 and multiplying it by 240 kg, one obtains 1,850 kg of paddy, or V$N 18,500, as the subsistence level of income.

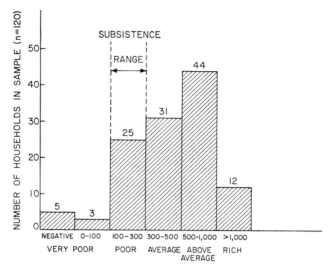

FIGURE 10.1   Family Net Income

holds had income levels at least two to three times their subsistence needs. Also, the distribution of the sample's income was in fact skewed toward the rich rather than the poor. It is not surprising that earlier efforts to establish a significant relationship between income and fertilizer use failed; it appears that very few families were so close to subsistence that they passed up investment opportunities in favor of immediate consumption expenditures.

By comparing the characteristics of the 8 very poor farmers with those of the 12 rich farmers it was found that the former group included 3 illiterate farmers, 3 GVN aid recipients, and 6 tenants, while the latter group included no illiterates, 10 aid recipients, and 5 tenant farmers. The average rice holding of the rich farmers was more than three times that of the very poor farmers. Nevertheless, 4 of the rich farmers were vegetable farmers who owned no land. The very poor group included the only two farmers who in the course of the interviews demonstrated that they were totally confused by the rapidly changing economic environment; both were illiterate and had no literate household member of adult age in their families.

Investment

To permit a close examination of the causes of the observed variations in income, the data are broken down by farmer type in Table 10.1.

TABLE 10.1 Income, Investment, and Other Variables

Category	Number in Sample[a]	Average Gross Income, Y_G (V$N 00)	Average Invest- ment, I (V$N 00)	Average Net Income, Y (V$N 00)	Average House- hold Size	Average Size of Rice Holding (ha)
1. Sample totals	120	732	282	450	7.7	2.00
2. LBD farmers	50	842	201	641	8.2	2.06
3. TCN farmers	70	653	339	314	7.4	1.95
4. Rice growers	57	808	188	620	7.9	2.08
5. Rice and vegetable growers	38	898	421	477	7.9	1.76
6. Vegetable growers	23	852	309	543	7.1	

[a] Categories 4, 5, and 6 do not total 120 because of incomplete investment data on 2 farmers.

Between LBD and TCN, LBD farmers enjoyed a greater net income (64,100 piasters versus 31,400 piasters) yet made a smaller average investment (20,100 versus 33,900). Therefore, even after the development of vegetable cultivation in TCN, it remained a poorer village relative to LBD. By comparing categories 4, 5, and 6 in the table, the reason for these results is evident. Rice growers invested less than the other two groups (18,800 versus 42,100 and 30,900 piasters), yet they received much higher net incomes than either rice and vegetable growers or vegetable growers (62,000 versus 47,700 and 54,300 piasters). In short, those who invested less earned more, or those who invested more earned less. Similarly, since off-farm investment opportunities were rare, it can be said that those who saved more earned less, or the rice growers saved less and earned more. There is one exception to this trend: Those who grew rice and vegetables invested more but earned less than vegetable growers or rice growers.

In Figure 10.2 an elasticity function is fitted for the three categories of farmer, relating gross income and total farm investment or savings. These equations are not identified but represent a linear combination of a savings function and a return on investment function (assuming that all income is from farm sources—actually about 80 percent was). Interpreted either way, the relevance of these equations to the present argument is the same. Written as savings (S) functions, they show that at the same level of income rice farmers are saving and investing a much

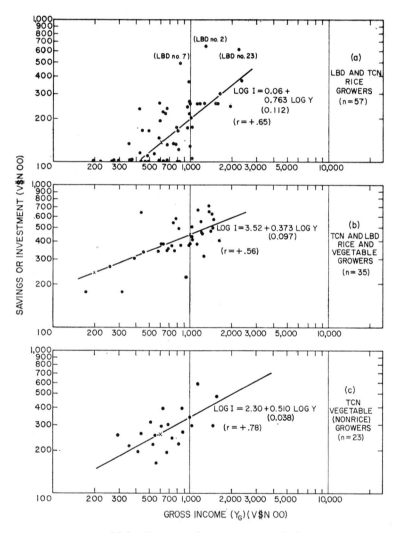

FIGURE 10.2 Income, Investment, and Savings

smaller share of their incomes than vegetable or rice and vegetable farmers.

rice only $\qquad$ $\log S = 0.06 + 0.763 \log Y$ $\qquad$ (10.1)
$(n = 57)$ $\qquad\qquad$ (0.118)

rice and vegetables $\qquad$ $\log S = 3.52 + 0.373 \log Y$ $\qquad$ (10.2)
$(n = 38)$ $\qquad\qquad$ (0.097)

vegetables only $\qquad$ $\log S = 2.30 + 0.510 \log Y$ $\qquad$ (10.3)
$(n = 23)$ $\qquad\qquad$ (0.088)

For example, at an income level of 60,000 piasters, a rice and vegetable farmer invests 36,500 piasters, a vegetable farmer 26,000 piasters, and a rice farmer only 13,900 piasters. At an income level of 100,000 piasters the respective investments are 45,000, 34,000, and 20,300 piasters.

Viewing the relationship as a return on investment function, we write the following equations:

rice only $\qquad$ $\log Y = -0.079 + 1.31 \log I$ $\qquad$ (10.4)

rice and vegetables $\qquad$ $\log Y = -9.49 + 2.68 \log I$ $\qquad$ (10.5)

vegetables only $\qquad$ $\log Y = -4.50 + 1.96 \log I$ $\qquad$ (10.6)

The small size of the rice intercepts as opposed to the large negative vegetable and vegetable and rice intercepts reflects the negligible initial capital investment required for rice cultivation compared with the heavy initial capital costs associated with vegetable farming. In the range of investments observed, the investment coefficients indicate a positive marginal product for capital in all cases but a much higher marginal product (at the same income level) for vegetable cultivation.

THE SUBSISTENCE OPTION VERSUS THE CASH OPTION

These results can be explained as follows. Rice growing, if the family has an adequate supply of land, is the preferred occupation; it requires a smaller labor input at less arduous tasks and gives a higher yield on the small amount of capital invested—the rice-capital coefficient is not a variable (except for fertilizer), and diminishing returns set in rapidly. Vegetable growing requires little land but a large amount of labor (at difficult tasks) and large quantities of capital (in effect, capital is substituted for land). If a farmer had an adequate supply of land to occupy his family labor at rice growing, he did not grow vegetables.[2] The explanation for this is threefold: two parts rational, one part non-rational.

First, employing 1966 methods of vegetable cultivation, farming with only hired labor was not a profitable enterprise. Vegetable growing was a family-unit, child-labor-using task; several farmers had attempted large-scale growing with hired labor but had been forced by the high cost and low efficiency of hired labor to cut back their operations to that size manageable by the family, employing hired labor for only mass-production tasks like harvesting. Second, from the consumption side, the well-endowed rice farmer had only a profit motivation and not a subsistence motivation to seek higher income—or, beyond subsistence needs, the utility of income declined. Third, several rice farmers said that their children would not "dirty their hands" at the difficult tasks of vegetable cultivation.[3] However, the last reason was probably a reflection of the first two reasons more than an indication of an outright refusal to work. This is true because some of those who grew only vegetables were former rice farmers who as refugees had no alternative (having no land) but to grow vegetables on small plots.

Contrasting the characteristics of the rice growers with the rice and vegetable growers, the major difference is in the smaller-size plot of the latter group (1.76 hectares) compared with the former (2.08 hectares). The family sizes of both groups were almost identical. Consider the farmer whose family supply of labor is not fully employed growing rice on his small plot. He may choose either to grow some rice and some vegetables or to specialize in vegetables and sublease land to other vegetable growers. Most farmers in this category chose the "subsistence option" of growing some rice and cultivating a vegetable plot of a size

[2] The vegetable growers' lower average age (43 years compared with the non-vegetable growers' 52 years) is a result of the inability of the limited supply of land to provide rice land for younger generations. This age difference, coupled with the fact that some vegetable farmers were in temporary housing as refugees, explains the small household size of this group.

[3] The wife of a landowner with five children, who in 1963 left 10 ha of land owned in a Viet Cong area and began renting a hectare of rice land in LBD, when asked why her family did not farm vegetables, replied, "My husband and children are accustomed only to indoor work, not to painstaking outdoor activities."

adequate to occupy the family nonrice labor supply rather than the "cash option" of vegetable growing. Doing this they sacrificed the advantages of specialization (the rice and vegetable growers obtained a lower return on their investments than either the rice or the vegetable farmers) in vegetable cultivation, while at the same time gaining access to a farming activity for which the return on investment was higher than the option they had of putting more capital in their rice plot.

To sum up, per household investments or savings were primarily dependent upon the opportunities for investment open to the household and were not determined by matters of individual preference. Each farmer started with his family labor supply and available land. If the supply of land was sufficient for rice cultivation to occupy his family's labor resources, he saved and invested only small amounts, for the reasons already outlined. If he saved more than he invested in rice cultivation, he may have participated in a *hui* as a creditor, but more likely he consumed this income because other farm investment opportunities gave a low return, and nonfarm investment opportunities were limited.

Therefore, any observation of the rice (prevegetable) economy of the Delta before 1963 would have given results similar to those in Figure 10.2 (a). Those with high levels of investment (respondents 2, 7, and 23) were special cases: no. 2 was a rice merchant, no. 7 purchased a cow after selling a buffalo, and no. 23 was a fish merchant. In general the scatter is inconclusive; in particular, it would be inappropriate to conclude from it that the farmers had a low propensity to save. As the results of Figure 10.2 (b) and (c) show, the amount farmers saved and invested was determined by the production opportunities open to them. Without such opportunities for the employment of capital (for example, vegetable growing), or under conditions in which, in Professor Schultz's terms, the price of sources of income streams is high, the incentive to save would be absent and savings low.[4]

These results also serve to remind us of the overwhelming economic role played by land in the prevegetable economy of the Delta. As seen in Equations 10.7 and 10.8, fitted from interview data, the land factor (L) appears as the predominant factor in rice production while fertilizer

[4] Theodore W. Schultz, *Transforming Traditional Agriculture* (New Haven, Conn.: Yale University Press, 1964), p. 84.

(F), representing capital, and labor (W), the hired and family labor available, are nonsignificant:

rice production
function

$$\log Y = 2.61 + 0.896 \log L + 0.116 \log W$$
$$\qquad\qquad\quad (0.120) \qquad\quad (0.142) \qquad\qquad\qquad (10.7)$$

($n = 57$)

$$+ 0.070 \log F$$
$$\quad (0.098)$$

vegetable
production
function

$$\log Y = 3.87 + 0.596 \log L - 0.134 \log W \qquad\qquad (10.8)$$
$$\qquad\qquad\quad (0.443) \qquad\quad (0.404)$$

($n = 23$)

$$+ 0.598 \log F$$
$$\quad (0.304)$$

In the vegetable equation both land and capital appear to be major contributors to vegetable production, although only the capital coefficient is significant at the .05 level. (Because rice output was measurable in kilograms, and rice and vegetable output only in the value of the crop sold, Equation 10.8 is a much weaker production relationship than Equation 10.7.)

Next, equations were fitted on the assumption that land was the determining factor of production. Equations 10.9 and 10.10 both show significant coefficients for land, and Equation 10.10's land (L) coefficient of 1.09 indicates positive returns to scale (or specialization) for vegetable cultivation. Using capital alone in a vegetable production function gives Equation 10.11, which provides additional evidence of the important role of capital in vegetable cultivation.

rice production
function
$$\log Y = 3.21 + 0.875 \log L \qquad\qquad (10.9)$$
$$\qquad\qquad\quad (0.084)$$

vegetable production
function
$$\log Y = 3.10 + 1.09 \log L \qquad\qquad (10.10)$$
$$\qquad\qquad\quad (0.343)$$

vegetable production
function
$$\log Y = 3.68 + 0.838 \log F \qquad\qquad (10.11)$$
$$\qquad\qquad\quad (0.235)$$

ECONOMIC ATTITUDES

The general obstacles to increased investment in farm activities were evident from responses to the question, "What is your most important production problem?" Of 110 replies, 31 cited water or irrigation, and 19 the availability of three inputs—sprayers, insecticides, and fertilizers —all three distributed through official outlets at official prices (the last two were also sold at higher prices by private dealers). The input problems ranged from the most common complaints by those wishing to buy a sprayer but unable to obtain one (several farmers had been on official waiting lists for two years) to dissatisfaction with the effectiveness of the available insecticides and the inconvenient operating hours of the official outlets. The third major problem was profitability, mentioned by 18 farmers. In addition, 17 replies cited a shortage of family labor or the high price of hired labor; 14 said they had no production problems; and 2 cited the corvée, 2 insecurity, 4 crop and animal diseases, and 3 a shortage of land.

Putting the question another way, farmers were asked to state the reasons for various nonchanges, including both nonchanges mentioned by themselves as desirable but not accomplished in 1966 and nonchanges specifically suggested in the interviews (why do you not raise pigs, more vegetables, and so on?). Of the 219 responses, 72 cited a shortage of family labor and the high cost of hired labor, 60 considered the particular activity unprofitable, 31 said they lacked the necessary land, and 22 said their land was not adequately irrigated for the suggested activity. Of the minor replies, 8 mentioned a lack of knowledge or experience, 16 said the necessary inputs were not available (for instance, a sprayer), and 2 said they were "too old" to undertake the suggested change.

The responses revealed a realistic assessment of existing economic conditions. Farmers were frequently asked to explain their reasoning. Almost every reply showed that the alternative had been seriously considered and rejected on sound financial grounds; for example: "The rice bran price is too high for expanded pig production"; "too many pigs die"; "using hired labor makes vegetable growing unprofitable"; "I have no family member to watch the buffalo"; and "my home plot is too small for pig raising."[5]

[5] Realistic though these obstacles were, they did not prevent planning for expansion in 1967. Of 116 replies to a question on planned 1967 farm activities, 70

Conspicuously absent from these replies were so-called noneconomic obstacles to change. As noted earlier, on three occasions families indicated that they had bypassed vegetable growing because the family's members were not willing to engage in such "painful and dirty" labor. A 70-year-old woman farmer who also was the keeper of the local pagoda of the Cao Dai sect in LBD stated that she raised no pigs because, "I am a religious person, and the killing of animals is forbidden to every religious person," but such inhibitions bothered none of the other 9 Cao Dai subjects interviewed. (Ten farmers said they had no religion, while the remaining 100 said they were Buddhists.) No evidence was found that religious considerations conflicted in any way with economic ones (except the case noted), nor did the economic behavior of the Cao Dai or nonreligious subjects differ from the Buddhist subjects.

Besides the frequently cited problem of families finding it difficult to save the small daily cash surpluses they accumulated, being tempted instead to expend them on "wasteful consumption expenditures," the most frequently specified (by 11 farmers) noneconomic obstacle to additional savings and investment was the temptation to gamble and drink. The farmers gambled on cock fights and card games, both flourishing activities in the dry season. One farmer said his economic welfare had improved over previous levels because vegetable growing permitted such a full utilization of his day that he had no time to gamble or drink. On the whole, activities like gambling did not appear to occupy a disproportionate time or absorb large expenditures.

Nor did family considerations inhibit economic activities. To the contrary, as we saw in Chapter 6, the strength of the family relationship was an important factor in the efficiency of the family production unit.

There was evidence that farmers at about 60 years of age became less anxious to experiment and risk capital for further production. Several older farmers said they were satisfied with their incomes because it was sufficient to meet their basic needs. One said that "the presenting and implementation of new ideas is the task of the young," and another stated that he did not want to rent more rice land because he preferred to avoid competition with others and to limit the jealousies of ambition.

---

planned no change, 41 planned to expand their activities (including 18 to grow vegetables, 14 to raise more buffalo, pigs, or chickens, and 6 to begin growing a second rice crop), and 5 planned to contract their farm activities—frequently because a family member had been drafted or had found a better nonfarm job.

A question designed to explore attitudes of economic motivation was commonly employed in the interview: "What changes in farm operations would you make if you had a free choice and the money?" The replies indicated that the question was interpreted in various ways. Twelve farmers could think of no reply. Other answers depended on whether the subject interpreted the question to mean a large amount of money or a small amount. Of the 98 responses, 34 said they would expand their farm operations (most frequently by buying a cow or a buffalo); 21 said they would buy land; 15 wanted to quit farming and become merchants or enter the transportation business (for example, with a Tri-Lambretta); 10 would purchase agricultural implements (for instance, a motor pump or sprayer); 8 said they wanted to develop an orchard; and 7 wanted to purchase consumption items, 1 to pay debts, 1 to give the money to his children, and 1 to buy gold.

From these replies, in combination with the farmers' responses to the opportunities offered by the motor pump, vegetable cultivation, and fertilizer use, a convincing case emerges for the economic rationality of the Vietnamese farmer. Social, religious, or personal inhibitions to work and the adoption of new ideas and techniques played a role probably no more significant than they would play in rural areas of the United States or Britain. The Vietnamese farmer, attempting to meet his family's basic subsistence needs, recognized few obstacles to his attainment of that goal. One farmer, unable to find the necessary land in one village, rented four different plots in three different villages and commuted by bicycle every day to farm each plot.

If any single group of attributes characterized the economic attitudes of the Delta farmer in 1966–1967, it was his open-mindedness toward, attentiveness to, and thorough understanding of his surroundings, attributes that, combined with his willingness to work, save, and invest, offer a strong base for future development. This conclusion is not altogether different from that of Gourou, writing about the Tonkin peasant over thirty years ago; he said: "The Tonkin peasant . . . shows great adaptability, understands the advantage of new procedures very quickly, and is easily moved by any impetus given him."[6] These views

---

[6] Pierre Gourou, *The Peasants of the Tonkin Delta*, trans. Richard R. Miller (New Haven, Conn.: Human Relations Area Files, 1955), p. 585.

can be usefully contrasted with the conventional one, stated eloquently
by Virginia Thompson, a British observer of the 1930s:

> The Annamites have distinct psychological as well as economic draw-
> backs as farmers. Their whole life is so impregnated with ritual and
> static Chinese philosophy that it makes antique methods meritorious
> simply because they are old. New crops, the regular care of animals,
> the use of fertilizers are all incurably repugnant to him. He is even
> suspicious of agricultural credit, that will extract him from the blood-
> sucking usurers. Rice-fields require hard work of a disagreeable kind,
> standing knee-deep in water and shooing off predatory animals for
> hours at a time—yet it lasts for only a brief while. This has developed
> the qualities of perseverance and industry, but it has done nothing to
> remedy the Annamite's total lack of initiative. The native farmer
> works within the strict orbit of his needs, which may be summed up
> in his philosophy that it is easier to do without something than to
> work for it. If his daily needs are satisfied, the Annamite takes no
> thought for the morrow.[7]

[7] Virginia Thompson, *French Indo-China* (New York: Macmillan Co., 1937), p. 161.

11   Notes on Economic Aid and Viet Cong Tax and Trade Policies

Introduction

In the previous chapters we have examined evidence of the influence of GVN and U.S. economic policies and programs on the rural economy. The role played by the several hundred million dollars of U.S. economic assistance provided each year[1] in stabilizing the economy at reasonable rates of inflation had a profound impact on the rural economy. This impact resulted in the low prevailing rates of interest (see Chapter 5) and in the availability of foreign exchange for the importation of commodities such as the motor pump and important agricultural inputs like fertilizer.

Similarly, Viet Cong policies played a central role in promoting rural economic change. Foremost among these policies were their land reform and rent reduction policies, followed by their labor policies that made it difficult to farm large holdings (Chapter 6) and thereby created incentives for subsistence-motivated investment (for example, in fertilizer) and innovation (for example, irrigation canal construction and the motor pump).

The purpose of this chapter is to complete the discussion of GVN-U.S. and Viet Cong economic policies and programs as they affected the rural economy. The chapter begins with a discussion of the role of GVN-U.S. aid programs, considers briefly the macroeconomic role of aid in the Delta, and ends with an extensive discussion of Viet Cong tax and trade policies.

[1] U.S. economic assistance in 1965 was $267 million; in 1966, $705 million; in 1967, $577 million (see USAID, ASB, 1966, p. 187).

The Role of Aid in the Village Economy

Because of the war, the economy was subjected to the most massive aid program ever devised. Every imaginable program received attention— from tenant farmers' unions, cooperatives, and farmers' associations, on the one hand, to pigsties, Australian chickens, and tons of imported rice, on the other. No attempt will be made here to evaluate these efforts, except to the extent that their successes and failures in the villages studied are representative of nationwide conditions and results.

The principal organization of official GVN agricultural assistance in LBD and TCN was the Farmers' Association. Its primary function was to distribute fertilizer and insecticides at subsidized prices. Through it were administered the NACO loan program, the crop protection program, the secondary-crop program, in-kind loans of sprayers, the pig program, and a rice-variety improvement program. Seventy-eight of the 120 farmers interviewed were members of the Farmers' Association. They paid an entrance fee of 120 piasters and had to be solvent farmers of good morality—not Viet Cong—and receive the village chief's recommendation. Apparently everyone who wanted to join was successful in obtaining membership. Those who did not still had access to low-price fertilizer (but not government loans or loans of sprayers); if the supply of fertilizer ran low, nonmembers purchased it on the private market. In 1966 the supply was adequate, so nonmembers presented their identification cards and received 300 kilograms per trip, while members could buy 600 kilograms per trip. Several farmers said they did not join because the Viet Cong opposed membership. A 24-year-old farmer chose not to join because he feared being drafted. In other cases, wives joined to avoid this risk.

Where possible, each hamlet had a local resident who received loan requests and applications for membership and passed out booklets and occasionally free commodities. His major task was to organize the farmers for occasional meetings at which they were given lectures on farming methods. In TCN a "4-T group"—those farmers wanting special instruction and anxious to undertake special projects—had been organized by Mr. Hoi,[2] who was responsible for its success. Its meetings were somewhat hindered by the farmers' reluctance to gather in groups,

---

[2] See chap. 7, footnote 8.

since such groups usually attracted the officials responsible for the draft and the corvée; however, to remove this uncertainty and promote attendance at his meetings, Hoi secured an agreement with the GVN whereby no draft or corvée would be implemented if the Provincial Agricultural Chief, District Chief, or Province Chief attended the meetings.

There are three important roles for a village-level aid program: It must assess local conditions precisely in order to define local problems; it must devise new techniques to solve these problems; and it must communicate new ideas and techniques to the farmers. In assessing local conditions, the official organizations were ineffective. Their failure was due to the conditions of insecurity and what farmers termed the "bookish approach" of city-dwelling agricultural agents. Few government officials recognized that the best way to find out about the farmer's problems was to ask him.

In the second task (developing new techniques), the official programs were again unsuccessful in most instances. The *soc nau* rice variety given to farmers in 1965 failed miserably, yet the *nang tra* variety was responsible for the successful 1966 and 1967 crops. Official efforts to halt the epidemics plagueing chickens and pigs failed. Insecticides did not prevent crop damage. The GVN fertilizer subsidy program, as opposed to the U.S.-funded fertilizer import program, was little more than a program to transfer income to the rural inhabitant. The subsidy was not necessary to encourage farmers to try fertilizer as a new input; all farmers were familiar with its use. Nevertheless, its sale at low prices did amount to an income transfer of 3,000 to 10,000 piasters per household, and if it is considered that this was desirable and unachievable by direct transfer means (considering possible corruption in handling funds), the subsidy may have been justified. On balance, because the government favored its inefficient distributors at the expense of efficient private distributors, causing the farmers to complain about poor distribution and sometimes about corruption, the fertilizer program appeared to hurt the government's cause more than the subsidy helped it.

The best example of a successful aid program was that discussed in Chapter 7, which assisted the farmers in solving their irrigation problems. The second vital developmental role played by the government was in maintaining local roads and replacing war-damaged bridges. In these cases, in which the needs were clearly defined, the government performed effectively.

In the task of communicating new ideas, the government's efforts met with mixed success. We have seen that both the Vietnamese and U.S. aid organizations failed to recognize the truly remarkable potential of the motor pump. In contrast, a Chinese agricultural team member was extraordinarily successful in acquainting TCN farmers with new vegetable varieties. A member of this team arrived in TCN in late 1962, seeking to promote the growing of field vegetables on off-season rice fields. At first he failed to convince anyone to try his seeds. He finally succeeded in introducing several melon and squash varieties because he persuaded Mr. Hoi, who had a reputation as a "pioneer" farmer in the village, to introduce the varieties. (Hoi proudly described himself as one who "experiments to find out.")

In the examples cited thus far we are led to two conclusions regarding the success of the various agricultural aid programs. First, the process of communication of ideas was largely informal, by word of mouth. Of 97 replies specifying sources of agricultural information in TCN, 55 mentioned covillagers, 15 cited Mr. Hoi, 7 specified the local Farmers' Association, 8 singled out relatives, 5 obtained information from the provincial radio programs, and 7 mentioned agricultural publications distributed by the government. In all except the last two cases, the means of communication was word of mouth. But a good idea travels fast, particularly if it emanates from a farmer considered by others to be more experienced than themselves.

Than Cuu Nghia village received ideas from throughout the Delta. For example, farmers found out from one young villager in the army at Can Tho that farmers in An Giang Province were growing a new vegetable variety. Frequent visits to Saigon by nearly every villager were the source of market information; often such trips were made to purchase farm items. In his 1958 survey Hendry found that only 16 percent of the heads of household in Khanh Hau had never visited Saigon (55 kilometers away) and that the rest made several trips there each year; 59 percent reported that they had gone to Saigon once or twice in 1957, and 25 percent reported going more frequently than that.[3]

[3] James B. Hendry, *The Small World of Khanh Hau* (Chicago: Aldine Publishing Co., 1964), p. 28.

Our second conclusion gives recognition to the role of particular "leading farmers" who were able to familiarize outsiders with local problems, capable of testing new methods, and willing to teach other farmers to use them. In short, find a good idea, convince a leading farmer of its value, and let the informal word-of-mouth communication system disseminate its possibilities.[4]

The Macroeconomic Role of Aid

By contrasting the upper Delta experience as seen in Dinh Tuong with lower Delta developments observed in Bac Lieu, we see two possible effects of aid on rural sector savings; in the upper Delta, aid increased savings, while, in the lower Delta, aid decreased savings as a share of income, though savings in absolute value increased. In the lower Delta new productive factors and new production opportunities were only marginally significant, whereas conditions in the upper Delta gave rise to a whole new range of production possibilities. Higher rural product prices made possible by increased government—USAID supported—expenditures released the lower Delta population from burdensome debts but did not open up new investment opportunities on an appreciable scale. Lower Delta families with higher incomes raised a few pigs, thereby increasing savings to buy and feed them for home consumption; but as we have seen, the profitability of pig raising did not warrant production beyond the scale sustainable from low-cost family food resources. Likewise, in general, aid to the lower Delta brought higher levels of income to the peasantry, but it did not increase markedly the level of investment or the volume of production.

The value of aid in the lower Delta could have been justified only

---

[4] A study of nineteenth-century Japanese extension efforts suggests a similar conclusion. Saburo Yamada in his "Changes in Output and in Conventional and Nonconventional Inputs in Japanese Agriculture since 1880," *Food Research Institute Studies*, vol. VII (1967), no. 3, pp. 371–413, finds that "the start of extension work in Japan was an intimate knowledge of the best traditional farming methods." After attempts to introduce Western methods in agriculture in the 1870s failed, a Meiji technology evolved that was designed to increase the efficiency of small-scale farming. The government took a major role in the diffusion of knowledge of these improved practices by organizing local agricultural improvement societies. In 1880 the Ministry of Agriculture and Commerce invited 110 "leading farmers" to Tokyo to consider measures for improving agricultural production (p. 407).

from a humanitarian viewpoint or, from a Keynesian viewpoint, if the increased consumption in the rural areas raised the savings rate in urban areas to provide investment for the clothing or building industries (as examples), whose products were in greater demand by rural inhabitants. If such investments had indeed taken place and activated otherwise idle capacity in the industrial sector (or attracted foreign private investment), as opposed to utilizing imported commodities requiring further aid to meet foreign exchange costs, then the aid may have raised the rate of investment for the economy as a whole.

It is more likely, however, in any economy with a predominantly agricultural base and an underemployed rural population, that increased rural prices provide purchasing power to the farmer that in turn permits the employment in the nonfarm sector of previously idle labor resources. But these newly acquired urban incomes are largely spent on food items that raise rural prices further if—as in the lower Delta—there was little prospect for increasing rural investment and output using existing techniques. In this case further food and investment good imports, requiring additional aid assistance, are necessary to provide the food for the expanded urban labor force and inputs for urban industries. Without further aid (which the GVN received), the government would have been forced either to expand the money supply and move the economy into an inflationary spiral or to end the boom by refusing to validate the wage requests of the nonrural sector.

If one is to escape the development dilemma by raising the absorptive capacity of a rural economy, techniques must be found to raise the productivity of available land and labor resources. We have seen that the obstacles to such increases can be both technological (the need for new highly productive factors of production) and institutional—"noneconomic" institutions can prevent the allocation of available resources in an optimum manner with respect to the immediately or easily available technological opportunities.

Viet Cong Taxes

All Viet Cong policies were not as conducive to an improvement in the peasants' material well-being as their land reform efforts. Foremost among the regressive policies were the taxes the Viet Cong levied on the rural population.[5] From an economic viewpoint, the implementation of this tax in 1964/65 was a major blunder of the movement; it lost for the Viet Cong much of the support in the rural areas that their land reform policies had gained.

Following their initial surge in strength from 1960 until 1962, the Viet Cong were not, as a potential government, forced to impose heavy financial burdens on the populace. In fact, most party members or guerrillas were self-supporting; they served in their native villages and continued to grow their own crops to sustain themselves and their families.

What small expenses the Viet Cong incurred during this period were met by revenues from the *dam phu* (contribution) system. In 1963 this system became a formal tax, or *thue*, of 10 percent on yearly net revenue. Businessmen paid 10 percent of their gross profits, and fishermen and farmers 10 percent of their yearly net income as estimated by party observers. In addition, the Viet Cong implemented a "rice bowl" policy in areas frequently traversed by Viet Cong units in need of rice for immediate consumption. Every household was urged to set aside at each meal the portion of rice that an additional party would have consumed. The "rice bowl" was then periodically emptied whenever local or regional troops passed through the village.

THE ORIGIN OF THE COMPREHENSIVE TAX

In late 1964, Viet Cong directives implemented a new tax program that set up elaborate and complete procedures for tax assessment and collection. The centerpiece of this new system was the agricultural tax, or, as it was commonly called, the troop support tax. Behind this program was the need for greatly increased Viet Cong revenues to support expanded military operations.

The decision by the Viet Cong and the North Vietnamese to counter U.S. and GVN military pressure by large-scale attacks was made some-

---

[5] I am indebted to Mr. David Elliott of the RAND Corporation (at My Tho), who in several discussions on the politics of low-level Viet Cong organizations advised me on the direction of my research on this subject. In particular, he suggested that I interview several ex-Viet Cong who had demonstrated special knowledge of economic conditions in Viet Cong areas; it was from later interviews with these people that I obtained much of the information on which this and the following sections are based.

time in 1964.[6] Evidently some controversy preceded this decision, as the positions of the Viet Cong, the North Vietnamese, the Chinese, and the Russians were weighed. The outcome favored movement into a stage emphasizing military activities (the strategy advocated by the North Vietnamese and successfully employed by the Viet Minh against the French) rather than continuing the guerrilla approach of the 1960– 1963 period (the strategy recommended by the Chinese). The advice of the North Vietnamese, being of more recent and similar origin and offering the prospect of victory within two years, was accepted.

Movement toward larger-scale military operations required more men and more money, both of which had to come from the population under Viet Cong control. A heavy manpower draft and burdensome production taxes were needed. As a step toward increasing revenues, the Viet Cong initiated a complete assessment of each villager's taxable capacity that was to serve as the basis for the taxes to support the war.

THE SYSTEM OF TAXATION

In late 1964, throughout the Delta, Viet Cong financial and economic cadres gathered villagers together in public meetings for a thorough assessment of each family's productive assets. The basis of this assessment was the family's earning capacity, embodied primarily in the land it farmed. The tactic of making this assessment publicly was conducive to an accurate estimate, because among the farmers in any village in the Delta there was complete knowledge of the quality of each farmer's soil, the water available, the yields commonly obtained, and other relevant factors. This collective assessment also guaranteed an accurate exemption allowance for families, since the number of dependents was common knowledge in the village.

Rice land was divided into two-crop and one-crop land. On two-crop land the assessment was on the basis of, for example, 150 *gia* of paddy production per year; on one-crop land it was 100 *gia* per year. Orchard land was also divided into two categories: first, land on which mangoes, tangerines, and the more lucrative fruit crops were grown; second, land producing bananas, coconuts, betel nuts, Malayan apples, or guavas— products that sold at a lower price. The assessment on first-quality orchard land was based on a real value of 1,000 *gia* per hectare, on

[6] Douglas Pike, *Viet Cong* (Cambridge, Mass.: The M.I.T. Press, 1966), p. 107.

secondary orchard land at 150 to 180 gia per hectare. Vegetable land was not listed as a separate category, primarily because vegetables required immediate access to GVN markets and were therefore not grown in the areas under Viet Cong control. The agricultural tax base was determined by crop production capacity alone. Other productive assets such as pigs, chickens, buffalo, oxen, and fishing gear were taxed separately or not at all.

Exemptions or deductions were granted on the basis of the number of family members in the household. Families were also permitted to deduct members serving the Viet Cong away from their home villages. Each household member (and absent Viet Cong family member) was granted a 12 gia of paddy yearly consumption deduction from the total crop production capacity of the household. After the total family deductions were subtracted from the household's crop production capacity, the residual was taxed at a rate determined from the Viet Cong tax table (Table 11.1).

TABLE 11.1 1966/67 Viet Cong Tax Schedule

Gia	%	Gia	%	Gia	%
5–10	6	41–50	14	101–110	26
11–15	7	51–60	16	111–120	28
16–20	8	61–70	18	121–130	30
21–25	9	71–80	20	131–140	32
26–30	10	81–90	22	141–150	35
31–40	11	91–100	24		

For example, a Delta rural household of eight members with the economic assets described in Table 11.2 had a net taxable capacity of 93 gia.

Applying this 93 gia figure to the Viet Cong tax schedule in Table 11.1, this family paid a 24 percent tax on its productive (not taxable) capacity of 189 gia, or it paid a tax based on the real value of approximately 45 gia, which at early 1966 prices was 4,950 piasters.

A FLEXIBLE TAX PROGRAM

The tax schedule in Table 11.1 was a flexible financial tool. Productive capacity was estimated in real terms (paddy equivalence) by converting the gross revenue from orchard land into a paddy equivalent using a

TABLE 11.2 An Example Household's Taxable Capacity

Amount of Land (ha)	Type of Land	Rate of Tax (*gia* per ha)	Taxable Capacity (*gia*)
0.5	two-crop rice	150	75
0.5	one-crop rice	100	50
0.4	second-quality orchard	160	64
Total productive capacity			189
Less 8 household deductions (each 12 *gia*)			−96
Net taxable capacity			93

paddy price at some point of time, probably December 1964, after which the relationship was fixed in real terms. The percentage of income tax applied was easily and frequently shifted. For example, the range of 7 to 25 percent in 1965 became a 6 to 35 percent range, as in Table 11.1, in 1966 when the war was escalated further.

The tax was highly progressive: Had the family in the example in Table 11.2 produced 100 gia, it would have paid no taxes, but if production increased 50 percent to 150 gia, it paid a tax of 16 percent; and if it increased another 33 percent to 200 gia, it paid a tax of 26 percent. Because the assessment was made in real terms, it was unitary in response to price increases and progressive in response to production increases above the subsistence level.

A PROGRAM FOR CONTESTED AREAS

Another system of economic classification, occasionally used to assess taxes before the 1964–1965 period but rather more widely used for political purposes, was that which classified families into landlords, rich farmers, middle farmers, poor farmers, and very poor farmers (see Table 11.3). Very poor farmers, poor farmers, and some middle farmers —the popular base of the revolution—were the targets of the efforts of Viet Cong cadres to develop support for communist programs such as the draft. The landlords and rich farmers were treated either passively or as the enemies of the revolution.[7]

In areas where the Viet Cong were not in complete control, this

[7] This system exhibits a not surprising similarity to that used during the communist revolution in China in the late 1940s. See William Hinton, *Fanshen: A Documentary of Revolution in a Chinese Village* (New York: Random House, Vintage Books, 1966), pp. 27–28.

TABLE 11.3 Viet Cong Political-Economic Classification

Class	Criteria	Tax Rate (%)
Landlord	greater than 5.0 ha	35
Rich farmer	greater than 2.5 ha	24
Middle farmer	1.0–2.5 ha	12
Poor farmer	less than 1 ha	5
Very poor farmer	less than 0.3 to 0.4 ha	0

simpler system of economic classification was used as the basis for tax assessment as well as for political mobilization. It was adjusted in 1965 to reflect the changes in income levels discussed earlier (namely, the improved position of the laborer vis-à-vis the actual farmer). Before 1965 the very poor farmer was defined by the Viet Cong as one who had no land to farm; that is, he worked as a hired laborer. But in 1965 this criterion was changed, and laborers were taxed. Only the newly defined very poor family—a family "without enough to eat"—was tax exempt. Laborers with "enough to eat" were classified in a taxable bracket and assessed a fixed proportion of their income (for example, 5 percent).

TAX COLLECTION

Within the villages, tax collection was the responsibility of the finance and economy section cadres of the village-level civilian organizations, who were assisted by other cadres, most notably the Farmers' Liberation Association, which, as the key village-level institution with a popular base, was responsible for giving support to the tax collection program. The period of tax collection was centered around the harvest, when the farmers were in their best financial position.

The Viet Cong tax program allowed for adjustments in payments for crop loss. For example, a 30 percent crop loss was allowed a 30 percent tax assessment reduction; a 50 percent loss, a 50 percent reduction; and a greater than 50 percent loss, an 80 percent reduction. Like the initial tax assessment, the estimate of crop loss was made at a village meeting, making it difficult to overstate the true loss.

The Viet Cong employed a variety of sanctions on villagers who refused to pay taxes or paid less than their assessed tax. Those who complained received political indoctrination ranging from low-key village propaganda meetings to more rigorous sessions deep in Viet Cong territory. Besides the inconvenience of attending these meetings, villagers were afraid that Vietnamese government and U.S. forces would assume they were Viet Cong and bomb or shell them, a threat that was amplified if one was forced to go into Viet Cong–controlled areas for "reeducation" sessions. More serious sanctions such as induction into the supply units supporting Viet Cong combat battalions were sometimes invoked. These involved even greater personal risk and served as a deterrent to tax deliquency.

Tax revenues varied from village to village. In 1966 they were often as high as a million piasters (approximately $9,000) for a village of 500 families (about 2,500 people). This was an average tax of $18 per family, representing a sizable financial burden for a family earning from $100 to $200 per year.

Tax revenues expended at the village level to maintain the local cadres and support local activities represented not more than 10 percent of total village tax revenues. For example, in one village 100,000 piasters were kept for local use from tax revenues totaling 1,400,000 piasters. Countrywide, 70 to 80 percent of 1965–1966 Viet Cong tax revenues reportedly came from the agricultural tax. The major COSVN expenditures were for troop support items such as food.

From the standpoint of the farmer's standard of living, the Viet Cong tax, at 10 to 20 percent of the peasant family's gross income, was one of the heaviest economic burdens he had to carry. (Even at this level, however, it represented less than half the rent paid by the farmer tilling land in GVN-controlled areas.) Either the political-military decision to escalate the war was made with an innocence of the implied eventual financial costs to the rural population, or those who made this decision were severely misled about the financial capacity and willingness of the villagers to meet these obligations. Although it had begun in the early 1960s as a contribution and was regarded as such by the farmers, by 1965 the Viet Cong tax had become, according to both refugees from Viet Cong areas and former Viet Cong officials, just another oppressive wartime burden.

Viet Cong Trade Policies

The market of the Delta economy knew no ideology nor did it support one military contestant or another. The continuous flow of products, factors of production, and people between GVN and Viet Cong areas, interrupted only by customs taxes imposed by the Viet Cong and checkpoint harassment by the GVN, is a measure of the resiliency of the traditional economy and those whose livelihood depended upon it. Efforts by both sides to impose autarky failed and, particularly for the Viet Cong, involved costly confrontations with the population.

We have seen that Vietnamese government efforts at "resource control" and selective aid-giving to GVN inhabitants were a mixed bag, often involving heavy economic-political costs not offset by military benefits. The outstanding example of such counterproductive policies were the controls exercised by the GVN over the sales of the motor pump.

Yet the Viet Cong were even more strongly opposed to the use of the motor pump. Their approach had a dual ideological basis. First, as we have seen, it was argued that every engine purchased assisted the Americans in waging war by providing them with needed money. This claim was often backed by elaborate calculations, using an estimate of total potential purchases of motor pumps multiplied by the price of each purchase and augmented by an estimate of gasoline import requirements to operate the engines. The second ideological premise of this policy was that it was important to promote communal use of capital equipment and oppose private capitalism. When it was found that the farmers refused to purchase items communally, they were encouraged, as a second best, to share motor pumps, using, for example, one for every five families. But this policy also failed. In the words of a former Viet Cong district official, "every sampan in Viet Cong areas has an engine, and even farmers who are brothers refuse to share a motor pump."

The Viet Cong attitude toward other commodities marketed from GVN areas was similarly inhibiting. For example, Viet Cong policy discouraged the use of chemical fertilizers; on the consumption side, the Viet Cong frowned on purchases of nylon shirts, rubber sandals, cigarettes, hats of synthetic materials, wristwatches, and fountain pens.[8] They argued that these items were unnecessary and that money spent on them aided the Americans. The Viet Cong were unaware or chose

---

[8] In several villages, incoming consumption items were taxed as much as 50% on value.

to ignore the fact that all of these items were produced within South Vietnam—except rubber sandals, which were of Japanese origin.

It was to the credit of village-level Viet Cong cadres that these restrictive trade policies were not generally carried too far once it became obvious that they were harmful to the villagers' interests. As a result, chemical fertilizers, insecticides, small motors, and various consumption items produced in GVN areas continued to flow, often unhindered, into Viet Cong areas. Even the communist propagandists were forced by the adamant demands of farmers, asserting their capitalistic prerogatives, to make temporary theoretical concessions. One high-level Viet Cong directive dated December 15, 1965 noted that the productivity of the feudalist landowner would be

> replaced by the individual productivity of the peasants as under capitalism. Not guiding peasants to progress is against the Revolutionary doctrine and thus causes trouble for our Revolution. Our Revolution asks a better life, wealth, productiveness for the peasant in order to support our fight against the American Empire. Instruction and guidance to make people join the collective activities is needed although right now individual productivity cannot be done without.[9]

Despite some flexibility, however, one farmer, a former resident of a Viet Cong secure village reported: "Without fertilizers the people got bad crops, and without the motor pump they could not grow a second rice crop." In this case the trade restrictions had been enforced and the population suffered.

THE VIET CONG CORVÉE

Although their ideology was often amended if it conflicted with the farmers' interests, the Viet Cong requirements that were established to meet immediate war needs were not so easily neglected. Villagers were frequently forced to perform laboring tasks for the Viet Cong. The war, not civilian economic improvement programs, had first priority. In 1965 the TCN district-level Viet Cong Farmers' Liberation Association listed its most significant accomplishments as (in descending order): the setting up of combat hamlets (erecting fortifications), digging spike pits and underground caches, acting as sentinels, providing

---

[9] From a USOM mimeographed report, September 6, 1966.

recruits, and assisting in the execution of the Viet Cong tax program. Much further down the list, in a secondary category, were the vital economic tasks of canal construction and cleaning.

VIET CONG SUBSISTENCE DIRECTIVES

By late 1965 the Viet Cong were facing serious shortages of locally produced items in their own areas. These shortages were the result of the movement of refugees to GVN areas, leaving their land idle, and the negative effect on production of the progressive Viet Cong tax discussed earlier. In the Delta, Viet Cong areas that had formerly been sources of significant agricultural surpluses became deficit areas. This development led to a strange mixture of Viet Cong trade policies.

For example, in 1966 a Viet Cong directive prohibiting the sale of buffalo from Viet Cong areas was promulgated on the reasoning that if the farmers sold their buffalo they would not be able to plow their fields. Farmers were also told that they would not be permitted to make a living from orchard cultivation but only from rice cultivation and pig raising. Taxes were imposed on exports of rice and live pigs (from 5 to 10 percent on value) and were paid by the farmer exporting them or by the buying merchant, depending on who carried them by the Viet Cong's movable customs collection point. Another Viet Cong subsistence directive required that villagers desiring to convert rice land to fruit production obtain a certificate of permission from the village cadre. It was rarely granted. In mid-1965 the inhabitants of some villages were directed not to sell paddy or pigs to GVN area markets; only sales of flowers, fruits, and vegetables were permitted. As economic conditions worsened in Viet Cong areas, the controls tightened. Villagers were limited in the amount of rice they could carry into GVN areas for milling (generally mills in Viet Cong areas had closed down or had been destroyed by GVN or U.S. forces) to that necessary for a month's family consumption. This regulation was intended to prevent villagers from selling their crops to merchants in GVN areas.

CONCLUSIONS

In nearly every case, these Viet Cong economic policies worked against the farmers' interests. The inability of the Viet Cong to provide a market for the commodities grown in the areas they controlled was a major liability and guaranteed that the autarkic Viet Cong policies either would be ignored or would harm the farmer.

In fact, a basic conflict existed between the communist ideology and the realities of the Delta economy. Viet Cong attempts to substitute the term "farmer" or "peasant" for that of "worker" in Marxist logic or even to place them side by side called for certain theoretical and organizational modifications that were never satisfactorily accomplished. According to one former Viet Cong interviewed, at the 1965 reorientation course for Viet Cong cadres held at the provincial level in Dinh Tuong, an instructor from the Viet Cong's COSVN encountered opposition when he said, "I fully agree that the farmers constitute the main force of the Revolution, but [they] will never be able to assume positions of leadership. . . . Only cadres coming from the worker class are qualified to do this. . . ." When questioned on his statement, he reportedly replied: "Although they constitute the main force of the Revolution, the farmers, because of their traditional way of life, are always inclined to do anything which helps them to improve their private property . . . they are easily excited . . . and discouraged." Workers, he stated, did not have this attachment to private property. Nonetheless, he conceded to his uneasy audience that it was possible for the farmer who overcame his attachment to private property to qualify for a position of party leadership.[10]

To one former high-level Viet Cong official, the farmers' attitude of self-interest was an important obstacle to party work. He stated: "Whenever their own interests are at stake, they will fight to defend them with great determination, but when they realize they will gain

[10] This ideological position is based on Marxism as practiced in the Soviet Union. The Vietnamese communists had studied the Soviet as well as the Chinese communist experience. This example illustrates that in an Asian environment the Soviet experience was less relevant than the Chinese example.

As early as 1926 Mao Tse-tung was modifying Marxism to suit what he perceived to be the paramount role the peasant would play in Asian revolutions in contrast to the role of the worker in Europe and Russia as argued by Marx. For an appreciation of Mao's thoughts, which seem to have matured while he was charged with the collection of land statistics for the Peasants' Committee of the Kuomintang in 1926, see Edgar Snow, Red Star Over China (New York: Grove Press, 1961 [Random House, 1938]), pp. 84–85. Also note André Malraux's interview with Mao in his Anti-Memoirs, trans. Terence Kilmartin (New York: Holt, Rinehart, and Winston, 1968), pp. 357–359.

more profit by changing sides they will do it eagerly." The farmers' self-interests often diminished their revolutionary fervor. The initial Viet Cong programs of 1960 were based on three appeals: land to the farmer tilling it, reunification of North Vietnam and South Vietnam, and "the building of a socialist regime in the South on the principles of democracy and equality for the people." This former Viet Cong official stated that, despite efforts to rally the people to the last two goals, most seemed to be interested primarily in seeing their living standards improve.

I 2 The Economics of Insurgency

United States Policy and Land Reform

A POLICY OF INACTION

After its noteworthy role in the post–World War II Japanese land reform as well as the crucial role of President Eisenhower's special representative, General Collins, in the Diem land reforms of 1955 and later,[1] it is not immediately obvious why the United States, in the 1960s, did not make land reform a centerpiece of its Vietnam policy. For an explanation, one is tempted by the conventional responses of disbelief in its importance, bureaucratic inertia, outright incompetence, or simply that other matters had a higher priority.

I received one of these explanations from the columnist Joseph Alsop, a long-time observer of Vietnamese affairs. On April 3, 1967, at dinner with Ambassador Lodge and Alsop at the ambassador's residence in Saigon, I suggested that one of the tragedies of U.S. policy in Vietnam was its failure to reform such obviously harmful social practices as the corvée and the collection of excessive rents, so common in GVN-controlled areas. Calling me a "wild-eyed liberal" who was "impervious to the facts," Alsop responded in the following terms. He drew on his experience in China, saying, "the corvée has always been employed in Asia; we used it to build airfields in China during the war. High rents have always been collected. The peasants expect it." Alsop simply did

---

[1] Price Gittenger, "Agrarian Reform," in Richard W. Lindholm, ed., *Viet-Nam: The First Five Years* (East Lansing: Michigan State University Press, 1959), p. 200.

not believe that land reform (or the corvée) was a major rural issue.[2]

Ambassador Lodge, who had listened to the exchange but did not comment, called me to his office two days later to hear my views again. After I explained my position, the ambassador offered two explanations. First, he noted that he had never received sufficient information on the points I raised. Then he said: "Since 1963 we have tried to hold this place together. Now I think it is time to turn to the social and economic problems you speak of, and the new team [Ambassadors Bunker and Komer who within a month replaced him] should be able to do so."[3]

I had encountered the instability, or "quiet life," view before in conversations with young political officers from the U.S. embassy in Saigon, who argued that a land reform would topple the Vietnamese government. However, when I asked these foreign service officers how many members of the (then) Constituent Assembly were landowners, they replied that this information was not available. While it was obviously true that many GVN officials were also landlords, no one had determined how many officials actually did own land, nor did anyone go to the trouble to ask those who did own land what their attitudes were—after the trauma of the 1960–1966 period—toward holding it or selling it. This suggestion that the GVN was incapable of executing a reform overlooked the fact that the Diem government, acting under U.S. and French pressure in 1954–1955, even before it had eliminated its political opposition, did in fact implement a land reform program that represented a truly revolutionary departure from the government's historical role as the protector of the landlord's interests.

The basic reason land reform was not pursued was that U.S. officials did not believe that land-based grievances were important. Efforts by the United States to solve the problem were little more than publicity

---

[2] Yet, in 1954, Alsop had reported from Ca Mau deep in the Mekong Delta that: "What impressed me most, alas, was the moral fervor they [the Viet Minh] had inspired among the non-Communist Viet Minh cadres and the strong support they had obtained from the peasantry" (*New York Herald Tribune*, December 3, 1954).

[3] Both Ambassadors Lodge and Komer were inclined to favor land reform. But each encountered significant staff opposition. The political section of the U.S. embassy in Saigon, with its concern for the stability of the Saigon government, was one of the major opponents of land reform.

exercises. Few U.S. officials seriously believed that the An Giang photographic project (see Chapter 3) represented a major land reform step. It was an easy technological tactic to obscure the problem.

What was surprising about the attitude of U.S. officials was their readiness to grasp at any technological or bureaucratic or even academic device as evidence of a solution to the land reform problem or as evidence that the problem was unimportant. Meanwhile, these officials ignored the obvious political implications of the existing GVN land policies—frequently reported to them by low-level advisers in the provinces.

The classic example of this readiness to accept academic and other concoctions as substitutes for a reform policy was suggested to me early in 1967 when I was told by high-level U.S. officials in Washington that a RAND Corporation study had found that land reform was not an important source of Viet Cong support. I was able to see this formerly classified document when it was published in June 1967.[4]

Its author, Edward J. Mitchell, employed linear regression analysis using six independent variables to explain variations in the extent of GVN control (by province) in South Vietnam, excluding the highland areas. He concluded:

> From the point of view of government control, the ideal province in South Vietnam would be one in which few peasants farm their own land, the distribution of landholdings is unequal, no [GVN] land redistribution has taken place, large French holdings existed in the past, population density is high, and the terrain is such that accessibility is poor.[5]

The implication of these results, which were immediately accepted by high-level U.S. officials in Saigon and Washington, was that the Viet Cong had made their inroads in owner-farmed rather than tenant-farmed areas. A corollary to this finding was that land tenure issues were not important grievances, or at least that such grievances had

---

[4] Edward J. Mitchell, "Land Tenure and Rebellion: A Statistical Analysis of Factors Affecting Government Control in South Vietnam," RAND Memorandum 5181–ARPA (Santa Monica, Calif., June 1967). Summarized in *Asian Survey*, vol. VII (August 1967), pp. 577–580; reported in *The New York Times*, October 16, 1967; and published as "Inequality and Insurgency: A Statistical Study of South Vietnam," in *World Politics*, vol. XX, no. 3 (April 1968), pp. 421–438.

[5] Ibid., *World Politics*, pp. 437–438.

not served as the basis for the support gained by the Viet Cong in the areas they controlled.

Because the study received widespread attention, it must be examined closely. It is immediately evident in Mitchell's specification of the independent variables employed that he had no precise knowledge of Vietnamese conditions. He noted that he had never been to Vietnam and wrote, "A precise interpretation of the empirical findings, however, cannot be made without a careful study in the field."[6]

Such an interpretation would reject his analysis. Every one of his variables that proved to be positively and significantly associated with GVN control—inequality, presence of French estates, extent of GVN land redistribution, population density, and the extent of tenancy—is a characteristic of the Delta provinces and not of the provinces of the coastal plains of Central Vietnam; and the extent of GVN control is, in many provinces, greater in the Delta than in the coastal plains. In other words, the differences found by Mitchell between these two groups of provinces can be explained by historical factors, factors of geographic proximity (namely, the Ho Chi Minh Trail), variations in topography, or the peculiar characteristics of the Annamite as opposed to the Cochinchinese.[7] These factors are not treated by Mitchell's model.

Another plausible explanation, also ignored by Mitchell, is that the observed variation in GVN control (the dependent variable) can be attributed to the North Vietnamese–Viet Cong strategy of the 1965–1966 period and before, a strategy that caused the conflict (and Viet Cong control) to be centered in Central Vietnam. The strategy's objective was to divide the country (where it is narrow, lightly populated, covered with jungle, easily supplied from the Ho Chi Minh Trail, and lightly defended by the South Vietnamese) along a line across Kontum and Pleiku provinces at the end of the Ho Chi Minh Trail to the province of Phu Yen on the coast.

Mitchell's mobility variable, the only variable that might have reflected one reason for the Viet Cong's concentration of effort in Central

[6] Ibid., RAND Memorandum, p. 33.
[7] See the perceptive comments of John T. McAlister, Jr., "The Possibilities for Diplomacy in Southeast Asia," *World Politics*, vol. XIX, no. 2 (January 1967), especially p. 293, where he discusses the importance of historical factors in explaining the role of Central Vietnam in the Viet Cong insurgency.

Vietnam—the greater freedom of movement in the jungles and high-lands of that area—was defined to include only plains and lightly forested hills, that is, the variable *excluded* dense forests, jungles, and paddy land, the dominant features of the Vietnamese countryside. Moreover, Mitchell completely excluded the highland provinces from his analysis. From this spurious beginning, he concluded that greater cross-country mobility meant less GVN control. Any U.S. soldier could have told him otherwise.

But even had Mitchell overcome the problems just cited, his model as specified could not possibly have shown what he purports to have demonstrated. Mitchell, in using GVN control as the dependent variable determined by the dependent variables—inequality of land distribution, accessibility, and so on—completely ignores what is known in econometrics as the identification problem. He assumes that causation in his equation runs from his independent variables to the dependent variable of GVN control; whereas the findings reported here indicate clearly that the causation runs the other way. That is, Viet Cong presence, and before that Viet Minh presence, led to institutional changes that redistributed land. Therefore, properly specified, Mitchell's model would explain the inequality of distribution by the extent of Viet Cong as opposed to GVN control, not the other way around. Mitchell's mistake is similar to that of one who, after observing that all who had the flu had been visited by doctors, concluded that the doctors caused the flu. The fact that land was more inequitably distributed in GVN areas than in Viet Cong areas did not mean that the Viet Cong gained control in areas of equitable land distribution but that, in the areas they controlled, the Viet Minh and Viet Cong through their land reform programs *caused* the land to be more equitably distributed.

Because of these shortcomings—an erroneously specified equation, poorly defined variables, disregard for historical factors, and neglect of post-1960 Viet Cong strategic and tactical decisions that in the 1964–1966 period drew troops *from* the densely populated high-tenancy areas of the Delta (often on the appeal of land reform) to fight in and control the jungle-covered highlands—Mitchell's analysis must be rejected.[8]

[8] Mitchell's effort to argue that in Vietnam the conditions of revolution are

Even a semiofficial American spokesman like Pike recognized that land was the single greatest issue of Viet Cong mass appeal.[9] This appeal was especially strong from 1960 until late 1964 when the Viet Cong enjoyed the accelerating success in the rural areas that gave credence to their claims to govern South Vietnam. The peasants were excited about the prospect of owning their own land; they were told they would become owners if the Viet Cong succeeded, and, by all appearances, through late 1964 the Viet Cong were succeeding.

Whatever path self-interest forced the farmer to choose, Viet Cong land redistributions and, of broader significance, the Viet Cong's role as a rent depressant were clear factors in the farmer's favor. In Chapter 3 it was estimated that eight million of the Delta's ten million people received economic benefits from Viet Cong land reform measures. Much of the rural support for Viet Cong policies can be attributed to the direct economic benefits or the promise of potential long-run gains that Viet Cong success offered. In contrast, the tenant had little incentive to support the Vietnamese government's policies because of the GVN's complicity with the landlord.

All these things considered, the reluctance on the part of GVN and U.S. officials to recognize the importance of the land reform issue and their readiness to accept technological, bureaucratic, or doubtful analytical substitutes instead is not a behavior subject to facile explanations. I can only suggest three possibilities.

---

analogous to those in eighteenth-century France or elsewhere, where the middle class rather than the peasant class revolted, is unconvincing. He fails to establish that insurgent revolutions are similar to those of Western Europe, nor does he establish that the predominantly rural societies of Asia resemble those of Western Europe in the eighteenth or nineteenth centuries, where the revolutions were urban led. His effort would have been better spent studying the rural revolutions in China and Mexico.

Writing of the Mexican revolution in 1910, François Chevalier has noted, "This reform was achieved essentially because the villagers were determined to throw off the crushing burdens imposed upon them and to recover all that they had lost." He concluded: "Possession of land appears to be an end in itself," and found that after the reform the peasant withdrew from politics to his parochial interests, a development experienced by the Viet Cong in Vietnam. See François Chevalier, "The *Ejido* and Political Stability in Mexico," in Claudio Veliz, ed., *The Politics of Conformity in Latin America* (London: Oxford University Press, 1967), pp. 158–191.

[9] Pike, *Viet Cong*, p. 276.

THE ROLE OF LAND IN A TRADITIONAL SOCIETY

First, Americans were incapable of recognizing the dominant role that land plays in a traditional rice economy and a rice-economy-based society. Coming from a capital-intensive economy, Americans did not attribute to the institutions of land tenure their true significance in the land-labor traditional economy of the Delta.

At issue is not simply the relative economic roles of capital and labor in U.S. and Asian societies. Far more was at stake with land in Vietnam; for if a man could not obtain a subsistence living by his own work except by becoming the virtual slave of his landlord, how could he have aspirations for a free society, a democracy, or a constitution? The Vietnamese peasant aspired to the right to survive; therein lay his dignity. No one has made this point more clearly than Mao Tse-tung:

> The first part of our struggle was a peasant revolt. The aim was to free the farmer from his overlord; to win not freedom of speech, voting or assembly, but the freedom to survive.[10]

The Americans offered the peasant a constitution; the Viet Cong offered him his land and with it the right to survive. Mao has also commented on the ferocity of the land-based revolt in China:

> *Everything arose out of a specific situation:* we organized peasant revolt, we did not instigate it. Revolution is a drama of passion; we did not win the people over by appealing to reason, but by developing hope, trust, and fraternity. In the face of famine, the will to equality takes on a religious force. Then, in the struggle for rice, land, and the rights brought by agrarian reform, the peasants had the conviction that they were fighting for their lives and those of their children . . . everywhere the soil was the specific situation. . . .[11]

AN IDEOLOGICAL DESIRE TO CONDEMN THE VIET CONG

The second possible reason for U.S. inaction on land reform was the fact that U.S. officials, in an unconscious effort to exhibit solidarity with the GVN against the Viet Cong, refused to credit the Viet Cong with the considerable social and economic benefits they provided to

---

[10] André Malraux, *Anti-Memoirs*, trans. Terence Kilmartin (New York: Holt, Rinehart, and Winston, 1968), p. 360.
[11] Ibid., pp. 360–361; Mao's emphasis.

millions of Delta inhabitants with their land reform programs. This view, that whatever the Viet Cong did to help the peasant was expedient, is evident in the writings of Pike, a part-time JUSPAO official. Like other Americans he could not accept the Viet Cong land reform program at face value. He said, "In many cases this [the Viet Cong program] amounted to a virtual bribe; the rural Vietnamese was offered the thing he wanted above all else: land."[12] Pike overlooked the fact that the peasant did accept these offers at face value. Who was the peasant, at the edge of starvation, for decades exploited by landlords and large-scale tenants and unexposed to the rhetoric of the cold war, to fear eventual communism or collectivization in the face of an immediate offer (in effect for twenty years) of a reasonable subsistence level of economic well-being?

To argue that the Viet Cong were opportunistic is not to argue that they were ineffective. They did formulate every issue in land terms. But they recognized that, under the prevailing economic conditions, land was the dominant factor of production and primary source of income. Collectivization efforts and work-exchange teams were a rare policy end. Perhaps they served an ideological purpose, but this function met needs at higher levels. At lower levels the Viet Cong's fixation on land mirrored the peasants' concern for the economic and social role that land played in Delta life. This land fixation kept the Viet Cong closely attuned to the farmers' problems and allowed the Viet Cong to recognize, for example, a major fallacy in the Diem strategic hamlet program: It forced tenants into the landlords' hands by limiting the supply of residential and near-home land—the most productive type (for pig, fruit, fish, and buffalo raising). The economic burden associated with the strategic hamlet program is evident in the fact that rents in the strategic hamlet area of LBD shot up five times after the Diem program was implemented in 1963.

Simply to imply that the Viet Cong were trying to buy off the peasant is to overlook the fact that the United States, with technology and capital, was trying to do precisely the same thing. Both Viet Cong efforts and U.S. efforts sought a worthy goal: higher and more equitably distributed rural incomes.

12 Pike, Viet Cong, p. 276.

The limitations of U.S. attitudes are adequately summed up in the JUSPAO "Guidance Paper" cited in Chapter 3:

> The conclusion to keep underlining is that the VC [Viet Cong] offer the poor peasant much less than the GVN even though they pose as the defenders of his interests. And to see what happens once the communists are firmly in the saddle, one has but to look at North Vietnam where the farmer is reduced to serfdom.[13]

This zeal of anticommunist propaganda is worthy of that of communist propaganda itself. The Viet Cong propagandist had only to reply: If you want to see what happens once the GVN are firmly in control, look at the present high rents and unsatisfactory tenure conditions in nearby GVN areas.

A BUREAUCRATIC EXPLANATION

Those Americans who stayed in Vietnam longer than the usual twelve-month tour or who inquiringly worked in the rural areas will not be surprised by the evidence on the role of land presented here. Unfortunately, few Americans fell into this category and, as one went to higher levels in the Saigon bureaucracy, not to mention the Washington bureaucracy, these issues were rarely considered. A bureaucratic explanation for the ignorance of U.S. policy on this subject is undoubtedly too simple; yet it cannot be ignored, and, with the ideological bias of the U.S. approach, fostered by a desire to condemn the Viet Cong, and the inadequate American appreciation of the role of land in Asia, it seems to explain the U.S. failure to give land issues the attention they deserved.

The Balance of Interests: Viet Cong versus GVN Economics

From July 20, 1960, the date of the resurgence of communism in the Delta (the beginning of the Viet Cong's General Uprising campaign), until late 1964, Viet Cong economic policies were of major benefit to the peasant, giving some evidence to support their stated interest in his "material well-being." The major ingredients of this effort were land reallocations and the lowering of rents. These reforms

[13] "Psyops Aspects of GVN Land Title and Land Tenure Programs," Guidance Paper no. 3 (March 20, 1967).

transferred significant wealth from the landlords to tenant farmers and workers. Viet Cong pressures to increase rural wages also brought substantial economic benefits to the rural worker. After the 1964 decision to conduct large-scale military operations, economic policies to improve the farmer's welfare were bypassed in favor of political, military, and financial policies designed to support the war.

The support gained by bold Viet Cong policies directed against the landlords was diminished by the burdens imposed by high taxes and draft demands initiated in 1964–1965. Income transfers from landlord to tenant were often offset by transfers from the tenant to the Viet Cong. Other Viet Cong policies, for example, their efforts to control the flow of traded goods, were not neutralized by GVN policies of equal negative impact. GVN rural taxes were, for practical purposes, nonexistent. Petty GVN hindrances such as controls on engine sales could be surmounted—except by the very poor—with patience and money. Even though the factors favoring the GVN were not those directly attributable to governmental activities, the prosperous wartime markets in GVN areas, the availability of jobs in GVN areas for potential refugees, and the advanced inputs that flowed from GVN area sources (public and private) tied the farmers' immediate interests to non–Viet Cong areas and were a severe nonmilitary blow to Viet Cong interests.

What all of this meant to the peasant—whether the GVN or the Viet Cong on balance brought more benefits to the peasantry, or whether the Viet Cong emphasis on land and labor was more efficient than the GVN-U.S. emphasis on capital and technology—is not easy to resolve. The problem is threefold. First, land played a social as well as an economic role. Its significance was deeply etched in the social and economic fabric of Delta society: No financial aid, however generously dispersed; no technology, whatever its productivity; no fertilizer, however low its price; and no propaganda, however smoothly applied, could obscure in the peasant's mind the social injustices he had suffered at the hands of those who, before 1946, controlled the land. Yet, in a way, just as the past was in the hands of the Viet Cong, the future favored the GVN.

From 1960 until 1965, Viet Cong policies held a great appeal for those who, before 1960, were at the edge of starvation. Even in

1966–1967 the subsistence tax exemption, allowed before the punishing Viet Cong tax was applied, satisfied many farmers. But it could not satisfy these farmers for long, nor could it satisfy many others who wanted higher incomes, who saw that the employment of capital and technology was a necessary production concession and who knew that the permissiveness of a reasonable tax structure was a vital personal incomes policy for whichever government claimed to provide the peasant with the greatest opportunity to advance economically.

On balance, these issues boiled down to an ideological struggle, not for the farmer but for the contestants. Could the Viet Cong compromise with capitalism on the issues of technology, capital, and trade? Could the GVN and the United States compromise with communism and recognize the importance of an equitable distribution of the Delta's land resources?

A QUESTION OF IDENTIFICATION

The Viet Cong were a movement of the masses; the GVN represented a movement of the elite, trying—with the prodding of the U.S. government—to reach the masses. With their emphasis on land, the Viet Cong had seized on a personalized issue and identified themselves with the problems of the majority of the rural populace. Meanwhile, in its treatment of the masses, the GVN committed innumerable blunders. Among these was the strategic hamlet program, under which families were herded into fortified outposts that they were forced to build as corvée labor. The Diem government never realized that the peasants were not enthusiastic about leaving their homes, gardens, orchards, and buffalo for the close living of the hamlet fortress. Diem's brother Ngo Dinh Nhu said: "Participation is considered a citizen's duty. . . . There is no reason for not participating. Contributions will also be necessary, to take the form of five to ten days of labor and from fifty to one thousand piasters from each citizen over the age of 18."[14] The Viet Cong recognized the abuses of this program; their bureaucracy was smaller and their interests lay closer to those of the rural inhabitant.

[14] Pike, *Viet Cong*, p. 67. For an earlier assessment of these same misconceptions as attributed to Diem himself in 1959 with regard to the "agroville program," see Joseph J. Zasloff, "Rural Resettlement in South Vietnam: The Agroville Program," *Pacific Affairs*, vol. XXXV, no. 4 (Winter 1962–63), p. 334.

When the GVN approached the people it did so through its own class, the official (usually a landlord). It was the poor farmers interviewed who supplied the corvée labor. One spoke of his "inability to maintain good relations with the officials"; another nervously said, "I am the victim of poor public administration." It was easy enough for strategic hamlet advocates to recognize, after their program failed, that Diem, with fewer resources, had tried to build, in two-thirds the time, sixteen times as many fortified hamlets as the British had built in Malaya.[15] But at the time the program was launched by decree on February 3, 1962, the advisers lacked a sufficient understanding of the rural economy to allow them to anticipate the abuses just described, and the GVN institutions did not have the means of bridging the gap between high-level officials and mass interests. In 1963 the Viet Cong did have these means. They correctly labeled the strategic hamlet as a "prison" that restricted peasant economic activities. The Viet Cong program's primary attribute was its ability to give quick policy recognition to outstanding rural grievances; this ability was a result of their identification with the peasant and their knowledge of his problems.

With its technology, the GVN received little "personalized" credit for what was in fact accomplished by the market. The GVN was responsible for maintaining the roads, ports, and other infrastructural facilities on which the market's operations depended, but these were impersonal accomplishments. At times the GVN did receive direct credit. Farmers in one village welcomed the GVN's return and its opening of the village road; in another they credited the GVN with replacing a blown bridge. One TCN farmer, when asked to compare living in a Viet Cong area with living in a GVN secure area, replied, "The Viet Cong have never helped or encouraged the farmers to dig canals; they interdict the distribution of motor pumps; and they tax all new productive activities." After the war intensified in 1965, it was not clear exactly to whom, on balance, the peasant, acting solely in his immediate economic interest, would give his support.

THE BALANCE OF TERROR

There is yet a final consideration. In the rural areas in 1965, there emerged a new determinant of the population's attitudes toward the

15 See Sir Robert Thompson, *Defeating Communist Insurgency* (New York: Frederick A. Praeger; London: Chatto & Windus, 1966), particularly pp. 121–140.

opposing sides. This was the question of physical security. The role of security is seen in the responses of the farmers to the question, "How does your family's economic condition differ from that of a family similar to yours but living in an insecure area?"

Twenty-four replies said they did not know, and 2 farmers did not respond. Of the remaining 94 replies, 63 percent said that the Viet Cong area was less secure; 19 percent said there was greater prosperity in GVN areas, primarily because of market proximity and greater security; 13 percent cited the Viet Cong taxes as the reason for their better position in a GVN area; 3 percent mentioned the Viet Cong corvée; and 2 percent maintained that economic conditions were better in Viet Cong areas.[16] In short, security was the overriding condition in the disfavor of Viet Cong areas compared with GVN areas. One TCN farmer and 1965 refugee from a nearby Viet Cong–controlled area fled

> because I could no longer live with the threats of shelling, bombing, firing from aircraft night and day, and ground fighting from sweep operations. Many fields over there are left to waste. Almost everyone has left his home village for Saigon or for more secure areas in which to make a living.

The balance of terror threatened to push the issues of land reform, technology, Viet Cong taxes, and everything else into the background. It was, in another farmer's words, because

> more working time is available here than in insecure areas so there is more income here. In an insecure area people do not care to plan to produce more than strictly necessary for subsistence. They have to plan always to be ready to take refuge. They do not want to invest to make more effort because they are afraid of not being able to recover the invested money. They don't like to borrow and risk bankruptcy.

It is obvious, then, that on economic grounds alone we can arrive at no conclusive statement on the Viet Cong–GVN struggle. We can only say that economic grievances, particularly those arising from land, played a major role in the growth of Viet Cong support in the Delta. Meanwhile, the GVN, the defender of the economy's infrastructure, with its more permissive wage and trade policies, received by association the

---

[16] Both of these farmers complained of the GVN corvée and noted that, because their incomes were at the subsistence level, they would not have had to pay Viet Cong taxes.

benefits of an open economy. Considering the 1960–1967 period as a whole, the Viet Cong enjoyed the greatest support for their programs in the 1960–1964 period,[17] before the war was escalated and Viet Cong taxes began to weigh heavily on the population. The GVN benefits reached the population after 1965 and flowed generously through 1967. But by mid-1967 the Viet Cong realized the importance of the balance of terror. In August 1967 both TCN and LBD farmers were warned of Viet Cong intentions to attack the secure and semisecure GVN areas; the Viet Cong executed their policy of terror at Tet in 1968. One interpretation of the Tet offensive and the ensuing campaign of terror against GVN areas is that it was designed to improve the relative attractiveness of living conditions in Viet Cong areas.

Old Realities and New Myths

In a provocative article entitled "Insurgency and Counterinsurgency: New Myths and Old Realities," Charles Wolf, Jr., an economist with the RAND Corporation, has provided the clearest statement yet to appear of what has recently been termed a "revisionist" attack on the accepted doctrine of insurgent movements.[18] Wolf rejects what he calls the "currently accepted doctrine" about insurgency, which "is that popular attitudes and popular support play the decisive role in enabling insurgent movements to get started, gain momentum, and erupt in 'liberation wars.' "[19] He says:

> I would be inclined to argue that an opposite position is both logically and empirically tenable. Effective insurgency and guerrilla activity can

[17] Pike reports that the size of the Viet Cong doubled between December 1960 and early 1961, doubled again by late 1961, and had doubled a third time by early 1962. He says that in early 1962 there were 300,000 NLF members, a figure that dropped by 50,000–100,000 after the fall of Diem. See Pike, *Viet Cong*, p. 115.

[18] Charles Wolf, Jr., *Yale Review*, vol. LVI (Winter 1967, published in December 1966), pp. 225–241. Reprints of this article were circulated in the U.S. Mission in Saigon in early 1967 and received widespread attention. To my knowledge, David Halberstam first applied the term "revisionist" in this context, although he used it to apply only to the land issue. He wrote: "Westerners have always believed that the Viet Cong's distribution of land to the peasants was basic to their early success. More recently there has been something of a revisionist attack on that theory, suggesting in effect that land was not that important to the Communist cause, and indeed it was a Western misconception of Vietnamese life." David Halberstam, "Voices of the Vietcong," *Harper's*, January 1968, p. 47.

[19] Wolf, "Insurgency and Counterinsurgency," pp. 225–226.

grow and gather momentum among a population that is passive or even hostile to the movement, *because of the structure and nature of transitional societies in the less-developed countries.*[20]

Then he concludes, "The growth of the Viet Cong and of the Pathet Lao probably occurred despite the opposition of a large majority of the populace of the two countries."[21]

Wolf's view deserves attention, despite the fact that he has offered no evidence to support it, because the evidence presented here clearly supports the so-called "accepted doctrine." Furthermore, whatever its merits, the revisionist view is widely held. We note, for example, that Wolf's view has marked parallels with those presented by Mitchell in the RAND publication cited earlier.[22] Due to RAND's influence, both through ex-RAND employees in high-level government posts and among government officials at large, on U.S. policy, there is a de facto case that, whether accepted or rejected, Wolf's view was thoroughly studied. It is interesting to note, for example, the similarities between the approach of Pike and that of Wolf. Pike has written that "the essence of the third-generation revolutionary guerrilla warfare in South Vietnam was *organization.*"[23] This statement bears a close resemblance to Wolf's conclusion: "Insurgency should be recognized *not* as an inscrutable and unmanageable force grounded in the mystique of a popular mass movement, but as a coherent operating system that can be understood structurally and functionally."[24]

Wolf does not define a "coherent operating system." Pike attempts to place a similar label on the Viet Cong; but, although one can grant the very important role organization has played in Viet Cong successes, it is difficult to see how organization could have gotten the Viet Cong the support they gained in the Delta without the major economic, political, and social grievances the movement sought to and actually did ameliorate.[25]

[20] Ibid., p. 227; Wolf's emphasis.
[21] Ibid.
[22] "Land Tenure and Rebellion."
[23] Pike, *Viet Cong*, p. ix; Pike's emphasis. Pike also wrote that "everything the NLF did was an act of communication" (ibid.; Pike's emphasis). One wonders if Pike noted Mao's view of the effectiveness of communications per se (i.e., propaganda), as related to Malraux: "People talk of propaganda, but propaganda produces supporters not soldiers" (Malraux, *Anti-Memoirs*, p. 359).
[24] Wolf, "Insurgency and Counterinsurgency," p. 241; Wolf's emphasis.
[25] The late Bernard Fall was always wary of such grossly oversimplified arguments.

As for Wolf's "old realities," Paret and Shy, in their perceptive survey of past guerrilla movements, maintain that "social pressure, at times even terror plays a role; but it requires an element of individual conviction to compel men to take part in this most punishing kind of combat."[26] Only wishful thinking could pursuade one that the Viet Cong movement, to which peasants have generously made even the most extreme sacrifices, was built on sham, or was in any major sense merely an organizational or communications accomplishment.

To the extent that the revisionist view emanated from the RAND Corporation and JUSPAO or those who relied on these organizations for their sources, it was the partial result of the limited research techniques employed by these two organizations. Both relied extensively on interviews with former members of the Viet Cong hierarchy—defectors and prisoners of war—who as part of the Viet Cong organization reflect a preoccupation with organizational and communication techniques and problems that were not representative of conditions at large among the population that supported the Viet Cong. The approach easily led one to the "infrastructural" view frequently alluded to by Americans who said, "What we need to do is to root out the Viet Cong infrastructure."

The revisionist view fits easily into the formal framework of U.S. policy on Vietnam. Once one ignored rural grievances, one tended to discount the civil war aspect of the Viet Cong struggle. It then became an easy step to connect one organization with other organizations, that is, the Viet Cong with the North Vietnamese Communist party, and arrive at Pike's conclusion that the General Uprising campaign of 1960 "was not the ordinary violent social protest" against, for example, "inadequate living standards" and "corrupt governments. Revolutionary

In his "Viet Nam in the Balance," *Foreign Affairs*, vol. 45, no. 1 (October 1966), he cited numerous political grievances against the GVN in reply to another "revisionist" contribution, by a CIA official, George A. Carver, Jr., which appeared in the April 1966 issue of *Foreign Affairs* ("The Faceless Viet Cong," pp. 347–372).

In this same article Fall wrote: "Hence, the certitude of a genuinely 'peasant-oriented' land reform including a freeze on land holdings already distributed by the Viet Cong, would do more to change the allegiance of the peasantry than possibly any other single counterinsurgency measure" ("Vietnam in the Balance," p. 5).

[26] Peter Paret and John W. Shy, *Guerrillas in the 1960's*, 2nd ed. (New York: Frederick A. Praeger, 1962), p. 19. The authors write, for example, of T. E. Lawrence, "Above all, he stressed the need for popular support if guerrillas are to maintain themselves for any length of time" (ibid., p. 24).

guerrilla warfare was quite different. It was an imported product. . . ."[27]

One of the more disturbing views held by revisionists is their view toward "economic and social improvement programs." Wolf writes:

> But again the crucial point is to connect a particular program with the kind of population behavior that the government wants to promote . . . projects that provide schools, dispensaries, roads, and other social services may be more effective than would economically more productive projects—for example, in agricultural development.[28]

In light of the evidence presented here, this view of aid is untenable. Instead, we are led to the conclusion that in an insurgent war it should be the policy of the counterinsurgency effort to give aid to the inhabitants of noncontrolled areas. For, to the extent that grievances are the source of discontent, and the insurgents gain support by appealing to these grievances, then policies to raise the incomes of the poor who are caught in the vicious circle of indebtedness and landlord control will tend to ameliorate the grievances and lessen insurgent support.[29] Anything (fertilizers, motor pumps, tractors, land reform, and the like) that helps the farmers and laborers to escape from these impoverished conditions should be pushed through the market, which ignores security considerations, into the insurgent-controlled areas.[30]

The Viet Cong employed institutional techniques that brought economic benefits to the population in areas of the Delta over which they had little control. The GVN, on the other hand, often cited "economic

[27] Pike, *Viet Cong*, pp. 32–33.

[28] Wolf, "Insurgency and Counterinsurgency," pp. 240–241.

[29] This lessening of insurgent support could come either by the diminished support of the population for the insurgent cause or by an increased willingness on the part of insurgent cadres to accommodate themselves to acceptable counterinsurgency policies.

[30] Not only does Wolf's view of aid to insurgent areas overlook the grievance-removing role of such aid, but it overstates the benefits, e.g., taxes, the insurgents might obtain from a more prosperous insurgent economy. In the case of the Viet Cong, higher incomes in insurgent areas would have made the Viet Cong tax, because it was progressive, a heavier burden than it actually was. Also, it is not clear that the Viet Cong war effort was constrained by a shortage of funds; that is, if their tax revenues increased, what benefits, otherwise denied them, would they have been able to purchase? Prosperity diminished the willingness of the population on either side to make time-consuming contributions to the war effort. In TCN, both GVN and former Viet Cong officials noted that the recently arrived prosperity made it difficult to draft people. Moreover, Viet Cong efforts were particularly dependent on "voluntary" contributions of labor to assist their war effort; therefore, when the opportunity cost of a farmer's time rose, he was less anxious to become a revolutionary.

warfare" considerations such as those outlined by Wolf and refused to allow aid to flow into Viet Cong–controlled areas. Fortunately, the market, primed by U.S. aid, overwhelmed the barriers erected by the GVN and frustrated the GVN's revisionist-like policy.

The Viet Cong example itself vindicates the conventional view that a successful insurgency can be and probably usually is a grievance-based movement. The revisionists receive no support. The "new myths" of organization, and so on, cannot obscure the "old realities" of the Delta economy that served as the basis for the success of the Viet Cong movement.

Appendix A:
Interviews

Agricultural Production Questionnaire

1–1. Identification: No. of Household ——— Name ———
                  Date of Interview: Month ——— Day ———

1–2. General comments (qualifications of respondent, general notes, etc.)

1–3. Farm change KEY. (Instructions: In the course of the interview as farm changes are encountered, record them by placing check(s) in the space below. Use this key as the basis for filling out the questionnaire insert—Section 2 on farm change.)

    A. Crop change (introduction of a new crop or expansion of an old crop involving over 10 percent of land or over one cong) ———

    B. Fertilizer use (used or ceased using for first time or change of more than one-fourth in amount used) ———

    C. Farm implements (use of new equipment in farming) ———

    D. Method of production (use of more or less labor in harvesting, planting, etc.) ———

    E. Variety of seed planted (use of variety not previously planted) ———

    F. Farm animals (new ones raised or 50 percent increase or decrease over number raised in 1965, e.g., pigs) ———

    G. Farm enterprises (introduction of or over 50 percent increase or decrease in fish, poultry) ———

    H. Structural change (new irrigation canal, land purchase, etc.) ———

    I. Other (specify) ———

Agricultural Production Questionnaire

1–4a. At this location, how much land do you own? ———mau

rent? ———mau

b. Do you own or farm any land at another location? (in 1966)

———mau owned at other locations

———mau farmed (by interviewee) at other locations

c. For how many years have you farmed this land? ——— years (est.)

d. How much land did you own and farm in 1965?

———————mau owned

———————mau farmed

1–5. What means of production do you own? and did you purchase last year? (Check from the list below, giving numbers where appropriate and adding items as needed.)

Item	Owned	Purchased Last Year
oxen plow (Cambodian)	———	———
plowing machine	———	———
harrow	———	———
threshing sledge	———	———
digging tool	———	———
roller	———	———
waterwheel		
sickle	———	———
motor pump	———	———
other (specify)	———	———

1–6a. Considering last year's crop of rice, vegetables, etc., did your activities in 1966 represent any significant change over 1965? (Specify, e.g., did the acreage or yield of the first or second crop fall or rise significantly, were new crops planted, were more crops planted, etc.?)

b. Now inquire of the subject concerning changes in the following areas and check the appropriate spaces if such changes were made.

——— use (20 percent change) of chemical fertilizer

——— changed plowing technique

——— use of more or less labor

——— use of a new variety of rice

——— use of insecticides

——— use of more water

——— use of a motor pump

c. How much chemical fertilizer did you use on the following crops in 1966?

first rice crop ——— kg   vegetables ——— kg

second rice crop ——— kg   other (specify) ——— kg

d. Does your use of fertilizer on the above crops in 1966 signify an important change (increase or decrease of one-fourth or more) over fertilizer use in 1965? (Specify crop on which change was made.)

e. Do you use organic fertilizer? ——yes; ——no. Percentage of total fertilizer used? ——%

Primary Agriculture (include all planted crops)

1–7a. Paddy—land area and production for last year's crops (1966):

	Area (ha)	Production (gia)
first crop	——	——
second crop	——	——
total	——	——

b. Of your 1966 paddy crop:
How much has been used to pay laborers?

——gia (in kind or cash equivalent)
to pay rent? ——gia (in kind or cash equivalent)
to pay debts? ——gia (in kind or cash equivalent)
sold for expenditures? ——gia
for other uses (specify)? ——gia
is in storage? ——gia

c. Of the quantity of paddy stored:
How many *gia* do you plan to sell? ——gia
How much will be consumed at home? ——gia

d. Of the paddy you plan to sell, in what month do you anticipate you will sell the largest portion? ——month of profitable sale. During what month of 1966 did you sell the largest portion of all paddy you sold in 1966? ——month

1–8a. How many *cong* did you devote to vegetable production in 1966? ——cong. In terms of the revenue received, which were the most important vegetables you cultivated in 1966? (List in order of importance.)

1.　　　　　　　　　　3.
2.　　　　　　　　　　4.

Estimate the total revenue you received from the sale of vegetables in 1966? V$N ——

b. If you were not a vegetable grower in 1966 and had to purchase those items you consumed from your own crop, how much would your family have had to pay? V$N ——

1–9. What changes do you plan in these areas (first rice crop, second rice crop, third rice crop, vegetables) in 1967? (Obtain a specific reply.)

1–10a. Did you use insecticides in 1966? ——yes; ——no.
Estimated total cost? V$N ——

b. How many *cong* of fruit land do you have? ————*cong* in fruit crops. What is your estimate of the revenue received from the sale of these fruit crops in 1966? V$N ————

Secondary Agriculture (include all noncrop items, fish, poultry, etc.)

1–11. Do you raise fish? ————yes; ————no (check one).
    If yes: What portion of fish production is consumed at home? ———— For the portion sold, what is the estimated yearly revenue? V$N ————
    If no: The farmer does not raise fish because:
        no fish pond ————
        plot is too small ————
        not interested ————
        no water available ————
        no capital ————
        too difficult to raise ————
        no time for care ————
        other (specify) ————

1–12a. Animals owned, sold, and consumed:

Item	Number Owned (1966 av)	Number Owned Greater or Less than 1965	Number Sold in 1966	Number Consumed at Home in 1966
oxen-buffalo				
pigs				
chickens				
ducks				

b. Do you sell chicken eggs? ———— duck eggs? ————.

1–13. Have you expanded or contracted any of the above activities (fish, animal, or poultry raising) in 1966? Explain.

1–14. What changes do you plan in these activities in 1967? Explain.
        The change being studied is ————————
        (use code, Section 1–3)

SECTION 2: INSERT ON FARM CHANGE

Note: Complete as many inserts on change as necessary to investigate all changes made.

2–1a. Why did you make this change? Or what did you expect from it? Explain.

b. If the reply is "more production," is this production to be used for home consumption ———— or for sale ————?

c. If it is to be used for sale, the resulting income is desired for what expenditures?

2–2. Why was this change not made earlier? Explain.

2–3. The initiative was taken by: the farmer ———; his wife ———; a son ———; the landlord ———; someone else (specify) ———.

2–4. How did you become aware of this new technique or crop? (Obtain a general reply; then determine more precisely the exact source, using the categories below. The objective is to differentiate between and to identify both the source—e.g., a friend, USAID, Farmers' Association, etc.—and the *means of communication*—word of mouth, village meeting, radio, newspaper, etc.)

2–5a. How was the change made?

Items Required (machinery, fertilizer, etc.)	Agent or Source (private, governmental aid, etc.)	Location of Agent	Estimate of Cost	Any Difficulty Obtaining Item
1.				
2.				
3.				
4.				
5. Payment to landlord or other special costs (explain)				

b. For those items purchased, the money came from:
i. sale of produce? ———
ii. sale of assets? ——— (e.g., gold, savings, hoards)
iii. a loan? ——— of an amount? V$N ——— at a monthly interest rate of ——— percent.
iv. another source not mentioned above? (Specify, e.g., wages.)

c. Who performed the task? Circle one or more of the following: the farmer, members of the family, friends, hired labor.

d. Did you encounter any technical problems in implementing the change? Explain.

e. Were you satisfied with the results of the changes you implemented? Explain (obtain a detailed statement, particularly if the subject's expectations were not met, e.g., the price of an item he intended to sell went down).

2–6. Were there other changes you would have wished to have implemented but which were not made?
a. The change desired? ——— (use "Farm change KEY" if possible)
b. The reason it was not implemented (e.g., no money, lack of

knowhow, shortage of labor, unable to obtain a needed item)?
Explain.

   c. Do you plan to implement this change in 1967?

2–7. What changes do you plan to make in 1967?

2–8. Nonchange. (Instructions: Select a change from the "Farm change KEY" that was *not* implemented or mentioned by the farmer and ask him why he has not adopted the change. Obtain a detailed reply if possible.)

   a. Change investigated (select from KEY) ————

   b. Response:

   c. Second change selected ————

   d. Response:

SECTION 3: FARM ENVIRONMENT

3–1. Aid programs (USAID and GVN):

Program	Is Aware of	How Influenced	Opinion
1. vegetable			
2. pig			
3. chicken			
4. fish			
5. new rice variety			
6. other			

3–2a. Were you able to purchase the desired amount of fertilizer last year? If no, explain (e.g., insufficient money, fertilizer not available, etc.)

   b. What amount of that fertilizer used was purchased at the official price? ————kg at official price. At the free market price? ————kg at free market price.

   c. Are you a member of the Farmers' Association? ————yes; ————no. If no, why are you not a member?

3–3. Rent: Do you pay rent on your farmland? ————yes; ————no. If yes:

   a. How was the rent determined?

   b. The actual rent paid per hectare in 1966?

     ————percent of crop   ————other (explain)
     (1st, 2nd, both?)   ————rent paid (specify in kind or
     ————fixed rate per   cash equivalent)
     hectare

   c. Has your rent increased or decreased in the period of the last two years? (1965–1966)

     ————increased; ————decreased; ————no change.

   If possible, determine the amount of change.

3–4a. The landlord: How much land does he own? ————hectares; ————unknown. Where does he live?————

b. Rent payment: Who collected your rent in 1966? ———landlord; ———landlord's agent; ———not collected; ———other. (Specify means of collection.)

3–5. Since many farmers in rural areas owe money, are you in debt? ———yes; ———no.

If yes:

a. To (check as appropriate):

———relative (R)	———NACO (N)
———landlord (L)	———Farmers' Association (F)
———storekeeper (S)	———cooperative (C)
———moneylender (M)	———other (specify)
———*hui* (H)	

b.

Debts (V$N)	To Whom (use code)	For What Use	Months Debt Has Been in Effect	Estimated Monthly Interest Rate
1.				
2.				
3.				

c. Do you expect debt position in 1967 to be (the same as), (better than), or (worse than) it was in 1966? (Circle one.)

d. If a change is expected, why?

3–6. What is your most common source of agricultural information?

3–7. Presently, what are your most important farm production problems? Explain.

3–8. What do you think about the use of mechanized farm implements?

3–9a. Economic welfare:

Over the past year, how has your family's economic position changed? ———it has not changed; ———it has improved; ———it has deteriorated.

b. Explain a.

c. How has the war affected your family's economic condition? Explain.

d. How does your family's economic condition differ from that of a family similar to yours but living in an insecure area? Explain.

3–10. What changes in farm operations would you make if you had a free choice and the money?

3–11a. When the war ends, how will your farm operations be affected? (Obtain the subject's reply, then present the problems below.)

b. If some prices go down (e.g., vegetables)?

c. If members of your family return home (e.g., from the army, from Saigon, from other nonfarm employment), what will they do?

3–12. In 1966, of the labor worked on your farm, how many man-days (est.) were performed by *hired* labor?

———man-days hired labor (1966).

Viet Cong controlled area

Huynh van Hoi's house

Bay The's house

Route 4 to Saigon

Route 4

Canal

J

L

N

Provincial

Abandoned airfield

C

Viet Cong controlled area

Major living area

Provincial road

Village office
and guardpost

Village guardpost

D

B

Tu Lu

Canal

Route 4

Viet Cong controlled area

Thay Hai's orchard and land

I

H

Route 4 to My Tho

Termination of natural stream

Than Cuu Nghia, January 8, 1967 (dry season)
Scale: 1 inch = approx. 1/3 km
See Figure 1.4 and chapters 1 and 7 for further details

— — — boundary of area studied

rice land

vegetable land

living areas and fruit trees

SECTION 4: FAMILY INFORMATION

4–1. How many people live in this household?———

Relationship to Interviewee	Sex M. F.	Age	Literacy (reads newspaper, letters)	Level of Education (P—primary, S—secondary)	Occupation (be specific)	For Off-farm Work, Estimated Monthly Nonfarm Income
1. Interviewee.						
2.						
3.						
4.						
5.						
6.						
7.						
8.						

4–2a. Are there any other members of the family who have recently (in the last two years) moved to urban areas or to other rural areas to work privately or to work for the GVN (military or civilian) or the U.S. government? ———yes; ———no.

Relationship to Interviewee	Present Occupation	Location	Number of Visits Home per Month
1.			
2.			
3.			

b. In the past year did you receive any money from your children or relatives living away from this household? ———yes; ———no. If yes, could you estimate the total amount you received last year? V$N ———

4–3. Do you receive income from the renting of farm animals or equipment (est.)? V$N ———; of land? V$N———; interest on loan to others? V$N ———.

4–4a. Type of house:
   i. thatched roof with thatched walls ———
      thatched roof with earth walls ———
      thatched roof with wooden walls ———
      tile roof with wooden walls ———
      tile roof with brick or cement walls ———
      other (specify) ———

ii. The floor is tile ———; cement ———; wood ———; dirt
———.

b. Does the household have? (Observe and record whenever possible.)

Item	Number presently owned	In 1966 did you buy any of these items for replacement or supplemental use?
wardrobe		
sewing machine		
pressure lamp		
set of chairs and table		
wristwatch		
bicycle		
motor bike or scooter		
brass worshiping items		
radio		
other (specify)		

4–5. What is the family's religion? ———
4–6. Did you make any improvements in your house last year? ———
yes; ———no.
If yes, specify what improvements and estimate the cost in 1966:
V$N ———.
4–7. Monthly cash expenditures (optional; fill in every five interviews if possible).

Item	Monthly Cash Expenditure	Item	Monthly Cash Expenditure
1. rice glutinous rice bread potatoes		9. household nonfood (fuel, soap, cooking oil)	
2. meats—pork, beef		10. clothing, cloth, etc.	
3. fish and fish preparations		11. medicines and medical care	
4. poultry and eggs		12. educational expense	
5. vegetables and fruit		13. worshiping ceremonies, weddings, funerals	
6. sauces (nuoc mam, etc.)		14. entertainment, including lottery and gambling	
7. beverages—tea, beer, ice		15. transporation	
8. tobacco, cigarettes, etc.		16. meals other than at home	

4–8. Have there been any significant changes in the last two years in the items your family consumes?

4–9. Have price changes affected the items you purchase? (Note changes in quality and quantity.)

Question Outline for Land Tenure Field Research

In each province studied, the objective is to collect information on certain issues related to the current tenure situation and possible land reform alternatives. The key issues and questions are:

A. ISSUES

1. Rent payment under existing conditions: Which farmers are paying rent (those living in GVN, contested, and Viet Cong areas) and how much rent (as a proportion of yield) are they paying?

2. The government's role: To what extent are government civilian and military officials involved in rent collection (back rents or otherwise) for absentee landowners? What constructive action has the government taken in land reform matters in the last six months?

3. The market for land: For recent rural land transactions, what price was paid, when, for what quality of land, from whom to whom? How much land is being diverted to new uses (vegetable crops, agricultural business, industrial, or military)? How did this affect values and tenure relationships?

4. The demand for land: Is there idle (abandoned) land in the province? How much? Is this due to insecurity and/or the labor shortage?

5. Landowner's role—absentee as opposed to owner-operator leasing part of his land: Does he provide credit to his tenant? By failure to grant permission, does he hinder the conversion of land into new crops or other uses or the building of irrigation ditches?

6. Landowner's attitudes: How was he affected by the Diem reforms (land confiscated, payments)? Has the Diem reform supplemented by Viet Cong pressures of the 1960–1967 period changed his attitude about holding land? Would he be willing to sell his land? Why or why not? Does he have nonland sources of income.

B. QUESTIONS

1. The government officials (land service chief and village officials):
   a. To what extent has the Diem reform been implemented and with what results?
   b. What land reform activities have been carried out in 1967? What are the obstacles to further reform progress? What is your per-

Appendix A

sonal opinion on the land reform issue? What should be done? By whom, at what level?

c. Are village officials collecting rent for absentee landowners?

2. The absentee landowner:
   a. How much land do you own? In what village?
   b. How have your rent collections varied, over the last six years and from area to area? Have you ever used village officials to collect your rents? What is the procedure?
   c. Were you affected by the Diem land reform? How (land confiscated, payments received)? What is your opinion about these results?
   d. Do you lend money to your tenants? Have you assisted them in constructing canals, farming new crops, etc.?
   e. Have you sold any land recently? Have your tenants approached you asking to purchase your land? Would you be willing to sell your land? (Why or why not?)
   f. What future plans do you have for your land?

Appendix B: Historical Data and Statistical Notes

Historical Data

TABLE B.1   Data on Rice Area Cultivated, Exports, and Prices

Year	Rice Area Cultivated (000 ha)	Rice Exports (000 MT) Cochinchina Rice	Indochina Paddy Equivalent	Rice
1860		57		
1868	215	133		
1879	349			
1880	522	284		
1881	614			
1882	686			
1883	763			
1884	694			
1885	743			
1886	754			
1887	818	320		
1888	820			
1889	875			
1890	854	439		
1891	911	360		
1892	972	506		
1893	926	605		
1894	1,134	570		
1895	1,026	525		
1896	1,058	440		
1897	1,115	600		775[b]

	Prices (V$N per 100 kg)			Population (000)	Cost-of-Living Index (Saigon working class, 1925 = 100)
	Paddy Wholesale	Rice, Saigon			
		No. 1[a]	No. 2[a]		
1860					
1868					
1879					
1880				1,679	
1881					
1882					
1883					
1884					
1885					
1886					
1887					
1888	1.68				
1889	2.10				
1890	1.87		3.47		
1891	2.02		3.80		
1892	2.10		3.97		
1893	1.88		3.62		
1894	2.12		3.86		
1895	2.36		4.12		
1896	2.76		4.80		
1897	3.00		5.19		

TABLE B.1 continued

Year	Rice Area Cultivated (000 ha)	Rice Exports (000 MT) Cochinchina Rice	Indochina Paddy Equivalent	Rice
1898	1,107	625		804[b]
1899	1,143	688		894[b]
1900	1,174	719		915[b]
1901	1,174	719		912[b]
1902	1,214	869		
1903	1,317	527		
1904	1,392	764		
1905	1,407	495		
1906	1,554	583		
1907	1,363	1,100		
1908	1,474	980		
1909	1,527	880		
1910	1,528	1,003		
1911	1,566	870		
1912	1,599	682		
1913	1,644			1,287
1914	1,703			1,419
1915	1,766			1,373
1916	1,800			1,345
1917	1,650			1,367
1918	1,650	1,189		1,620
1919	1,750	636		967
1920	1,752	840		1,188
1921	1,714	1,138		1,720
1922	1,780	920		1,440
1923	1,788	733	1,770	1,340
1924	1,818	772	1,660	1,230
1925	1,880	935	2,000	1,520
1926	1,950	1,070	2,200	1,597
1927	2,056	1,058	2,260	1,666
1928	2,114	1,100	2,390	1,798
1929	2,113	870	1,970	1,472
1930	2,214	804	1,530	1,122
1931	2,051	650	1,320	960
1932			1,620	1,214
1933			1,750	1,289

TABLE B.1   continued

	Prices (V\$N per 100 kg)			Population (000)	Cost-of-Living Index (Saigon working class, 1925 = 100)
	Paddy Wholesale	Rice, Saigon			
		No. 1[a]	No. 2[a]		
1898	3.02		5.31	2,263	
1899			5.09		
1900			5.16	2,937	
1901			5.16		
1902			5.69		
1903			7.61		
1904			5.45		
1905			5.90		
1906			5.55		
1907			6.08		
1908			6.38		
1909			5.65		
1910			6.62		
1911			7.66		
1912			8.89		
1913	3.81		5.98		
1914	3.54		5.58		
1915	3.69		6.04		
1916	3.52		5.70		
1917	3.03		4.88		
1918	3.57		5.98		
1919	6.69		11.01		
1920	6.48	12.7	11.53		
1921	4.31	8.7	7.77	3,788	
1922	4.39	8.2	7.63		
1923	5.52	9.26	8.85		
1924	6.41	10.54	10.18		
1925	5.90	10.04	9.60		100
1926	6.55	10.95	10.37	4,100	99
1927	6.15	10.63	9.74		103
1928	5.55	9.58	8.92		106
1929	7.11	11.58	11.07		113
1930	6.90	11.34	10.87		121
1931	3.86	6.72	6.19	4,484	105
1932	3.10	5.49	5.12		92
1933	2.29	4.07	3.89		85

TABLE B.1   continued

| | Rice Area Cultivated (000 ha) | Rice Exports (000 MT) | | |
| | | | Indochina | |
Year		Cochinchina Rice	Paddy Equivalent	Rice
1934			2,080	1,513
1935		1,530	2,320	1,748
1936		1,560	2,360	1,763
1937	2,200	1,350	2,030	1,529
1938	2,300		1,410	1,054
1939		1,680	2,210	1,673
1940	2,300	1,467	2,260	1,586
1941			1,400	944
1942	2,303		1,450	974
1943	2,204		1,510	1,024
1944	1,987		740	499
1945	1,715	492	68	45
1946	1,330		160	109
1947	1,316			
1948	1,103			
1949				
1950	1,237			
1951	1,288	272		
1952	1,349	152		
1953	1,541	102		
1954	1,572	160		
1955	1,803	69		
1956	2,060	0		
1957	2,125	184		
1958	1,702	113		
1959	1,810	246		
1960	1,749	346		
1961	1,823	154		
1962	1,925	84		
1963	1,965	323		
1964	1,959	49		
1965	1,877	(130) ⎫		
1966	1,819	(434) ⎬ imports		
1967		(860) ⎭		

TABLE B.1   continued

	Prices (V$N per 100 kg)			Population (000)	Cost-of-Living Index (Saigon working class, 1925 = 100)
	Paddy Wholesale	Rice, Saigon			
		No. 1[a]	No. 2[a]		
1934	1.88	3.26	3.09		78
1935	2.48	4.19	3.96		78
1936	2.99	4.97	4.74	4,616	79
1937	4.74	7.86	7.59		94
1938	6.61	10.63	10.08		107
1939	5.56	9.27	8.55		110
1940	7.56	13.20	12.15		128
1941	6.55	10.46	9.89		140
1942	6.89	10.23	9.74	5,400	180
1943	6.93	11.70	11.20	5,578	236
1944	8.67	15.53	14.84		361
1945	12.79	24.92	23.48		506
1946	32.00	75.00	65.00	5,579	1,703
1947					
1848				5,625	
1949					
1950	142	218			
1951	154	231		5,737	
1952	246	363		5,762	
1953	266	401		6,004	
1954	147	334		5,601	
1955	222	455		7,089	
1956	301	457		7,642	
1957	283	435		7,813	
1958	304	483		8,152	
1959	252	384		8,908	
1960	262	396		9,111	
1961	350	553			
1962	335	517			
1963	316	532			
1964	343	563		9,405	
1965	275	654			
1966					
1967					

Sources: See "Statistical Notes," pp. 264–267.
[a] No. 1 rice is first-quality, whole-grained rice; no. 2 rice contains broken grains.
[b] Rice exports rather than paddy.

Appendix B

Statistical Notes to Table B.1 and Text

RICE AREA CULTIVATED

Figures for 1868 and 1879–1931 are from Yves Henry, *Economie agricole de l'Indochine* (Hanoi: Imprimerie d'Extrême-Orient, 1932), pp. 272–274; the 1938 figure is from Erich H. Jacoby, *Agrarian Unrest in Southeast Asia* (New York: Columbia University Press, 1949), pp. 159–160, who cites *Bulletin Economique de l'Indochine*, vol. II (1938), p. 747 (report of the Inspector General of Agriculture), as source; 1940 from Jacoby, *Agrarian Unest*, p. 153; 1937 from Charles Robequain, *The Economic Development of French Indo-China*, trans. I. A. Wood (London and New York: Oxford University Press, 1944), p. 220; 1942 from Gouvernement Général de l'Indochine, Direction des Services Economiques, *Annuaire statistique de l'Indochine, 1941–1942*, p. 166; 1943–1946 figures from ibid., *1943–1946* (Hanoi, 1948), p. 91; 1944 and 1950–1953 from USAID, *ASB, 1958*, p. 63; 1954–1965 from Republic of Vietnam, Ministry of Agriculture, Agricultural Economics and Statistics Service, *Agricultural Statistics Yearbook, 1965* (Saigon, 1966), p. 34 (1954–1957 data are estimates of the GVN Directorate of Agriculture, and 1958–1965 data are results of surveys carried out by the Agricultural Economics and Statistics Service). USAID, *ASB, 1958*, p. 62, states that the area in cultivation is overstated for 1956–1958.

POPULATION

Figures for 1880 and 1900 are from Robequain, *Economic Development of French Indo-China*, p. 220; 1898 figure is from A. Galy, "La production, la consommation et l'exportation des riz en Cochinchine et au Cambodge," *Bulletin Economique de l'Indochine*, November 1899, p. 606; 1921 figure is from the first general census, completed in 1921 and reported in "La population de l'Indochine," ibid., 1922, pp. 163–165 (which gave a population of 18,983,203 for Indochina and 3,788,201 for Cochinchina); 1931 and 1936 population data from *Annuaire statistique de l'Indochine, 1936–1937*, p. 19; 1942 from ibid., *1941–1942*, p. 166; 1946 and 1948 from ibid., *1947–1948*, p. 19; 1943 and 1951–1957 from USAID, *ASB, 1958*, p. 3, for Southern Region (approximating Cochinchina); and 1958–1960 are from ibid., *1966*, p. 3.

EXPORTS

Buttinger writes, "The export of rice had been forbidden in precolonial Vietnam" (see Joseph Buttinger, *Vietnam: A Dragon Embattled* [London: Pall Mall Press, 1967], p. 165), with surpluses of the south feeding the north. He adds that after the French took control of Saigon harbor in 1860, 57,000 tons were exported; in 1870, 229,000 tons; and in 1877, 320,000 tons, implying that the figures refer to rice (not paddy) exports but not saying so or revealing his sources (ibid., pp. 165–166). The 1868 figure of 133,000 tons is from Jean Goudal, *Labour Conditions in Indo-China* (Geneva: International Labour Office, 1938), p. 200, and that for 1880 is from Robequain, *Economic Development of French Indo-China*, p. 220. More confidence can be placed in the 1890–1898 figures from *Annuaire statistique de l'Indochine, 1939–1940*, p. 304, which are given in total tonnage in terms of rice and derivatives. At that time, exports were mostly in paddy, as the 1899–1912 figures (from ibid.) converted to paddy equivalent and compared with a continuation of the 1890–1898 figures demonstrate. Therefore, the 1890–1898 series has been converted to a paddy series by adjusting the total rice derivatives statistics by an average of the difference of these two series over the 1899–1912 period for which both data are available. The conversion factor is 0.8 from the fourteen comparisons ranging from 0.805 to 0.742, which decline toward 1912, indicating an increasing proportion of rice exports compared with paddy exports in later years. A conversion factor of 0.62 was used to convert these paddy results to rice equivalents. Comparing these figures with those from Galy, "La production, la consommation et l'exportation des riz," p. 598, for rice exports through Saigon from Cochinchina and Cambodia (1894, 638; 1895, 631; 1896, 557; 1897, 639; and 1898, 723), the results are consistent. Robequain, in *Economic Development of French Indo-China*, p. 275, gives figures of 759,000 tons for exports from Cambodia and Cochinchina and 719,000 tons for Cochinchina alone in 1901. Exports in total tonnage and in equivalent paddy net weight for 1913–1946 are from *Annuaire statistique de l'Indochine, 1943–1946*, p. 277. Exports for 1951–1955 are given in paddy in USAID, ASB, 1958, p. 63. A conversion factor of 0.66 was used (see ibid., p. 61) to convert to rice. In 1956, rice exports were prohibited. Data for 1957–1964 are from ibid., *1964*, p. 84. Paddy rice imports of 0.4, 41.8, 24.6, and 5.1 (000 MT) were reported for 1955–1958, respectively, in ibid., *1958*, p. 62. In 1965, exports were banned, and 129,593 tons were imported; in 1966, 434,194 tons and in 1967, approximately 860,000 tons were imported (ibid., *1966*, p. 111).

PRICES

Paddy prices for 1888–1898 are from Galy, "La production, la consommation et l'exportation des riz," p. 607, and are given in paddy prices per picul converted by 100/68 to price per kg; for 1913–1941, *Annuaire statistique de l'Indochine, 1939–1940*, p. 290; for 1942–1946, ibid., *1943–1946*, p. 299; for 1950–1957, USAID, ASB, 1958, p. 35; and for 1958–1965, *Agricultural Statistics Yearbook, 1965*, p. 108. Rice no. 1 prices, 1920–1946, are from *Annuaire statistique de l'Indochine, 1943–1946*, p. 299, and 1950–1965 prices are from *Agricultural Statistics Yearbook, 1965*, p. 108. Rice no. 2 prices for 1890–1941 are from *Annuaire statistique de l'Indo-*

chine, 1939–1940, p. 303, and 1942–1946 prices are from ibid., *1943–1946,* p. 299.

COST-OF-LIVING INDEX

Saigon working-class general index weights: food, 55; housing, 20; other, 25. Figures for 1925–1946 are from *Annuaire statistique de l'Indochine, 1943–1946,* p. 301.

YIELDS

The available evidence indicates that yields declined in Cochinchina during the period of settlement, although caution is in order, as yields in Vietnam are the object of notoriously poor calculations and assumptions. Before 1946 no systematic process was employed to determine yields. Since 1946, when a capability for such a systematic assessment has existed, especially in the 1960s, security conditions have been such that the technique could not be employed on a Delta-wide basis. Still, one would expect that yields would drop as the extensive margin was reached and lands of inferior quality were brought into cultivation. Postwar statistics do show that yields have tended to fall in years when the area in cultivation rose markedly, for example, in 1953 compared with 1952 and in 1957 compared with 1956, and to rise when the cultivated area fell sharply, for example, in 1958 compared with 1957. Over the long term, yields in the post–World War II period were steady at the 1.3 MT per ha range until the late 1950s, when they jumped to over 2.0 MT per ha. This increase, largely the result of the application of fertilizers for the first time on a large scale, was the first reversal of a long-term steady or declining yield trend dating from the 1900 to 1920 period. Until 1930 this trend can be explained by the bringing into production of lower-quality or marginal lands.

Galy, in the *Bulletin Economique de l'Indochine* of November 1899, stated that he used a "very approximate" figure of 1.8 MT per ha in his calculations for Cochinchina, which was slightly below that then in use by the Directorate of Agriculture. He compared this yield with 2.2 MT in Cambodia, a figure he used with "much certainty." (See Galy, "La production, la consommation et l'exportation des riz," p. 606.)

In an article in the March 1899 issue of the same journal, another writer, describing the conditions of settlement in Go Cong Province, cites an average crop yield of 80 to 100 *gia* (1.6 to 2.0 MT) for first-quality rice land and 60 to 80 *gia* (1.2 to 1.6 MT) for second- and third-quality rice land ("La culture du riz a Gocong," p. 304). According to Galy, of the 1,107,-471 ha in cultivation in Cochinchina in 1898, 632,047 ha (57.2%) were rated as first quality; 269,712 ha (24.3%) as second quality; and 205,710 ha (18.5%) as third quality, making a high-yield figure of 1.8 MT plausible ("La production," p. 607).

But general writers on economic matters in Indochina use a variety of figures for later dates. Goudal, in the late 1930s, in *Labour Conditions in Indo-China*, p. 87, used 1.6 MT per ha; Le Thanh Khoi, in *Le Viet-Nam* (Paris: Editions de Minuit, 1955), p. 416, used 1.2 to 1.3 MT per ha for the same period, comparing it (unfavorably) with 3.6 MT in Japan, 2.5 MT in China, and 1.6 MT in Thailand. Robequain, in *Economic Development of French Indo-China*, p. 416, used a 1.2 MT figure for 1928, saying that yields had probably not increased much since that date. Henry, the foremost agricultural expert of his day, writing in 1932, used an average yield statistic of 1.34 MT per ha for 1931 (see *Economie agricole de l'Indochine*, p. 272).

For the calculations in the text, a figure of 1.6 MT per ha is used for the 1880 to 1910 calculations, and 1.4 MT for calculations applying from 1920 until 1945. Because the farmers interviewed by the author consistently stated that during the 1945–1955 period yields were at 1.3 MT per ha, that figure was used.

The yields given in the *Annuaire statistique de l'Indochine* (method of calculation unclear) are as follows: 1919–1922 average, 1.35 MT (*Recueil de statistiques, 1913–1922*, p. 111); crop year 1942/43, 1.4 MT (*1941–1942*, p. 88); 1943/44, 1.2 MT; 1944/45, 1.1 MT; 1945/46, 1.2 MT; 1946/47, 1.2 MT (*1943–1946*, pp. 90–91); 1947/48, 1.3 MT; and 1948/49, 1.2 MT (*1947–1948*, p. 97).

After 1957 a yield of 2.0 MT per ha in a normal year can be used with some confidence. The yield results reported in USAID, *ASB, 1958*, for 1950 to 1958 range from 1.2 to 1.5 MT per ha, with a median of 1.3 MT. The results reported in ibid., *1966* (p. 103) for the same Southern Region (roughly, Cochinchina) from 1959 to 1965 range from 2.1 to 2.4 MT per ha, with a median of 2.1 MT. If these results are accepted, a dramatic increase in yields must have taken place in the late 1950s. The plausible cause for the higher yields was the increase in fertilizer use during that period. Between 1951 and 1958, annual fertilizer imports rose from 16,000 MT to 52,000 MT for all of South Vietnam (USAID, *ASB, 1958*, p. 77).

Bibliography

"L'automobile en Indochine," *Bulletin Economique de l'Indochine*, March 1934, pp. 1357–1375.

Balogh, Thomas. *The Economics of Poverty*. London: Weidenfeld and Nicolson, 1966.

Bernard, Paul. *Le problème économique indochinois*. Paris: Nouvelles Editions Latines, 1934.

Blaug, M. "A Survey of the Theory of Process-Innovations," *Economica*, vol. n.s. 30 (February 1963), pp. 13–32.

Boeke, J. H. *Economics and Economic Policy of Dual Societies*. New York: Institute of Pacific Relations, 1953.

Buttinger, Joseph. *The Smaller Dragon: A Political History of Vietnam*. New York: Frederick A. Praeger, 1958.

———. *Vietnam: A Dragon Embattled*. 2 vols. New York: Frederick A. Praeger; London: Pall Mall Press, 1967.

Carver, George A., Jr. "The Faceless Viet Cong," *Foreign Affairs*, vol. 44 (April 1966), pp. 347–372.

Cho, Yong Sam. *"Disguised Unemployment" in Underdeveloped Areas, with Special Reference to South Korean Agriculture*. Berkeley and Los Angeles: University of California Press, 1963.

Clark, Colin, *Population Growth and Land Use*. New York: St Martin's Press; London: Macmillan & Co., 1967.

———, and Margaret Haswell. *The Economics of Subsistence Agriculture*. 2nd ed. New York: St Martin's Press; London: Macmillan & Co., 1966.

Cole, Allan B., ed. *Conflict in Indo-China and International Repercussions: A Documentary History, 1945–1955*. Ithaca, N.Y.: Cornell University Press, 1956.

"Le commerce de légumes de Dalat," *Bulletin Economique de l'Indochine*, 1935, pp. 1027–1034.

Cooper, J. L. "Land Reform in the Republic of Vietnam." Mimeographed. Saigon: USOM, March 1966.

"La culture du riz à Gocong," *Bulletin Economique de l'Indochine*, March 1899, pp. 303–307.

Davis, R. E. "An Analysis of the Property Tax in Vietnam." Mimeographed. Saigon: USOM, March 1965.

De Feyssal, P. *L'endettement agrarie en Cochinchine*. Hanoi: Imprimerie d'Extrême-Orient, 1933.

Dovring, Folke. "Unemployment in Traditional Agriculture," *Economic Development and Cultural Change*, vol. 15, no. 2 (January 1967), pt. I, pp. 163–173.

Dumarest, André. *La formation des classes sociales en pays annamite*. Lyon: Imprimerie P. Ferréol, 1935.

Eckaus, Richard S. "The Factor Proportions Problem in Underdeveloped Areas," *American Economic Review*, vol. XLV, no. 4 (September 1955), pp. 539–565.

————. "Notes on Invention and Innovation in Less Developed Countries," *American Economic Review*, vol. LVI, no. 3 (May 1966), pp. 98–109.

Enke, S. "Economic Development with Unlimited and Limited Supplies of Labour," *Oxford Economic Papers*, vol. n.s. 14 (June 1962), pp. 158–172.

Falcon, Walter P. "Farmer Response to Price in a Subsistence Economy: The Case of West Pakistan," *American Economic Review*, vol. LV, no. 3 (May 1964), pp. 580–591.

Fall, Bernard B. *The Two Viet-Nams: A Political and Military Analysis*. 2nd ed. New York: Frederick A. Praeger, 1966; London: Pall Mall Press, 1967.

————. "Viet Nam in the Balance," *Foreign Affairs*, vol. 45, no. 1 (October 1966), pp. 1–18.

Fei, John C. H., and Gustav Ranis. *Development of the Labor Surplus Economy: Theory and Policy*. New Haven: Yale University Press, 1964.

Firth, Raymond William, and B. S. Yamey, eds. *Capital, Saving and Credit in Peasant Societies: Studies from Asia, Oceania, the Caribbean and Middle America*. Chicago: Aldine Publishing Co.; London: Allen & Unwin, 1964.

Food and Agriculture Organization. *The Economic Relationships Between Grains and Rice*. Commodity Bulletin Series, no. 39. Rome, 1965.

————. *Statistics of Crop Responses to Fertilizers*. Rome, 1966.

Galy, A. "La production, la consommation et l'exportation des riz en Cochinchine et au Cambodge," *Bulletin Economique de l'Indochine*, November 1899, pp. 598–612.

Geertz, Clifford. "The Rotating Credit Association: A 'Middle Rung' in Development," *Economic Development and Cultural Change*, vol. X, no. 3 (April 1962), pp. 241–263.

Goldsen, Rose K., and Max Ralis. "Factors Related to Acceptance of Innovations in Ban Chan, Thailand." Mimeographed. Cornell Thailand Project, Interim Reports Series, no. 3. Ithaca, N.Y., 1957.

Gotsch, C. H. "Technological Change and Private Investment in Agriculture: A Case Study of the Pakistan Punjab." Ph.D. dissertation, Harvard University, 1966.

Goudal, Jean. *Labour Conditions in Indo-China*. Geneva: International Labour Office, 1938.

Gourou, Pierre. *The Peasants of the Tonkin Delta: A Study of Human Geography*. Translated by Richard R. Miller. New Haven, Conn.: Human Relations Area Files, 1955. First published as *Les paysans du Delta tonkinois: Etude de géographie humaine*. Paris: Editions d'Art et d'Histoire, 1936.

————. "The Standard of Living in the Delta of Tonkin." Mimeographed. Paper given at the Ninth Conference of the Institute of Pacific Relations, Hot Springs, Virginia, January 1945.

Gouvernement Générale de l'Indochine, Direction des Services Economiques. *Annuaire statistique de l'Indochine, 1936–1937; 1939–1940; 1941–1942; 1943–1946; 1947–1948*. Hanoi, 1938, 1942, 1945, 1948, 1949.

Hagen, Everett E. *On the Theory of Social Change: How Economic Growth Begins*. Homewood, Ill.: Dorsey Press, 1962.

Halberstam, David. "Voices of the Vietcong," *Harper's*, January 1968, pp. 45–52.

Hall, D. G. E. *A History of South-East Asia*. 2nd ed. New York: St Martin's Press, 1964; London: Macmillan & Co., 1966.

Haswell, M. R. *The Economics of Development in Village India*. London: Routledge & Kegan Paul, 1967.

Hendry, James B. *The Small World of Khanh Hau*. Chicago: Aldine Publishing Co., 1964.

Henry, Yves. *Documents de démographie et riziculture en Indochine*. Hanoi: Imprimerie d'Extrême-Orient, 1928.

————. *Economie agricole de l'Indochine*. Hanoi: Imprimerie d'Extrême-Orient, 1932.

Herdt, Robert W., and John W. Mellor. "The Contrasting Response of Rice to Nitrogen: India and the United States," *Journal of Farm Economics*, vol. 46 (February 1964), pp. 150–160.

Hickey, Gerald Cannon. *Village in Vietnam*. New Haven, Conn.: Yale University Press, 1964.

Hopper, W. David. "Allocation Efficiency in a Traditional Indian Agriculture," *Journal of Farm Economics*, vol. 46 (August 1965), pp. 611–624.

Huy-Loc, Pham. "For the Suppression of Usury," *L'Annam Nouveau* (Hanoi), December 13, 1936.

International Rice Research Institute. *Annual Report, 1966*. Los Banos, the Philippines, 1966; also attached "Statistics for Rice Research."

Jewkes, John, David Sawers, and Richard Stillerman. *The Sources of Invention*. New York: St. Martin's Press; London: Macmillan & Co., 1958.

Jorgenson, Dale W. "Surplus Agricultural Labour and the Development of a Dual Economy," *Oxford Economic Papers*, vol. n.s. 19 (November 1967), pp. 288–312.

Kato, Yuzuru. "Factors Contributing to the Recent Increase of Productivity in Japanese Agriculture," *Journal of Development Studies*, vol. 2, no. 1 (October 1965), pp. 38–58.

Khoi, Le Thanh. *Le Viet-Nam: Histoire et civilisation, le milieu et l'histoire.* Paris: Editions de Minuit, 1955.

Kindleberger, Charles P. *Foreign Trade and the National Economy.* New Haven, Conn. Yale University Press, 1962.

Lewis, W. Arthur. "Economic Development with Unlimited Supplies of Labour," *Manchester School*, vol. n.s. XXII (May 1954), pp. 139–191.

Lindholm, Richard W., ed. *Viet-Nam: The First Five Years.* East Lansing: Michigan State University Press, 1959.

Little, I. M. D., and J. M. Clifford. *International Aid: A Discussion of the Flow of Public Resources from Rich to Poor Countries.* London: George Allen & Unwin, 1965; Chicago: Aldine Publishing Co., 1966.

Long, Millard. "Interest Rates and the Structure of Agricultural Credit Markets," *Oxford Economic Papers*, vol. n.s. 20 (July 1968), pp. 275–288.

McAlister, John T., Jr. "The Possibilities for Diplomacy in Southeast Asia," *World Politics*, vol. XIX, no. 2 (January 1967), pp. 258–305.

Mathur, Ashok. "The Anatomy of Disguised Unemployment," *Oxford Economic Papers*, vol. n.s. 16 (July 1964), pp. 161–193.

Mellor, John W. "The Use and Productivity of Farm Family Labor in the Early Stages of Agricultural Development," *Journal of Farm Economics*, vol. 45 (August 1963), pp. 517–533.

Mitchell, Edward J. "Land Tenure and Rebellion: A Statistical Analysis of Factors Affecting Government Control in South Vietnam." RAND Memorandum 5181–ARPA. Santa Monica, Calif., June 1967. Also published as "Inequality and Insurgency: A Statistical Study of South Vietnam," *World Politics*, vol. XX, no. 3 (April 1968), pp. 421–438.

Moorman, F. R. *The Soils of Vietnam.* Saigon: Ministry of Agriculture, 1961.

Myint, H. "The Gains from International Trade and the Backward Countries," *Review of Economic Studies*, vol. XXII (1954–1955), pp. 129–142.

Nelson, Richard R. "The Economics of Invention: A Survey of the Literature," *Journal of Business*, vol. XXXII (April 1959), pp. 101–127.

Nurkse, Ragnar. *Problems of Capital Formation in Underdeveloped Countries.* London: Oxford University Press, 1953.

Olivera, Julio H. G. "On Structural Inflation and Latin American Structuralism," *Oxford Economic Papers*, vol. n.s. 16 (November 1964), pp. 321–332.

Oshima, Harry T. "Food Consumption, Nutrition, and Economic Development in Asian Countries," *Economic Development and Cultural Change*, vol. 15, no. 4 (July 1967), pp. 385–397.

Paglin, Morton. " 'Surplus' Agricultural Labor and Development: Facts and Theories," *American Economic Review*, vol. LV, no. 4 (September 1965), pp. 815–833.

Paret, Peter, and John W. Shy. *Guerrillas in the 1960's.* 2nd ed. New York: Frederick A. Praeger, 1962.

Pepelasis, Adam A., and Pan A Yotopoulos. *Surplus Labour in Greek Agriculture, 1953–1960.* Athens, 1962.

Pike, Douglas. *Viet Cong: The Organization and Techniques of the National Liberation Front of South Vietnam.* Cambridge, Mass.: The M.I.T. Press, 1966.

"La Plaine des Joncs et son exploitation agricole," *Bulletin Economique de l'Indochine*, October 1898, pp. 113–119.

"La population de l'Indochine," *Bulletin Economique de l'Indochine*, March 1922, pp. 163–165.

Republic of Vietnam, Ministry of Agriculture, Agricultural Economics and Statistics Service. *Agricultural Statistics Yearbook, 1964.* Saigon, 1965. Ibid., *1965.* Saigon, 1966.

———. *Census of Agriculture, 1960–1961.* Saigon, 1964.

Robequain, Charles. *The Economic Development of French Indo-China.* Translated by I. A. Wood. London and New York: Oxford University Press, 1944.

Rogers, Everett M. *Diffusion of Innovations.* New York: The Free Press, 1962.

Rosenstein-Rodan, P. N. "Disguised Unemployment and Underemployment in Agriculture," *Monthly Bulletin of Agricultural Economics and Statistics*, vol. VI, nos. 7/8 (July/August 1957), pp. 1–7.

Schultz, Theodore W. *Economic Crises in World Agriculture.* Ann Arbor: University of Michigan Press, 1965.

———. *Transforming Traditional Agriculture.* New Haven, Conn.: Yale University Press, 1964.

Seers, Dudley. "A Theory of Inflation and Growth in Under-Developed Economies Based on the Experience of Latin America," *Oxford Economic Papers*, vol. n.s. 14 (June 1962), pp. 173–195.

Smith, Arthur H. *Village Life in China.* New York: F. H. Revell Co., 1899.

Smith, Paul F. *Consumer Credit Costs, 1949–59.* Princeton, N. J.: Princeton University Press, 1964.

Solo, Robert. "The Capacity to Assimilate an Advanced Technology," *American Economic Review*, vol. LVI, no. 2 (May 1966), pp. 91–97.

Stout, B. A. *Equipment for Rice Production.* FAO Agricultural Development Paper, no. 84. Rome: Food and Agriculture Organization, 1966.

Stroup, Robert H. "Rural Income Expenditure: Sample Survey." Mimeographed. Saigon: USOM, Economic and Planning Division, 1965.

Sturt, Daniel W. "Producer Response to Technological Change in West Pakistan," *Journal of Farm Economics*, vol. 47 (August 1965), pp. 625–633.

Swift, M. G. *Malay Peasant Society in Jelebu*. New York: Humanities Press; London: Athlone Press, 1965.

Thompson, Sir Robert. *Defeating Communist Insurgency: The Lessons of Malaya and Vietnam*. New York: Frederick A. Praeger; London: Chatto & Windus, 1966.

Thompson, Virginia. *French Indo-China*. New York: Macmillan Co.; London: George Allen & Unwin, 1937.

United States, Agency for International Development (USAID), Office of Joint Economic Affairs. *Annual Statistical Bulletin* for 1958 through 1966. Saigon, 1959–1967.

Usher, Dan. "Thai Interest Rates," *Journal of Development Studies*, vol. 3 (April 1967), pp. 267–279.

Warner, Denis. *The Last Confucian: Vietnam, South-East Asia, and the West*. New York and London: Macmillan Co., 1963.

Wolf, Charles, Jr. "Insurgency and Counterinsurgency: New Myths and Old Realities," *Yale Review*, vol. LVI (Winter 1967, published December 1966), pp. 225–241.

Yamada, Saburo. "Changes in Output and in Conventional and Nonconventional Inputs in Japanese Agriculture since 1880," *Food Research Institute Studies*, vol. VII (1967), no. 3, pp. 371–413.

Yang, Lien-Shen. "Buddhist Monasteries and Four Money-Raising Institutions in Chinese History," *Harvard Journal of Asiatic Studies*, vol. 13 (June 1950), pp. 174–191.

Young, Allyn. "Increasing Returns and Economic Progress," *Economic Journal* (London), vol. XXXVIII (December 1928), pp. 527–542.

Zasloff, Joseph J. "Rural Resettlement in South Vietnam: The Agroville Program," *Pacific Affairs*, vol. XXXV, no. 4 (Winter 1962–63), pp. 327–340.

Index

Agency for International Development, see U.S. Agency for International Development (USAID)
Agrarian policy, Viet Cong, 63–64
"Agrarian Policy of the Party," 63–64
Agricultural Affairs Committee (AAC), 70–71
Agricultural Development Bank, 111n
Agricultural production, 16, 17, 75–103, 215
  and plot size, 142–144
  and Viet Cong tax policy, 219–220
  see also Agriculture
Agricultural tax (troop support tax), Viet Cong, 217–219, 222. See also Taxes, Viet Cong
Agriculture, 2–4
  primary, 76–88
  secondary, 88–94
  in traditional society, 234
Aid programs, 1, 17, 211–216
  and fruit cultivation, 89
  GVN-U.S., 211, 237
  macroeconomic role of, 215–216
  role in village economy, 212–215
  see also U.S. Agency for International Development
Alsop, Joseph, 228–229
An Giang Province, 53, 56, 214
  land identification program in, 69–70, 230
  rent-security relationship in, 61
An Xuyen Province, 53
Annam, 7n, 20, 46–47
Ardener, Shirley, 109n
Assassination, 55, 59, 161

Attitudes, 25, 74
  economic, 207–210
  and physical security, 239–241
Automobiles, 48–49

Bac Lieu City, 55
Bac Lieu Province, 5, 13, 17, 21, 40, 215
  French schools in, 24
  Phuoc Long district, 53, 55, 67
  population density of, 34–35
  rent collection in, 67–68
  research into land problems, 53
  and Viet Minh, 55
Bali, 43, 44, 45
Balogh, Thomas, 3, 5
Bernard, Paul, 31n, 40n
Blaug, M., 176
Boeke, J. H., 3, 4
Buddhism, 208
Buffalo, 75, 225
  production, 91–92
  as store of wealth, 92–93
Bunker, Ellsworth, 229
Buttinger, Joseph, 21n, 41n, 46–47, 49n, 95n, 105

Ca Mau Peninsula, 5, 21, 229n
Canals, man-made, 5, 23, 48, 50, 95, 152, 154. See also Irrigation
Cao Dai sect, 208
Capital, 1, 17, 104–122, 151, 185, 237
  credit institutions, 109–114
  the hui, 114–122

Capital (*continued*)
  interest rates and indebtedness, 105–108
  and opening of Delta for cultivation, 23
  and rice production, 84
  and vegetable cultivation, 87
Carver, George A., 243n
Cease-fire (1954)), 10
Census, population, 37
Central Office of the National Liberation Front (COSVN), 63, 64, 222, 226
Central Vietnam, 231–232
Chen Han-seng, 106n
Chevalier, François, 233n
Chickens, 75, 94
China, 18n–19n, 218, 220n, 234
Cho, Yong Sam, 136
Clark, Colin, 38n, 97
Cobb-Douglas production function, 123
Cochinchina, 5
  closing of frontier, 21
  decline in income, 35, 39, 42–45
  French failures, 49–52
  French sovereignty, 19
  pre-French legacy, 46–49
  rice cultivation, 21, 35
  settlement of, 19–23, 50
  usury, 105
Cole, Allan B., 56n
Collectivization, 236
Collins, General Lawton, 228
Combat hamlet, 11, 98
Commodity Import Program, U.S., 84, 174
Communication
  and diffusion of motor pump, 172–174
  and village-level aid program, 213–215
Consumption
  and aid programs, 216
  mass, 21
  of rice, 37–39
  and Viet Cong trade policy, 223–224
Corvée, 46, 47, 129–130, 213, 224–225, 238
  and U.S. policy, 228–229
Cost-of-living index, 1, 2
COSVN, see Central Office of the National Liberation Front
Cotton, T. A., 120n
Council of Notables, 47, 64

Credit, 31, 104–105
  and acceptance of motor pump, 170
  hui, 114–122
  institutions, 109–114
Crop failure
  and "tolerance," 32
  and Viet Cong taxes, 221
Crop rotation, 79

Dalat, 85
Dam phu (contribution) system, Viet Cong, 217
Data collection, 13–17
Davis, R. E., 66n
Death rate, 18
Debts, see Indebtedness
Diem, Ngo Dinh, land reform program of, 24, 57–58, 66, 70, 71
  abuses of, 58
  Ordinance Fifty-seven, 57
  Ordinance Seven, 57
  Ordinance Two, 57
  resurrection of, 68–69
  strategic hamlet program, 235, 238–239
  and trend to smaller holdings, 72
  and U.S. policy, 228–229
Diesel pump, 165–166, 168. See also Motor pump
Dinh Tuong Province, 5, 7–9, 13, 17, 40, 215, 226
  Ben Tranh district, 10
  Cho Gao district, 12, 67, 102
  exports, 101
  population, 34
  rent collection in, 67, 68
  research into land problems, 53
  Viet Cong in, 59–60
  Viet Minh in, 55
Double-cropping, 77–78, 151, 187
  and fertilizer use, 195
Draft
  military, 9, 125, 213
  Viet Cong, 218, 220, 224, 237
Drainage, 23, 151–152
Dumarest, André, 47

Eckaus, Richard S., 25, 135, 177
Economic policies
  French colonial, 49–50
  GVN, 236–238, 244–245
  Viet Cong, 238–239
Economic stabilization, 211
Education, colonial efforts in, 49

Index

Eisenhower, Dwight D., 228
Elliott, David, 131n, 217n
Enke, S., 135
Export, exports,
    determination of, 32–34
    market, 18, 21–23
    model, 34–39
    of rice, 32–37, 260, 262
    trends in, 101

Factor markets, 4, 16
    Viet Cong failures with, 225–226
Falcon, Walter P., 193n, 194n, 197
Fall, Bernard, 46n, 49n, 242n–243n
Family, 11, 15–16, 208
    Malthusian margin, 26–27
    as production unit, 123, 139–142, 145,
      147–148
    and Viet Cong tax policy, 218–219
Farm household, defined, 14n
Farm production interviews, 13–14, 246–
    255
Farmers' Association, GVN, 158n, 159,
    161, 212, 214
Farmers' Liberation Association, 221,
    224–225
Fei, John C. H., 135
Fertilizer, 15–17, 50n, 148, 180–197,
    211
    determinants of use, 188–193
    distribution of, 212
    GVN subsidy program, 213
    and increased rice production, 77, 113–
      114, 151
    and insecticide use, 185–187
    profit explanation of use, 188–191
    subsistence explanation of use, 191–
      193
    variations in yield response, 180–181
    Viet Cong opposition to use of, 223–
      224
    yield response, 181, 183–188
Fish, 75, 90–91
Food and Agriculture Organization, 38n,
    181n
France, 19, 99
    "exploitation" of Vietnam, 46–47
    failures in Vietnam, 49–52
    Ministry of Colonies, 99
    and settlement of Cochinchina, 21
    successes in Vietnam, 47–49
    withdrawal from Vietnam, 53
Frankel, S. H., xiii

Free land concession, French decree
    (1874), 50
Fruit, 73, 75, 88–90, 218, 225

Ganay, M., 106n
Geertz, Clifford, 109n
General Uprising (1960), 60, 112, 236,
    243
Geneva Peace, 56
Gia Dinh Province, 14, 19, 39
Giap, Vo Nguyen, 53
Gittenger, Price, 57n, 228n
Go Cong Province, 28, 40, 152n
Goldsen, Rose K., 173n
Gotsch, C. H. 165n
Goudal, Jean, 28, 32n, 48n, 105
Gourou, Pierre, 43n, 51, 93, 209
Grand Council of the Economic and Fi-
    nancial Interests of Indo-China, 113
Guerrillas, 131, 217, 218, 241–245
GVN (South Vietnamese government),
    8, 55, 56, 102, 211, 216
    aid at village level, 212–215
    economic policies, 236–238, 244–245
    elite identification, 238–239
    and Farmers' Associations, 212, 213
    fertilizer subsidy program, 213
    and irrigation, 162–163
    labor policies, 129–130
    as loan source, 111–114
    and rent determination, 59–60, 199
    resistance to motor pump, 174, 223
    response to Viet Cong land reform
      program, 66–71
    and taxes, 66, 223
    and U.S. policy, 229–233

Hagen, Everett E., 3, 4
Hall, D. G. E., 19n
Harvesting techniques, 42–45, 83
    and population density, 43
Haswell, Margaret, 38n, 97, 150n
Hendry, James B., 4, 8, 41n, 43n, 49, 55,
    57, 62n, 80, 81n, 92, 97, 99, 106–
    107, 165n, 214
    on labor, 125, 126
    on use of fertilizers, 186
Henry, Yves, 31n, 40, 41n, 51, 62n, 72n
Herdt, Robert W., 182–183, 197
Hickey, Gerald Cannon, 8, 79n, 87n, 90
Hinton, William, 59, 220n
Ho Chi Minh, 55n, 231
Hoi, Huynh van, 161n, 212–213, 214
Hué, 7n, 128n

Hui, 109n, 114–122
  bidding process, 118
  comparative interest rate, 121–122
  interest rate (1966–1967), 118–121
  members, 115–118
  organization of, 114–115
Huy, Truong Binh, 23, 24, 25, 30n
Huy-Loc, Pham, 105n

Ideology, 224, 226–227, 234–236, 238
Imports, fertilizer, 181
Income, 17, 18–52, 75–76, 198–200
  and aid programs, 215
  decline in real, 35, 39
  of farm laborer, 40, 42
  and fruit cultivation, 88–89
  and land utilization, 74, 76
  and new harvesting technique, 42–43,
    45
  opportunities, 133–135
  from rentals, 31–32
  and rice production, 76
  and vegetable cultivation, 87–88
Income tax, Viet Cong, 219–220
  deterrents to delinquency, 221
  see also Taxes, Viet Cong
Indebtedness, 106, 107–108, 215
  and fertilizer use per hectare, 113
India, 97, 145, 147, 180, 197
Indochina, see Vietnam
Inflation, 211
Innovation, 169, 211
  motivation for, 153, 157
Insecticides, 15, 84, 213
  distribution of, 212
  and fertilizer use, 185–187
  and fish production, 91
  and Viet Cong policy, 224
Insects, 186–187
Insurgency
  grievance base of, 244–245
  and rural economy, 1–2
Interest rates, 104–105, 113, 211
  of the *hui*, 118–122
  1945–1965, 106
  1966–1967, 106–107
  pre-1945, 105–106
International Rice Research Institute
  (IRRI), Los Banos, Philippines,
  79n, 180n
Interviews, 13–15, 246–256
  landlord, 13, 16–17, 255–256
  reliability of response, 15–16
  tested, 14

Investment, 17, 27, 201–210
  and aid programs, 215–216
  attitudes, 207–210
  decisions, 1
  and loans, 113–114
Irrigation, 17, 31, 50, 80, 151–163, 213
  community efforts, 159–160
  and fruit cultivation, 89
  and increased rice production, 77
  and labor shortage, 144
  landlord opposition to, 156–157
  in LBD, 154–157
  and local organization, 161–162
  in TCN, 157–159
  and the war, 160
  see also Canals; Drainage

Japan, 38, 50, 73, 138, 178, 180, 181
  extension work, 215n
  land reform, 228
Java, 43, 44, 45
Jewkes, John, 176
Joint U.S. Public Affairs Office
  (JUSPAO), 69, 235, 236, 243
Jorgenson, Dale W., 135

Kato, Yuzuru, 180n
Khanh Hau, 8, 90, 214. See also Hendry,
  James B.; Hickey, Gerald Cannon
Khoi, Le Thanh, 21n
Komer, Robert, 229
Ky, Nguyen Cao, 68–69

Labor, 17, 123–150, 151, 185
  boycotts, 63
  and capital use, 84
  and community efforts, 159–161
  the *corvée*, 129–130
  and cultivation of Delta, 23
  and diversification of rice varieties, 79,
    80
  and family, 123, 139–142, 145, 147–
    148
  and family earnings, 133–135
  GVN policies, 129–130
  and harvest wage, 131–132
  and harvesting techniques, 42–45, 83
  market, structural changes in, 125–127
  for rice field preparation, 81–82
  and rice seedling transplanting, 82–83
  scarcity of, 1
  seasonal demand for, 138–139
  seasonal migration of, 40
  and size of plot, 142–144, 147–148

Labor (*continued*)
supply, 124–125
surplus, 1
and vegetable cultivation, 86, 87
Viet Cong exchange, 130–131
Viet Cong policies, 129–130, 132, 211
wages, 127–128, 132
working conditions, 128–129
Labor-exchange association, Viet Cong, 130–131
Land, 18–52
attitudes toward, 74
concessions, 50–51
French-owned, 50–51
redistribution of (1954), 10, 154
role in traditional society, 234
in tenant-landlord relationship, 29–31
utilization, 73–74
values, 61–62
and Viet Minh, 55
see also Viet Cong, and land reforms
Land reform, 16
Diem government, 24, 57–58, 66, 68–69
GVN opposition to, 66–71
United States policy toward, 228–236
Viet Cong, 58–65, 211, 216
Viet Minh, 10, 55–57
Land tenure, 4–5, 53–74
GVN response, 66–71
and land use, 72–74
1945–1960, 53–58
and U.S. policy, 230–231, 234
and vegetable cultivation, 86
and Viet Cong reforms, 58–65
Landholding, 3
accumulation of large, 28–29
attitudes toward, 25
and Diem's Ordinance Fifty-seven, 57
fragmentation of, 27, 42
and land use, 72–74
size of, 14
and Viet Cong taxes, 11
Landlord, 8n, 18, 52, 151
and Diem land reform, 58
estate management, 31
institutionalization of system, 17
interviews, 13, 16–17, 255–256
and irrigation, 156–157
and maximizing revenues, 31–32, 39
opposition to fruit cultivation, 90
as source for loans, 111
-tenant relationship, 29–31
and Viet Cong, 59, 62, 237

and Viet Minh, 55, 56, 62
and village attitudes, 161
Landowners, 10, 21
French policy toward, 51
and irrigation, 154
and Viet Cong reforms, 61–62
and Viet Minh land redistribution, 56
Lawrence, T. E., 243n
LBD, see Long Binh Dien
Lewis, W. Arthur, 135
Lindholm, Richard W., 57n, 228n
Literacy, 49
Loans, 107
cooperative (*hui*), 114–122
government, 111–114
green-crop, 109–110
sa mai, 109–110
sources and conditions of, 111
Lodge, Henry Cabot, 228–229
Long, Millard, 104n
Long An Province, 8, 28, 40, 63, 88, 132
Long Binh Dien, (LBD), 9, 12, 15
Agricultural Affairs Committee, 70, 71
fertilizer use in, 183–188
government loan program, 112
hamlets, 12
introduction of new rice varieties, 80
irrigation developments in, 154–157
land redistribution in, 63
and motor pump, 172
population of, 12
production, agricultural, 75–77
and rent collection, 67
and rent-security relationship, 60–61
trend to smaller holdings, 72
vegetable cultivation, 88
working conditions in, 128

McAlister, John T., Jr., 231n
Malaya, 43–45
Malraux, André, 226n, 234n
Malthusian evictions, 25–28
Mao Tse-tung, 226, 234
Marketing, 17, 99–103
and GVN, 239
rice, 7, 99–100
Marxism, 226
Mathur, Ashok, 135
Medicine, 21, 48
Mekong River, 5, 85, 152, 154–155
Mekong River Delta, 1–2, 5–12, 48
area under cultivation, 54–55
economic conditions, post-1930, 45
before French arrival, 19–20

Mekong River Delta (*continued*)
  harvesting techniques in, 43–45
  irrigation, 151–152
  lower Delta, 5
  settlement of, 20–21, 95
  transport, 95
  upper Delta, 5
Mellor, John W., 147n, 182–183, 197
Merchants, 10
  as source of loans, 111
  and the war, 101–103
Mexican revolution (1910), 233n
Military operations, 217–218
Miller, Richard R., 105n
Minh Mang, emperor, 19–21
Ministry of Agriculture, 54n, 68, 180n
Mitchell, Edward J., 230–233, 242
Money markets, 3, 5
Moneylenders, 3, 24, 27, 31, 106, 109
  as major source for loans, 111
Moorman, F. R., 181
Mortgage loan, 28n, 46
Motor pump, 12, 77, 78, 84, 164–179,
  211
  diffusion of, 169–176
  invention of, 166–168
  resistance to, 174, 214, 223
  and vegetable cultivation, 84, 85, 88
  see also Irrigation
My Tho, 9, 10, 11, 12, 19n, 158
  ceded to French, 19

National Agricultural Credit Organization
  (NACO), 111n–112n, 212
  procedure for obtaining loans, 112n
National Institute of Statistics, Saigon,
  38n
National Liberation Front (NLF), 56,
  63, 65
Nelson, Richard R., 177
Nep (glutinous) rice, 80
Nhu, Ngo Dinh, 238
North Vietnam, 20n, 218, 243
Nurske, Ragnar, 135

Ong Van market, 12
Orchard land, tax assessment of, 218–219
Oshima, Harry T., 38n
Oxen, 75
  production, 91–92
  as store of wealth, 92–93

Paddy defined, 24n
Paglin, Morton, 133, 145–147

Pakistan, 165, 180, 197
Paret, Peter, 243
Pasquire, Pierre, 113
Pasteur Institute, branch at Nha Trang,
  48
Peasantry, 65, 66
  and Viet Cong economic policy, 236–
  238
Pepelasis, Adam A., 136
Philippines, 50, 178
Pigs, 75, 93–94, 215, 225
Pike, Douglas, 65n, 218n, 233, 235,
  238n, 241n, 242, 243
Plain of Reeds, 5, 12, 19, 158n
Popular Forces, 8
Population, 5, 9, 18
  of Bac Lieu, 34–35
  and capital-intensive harvesting techniques, 43
  of Cochinchina, 19, 21
  of Dinh Tuong, 34
  farm, 14
  of Long Binh Dien, 12
  of Than Cuu Nghia, 10
Primogeniture, 27n
Productivity, agricultural
  and fertilizer, see Fertilizer
  landlords' attitudes on, 31
  and loan program, 113
  and motor pump, 164–165, 170–171
  and production techniques, 1, 18, 216
Propaganda, 9, 11, 237
"Psyops Aspects of GVN Land Title and
  Land Tenure Programs," 69, 236
Pump, see Diesel pump; Motor pump

Railroads, 48, 95
Ralis, Max, 173
RAND Corporation, 217n, 230, 242 ,243
Ranis, Gustav, 135
Reform, land, see Land reform
Rent, 10, 18, 24, 56, 151
  collection by village officials, 67–68
  and Diem land reform program, 57
  and fertilizer use, 195–196
  GVN collection of, 66–67
  and maximizing revenues, 31–33
  and security, 60–61
  and strategic hamlet program, 235
  and U.S. policy, 228
  and Viet Cong, 59–61, 62, 64, 211
  and Viet Minh, 55
Republic of Vietnam, see Vietnam
Revenue, maximization of, 25, 31–32

Index

Revisionist, 241–245
Revolutionary Development Cadre Team
    8, 10
Rice, 73, 75, 203–206
    bottleneck to use of new techniques,
        80–81
    use of capital, 84
    crop sales, 100
    cultivation per capita, 35
    in diet, 37–39
    evolution of culture, 17
    export of, 32–37
    export model, 34–39
    fertilizer, and yield, 180–197
    field preparation, 81–82
    French failures, 49–51
    glutinous, 31n, 37
    harvesting, 83
    harvesting techniques, 42–45
    and insecticide use, 185–186
    and maximization of landlords' revenue,
        31
    merchants, and war, 101–103
    milling, 99
    price index, 1
    production, 7, 76–80
    role of international price of, 33–34
    seedling transplanting, 82–83
    varieties, 78–81, 151, 187, 213
"Rice bowl" policy, Viet Cong, 217
Roads, 95
    building of, 48–49
    government role in maintaining, 213
Robequain, Charles, 32, 48, 100n, 105,
    122
    on irrigation, 152
Rogers, E. M., 169
Roosevelt, Franklin D., 46n
Rosenstein-Rodan, P. N., 133
Rubber plantations, 51, 64

Saigon, 5, 12, 84–85, 214
    French capture of (1859), 19
    and Viet Cong land reform, 66
Savings, 93–94, 118, 202–203
    and aid programs, 215–216
    noneconomic obstacles to, 208
Schultz, Theodore W., 2n, 3–5, 179,
    205n
Security, 60–61, 239–241
Seers, Dudley, 3n, 104n
Settlers, 23–24, 42
Shy, John W., 243
Smith, Arthur H., 114n

Smith, Paul F., 105n
Smithies, Arthur, xiii
Snow, Edgar, 226n
Soil conditions, 187–188
Solo, Robert, 178n
South Korea, rice economy of, 180, 181
South Vietnam, see GVN
Stout, B. A., 175
Strategic hamlet program, 58, 88, 90n, 94
    and Diem policy, 235, 238–239
Stroup, Robert H., 14n
Swift, M. G., 43, 45

Taiwan, 38n, 178, 180, 181
Tam Hiep, 98
Tan Duyet village, 21, 53, 55
Tan Hiep, 59, 159, 161n
Taxes, Viet Cong, 9, 11, 12, 17, 216–
    222, 237, 240–241
    assessment, 217–219
    collection of, 221–222
    in contested areas, 220–221
    customs, 223
    deductions, 218, 219
    flexibility of, 219–220
    origin of comprehensive tax, 217–218
    policies, 17, 63, 216–222
    system of, 218–219
    variation in revenue, 221
    see also Income tax, Viet Cong
TCN, see Than Cuu Nghia
Technology, 1, 5, 17, 52, 237
    colonial, 50
    and disguised unemployment, 137–138
    intermediate, 178–179
    in land reform programs, 69–70
Tenancy, 18, 55
    competition for right of, 33
    and development of Delta, 23–25
    and Diem land reform program, 57
    and disguised unemployment, 137
    as means of exploitation, 25–34
    and Viet Minh, 56
    see also Land tenure
Tenant
    and Diem reform, 58
    -landlord relationship, 29–31
    and rent collection by village officials,
        68
    and Viet Cong reforms, 58–59
Tenant farmers' unions, 212
Terror, 239–241, 243
    and Viet Cong, 59
    and Viet Minh, 55, 56, 57

Tet, 94, 109
  1963, 88
  1968, 241
Thailand, rice economy of, 180
Than Cuu Nghia (TCN), 9, 10–12, 214
  agricultural production, 75–77
  fertilizer use in, 183–188
  hamlets, 10–11
  interviews in, 14
  irrigation in, 157–159
  land redistribution, 63, 66
  motor pump, 172–173
  number of households, 14
  population of, 10
  trend to smaller holdings, 72–73
  vegetable cultivation in, 85
  Viet Cong activities in, 11–12, 59
  working conditions, 128
Thompson, Sir Robert, 239n
Thompson, Virginia, 47, 48n, 49, 105, 210
"Tolerance," landlord, 32, 70
Tonkin Delta, 20, 43, 46, 209
Trade policies, Viet Cong, 17, 222–227
  subsistence directives, 225
Transport, 17, 94–99, 151
  cost comparisons, 96, 97
  motorization of, 95
  and the war, 98–99
Tri-Lambretta, 91, 92, 95
Troop support tax, Viet Cong, 217–219, 222. See also Taxes, Viet Cong

Underdeveloped countries, 176–179
Unemployment
  ceteris paribus clause, 136–138
  disguised, 1, 17, 135–150
  and seasonal demand for labor, 138–139
UNESCO, 90
U.S. Agency for International Development (USAID), 69, 215
  Commodity Import Program, 84, 174
  encouragement of fertilizer use, 181
  and irrigation, 162
  Irrigation and Rural Engineering Branch, 169, 174–175
United States army, Ninth Infantry Division, 11
United States government (USG), 8, 211, 243
  fertilizer import program, 213
  and land reform, 69–70, 228–236, 238
U.S. Information Agency, 174

Usury, 46, 104–106

Vegetables
  average plot holding, 85, 86
  crop calendar, 88
  crop diversification, 78
  cultivation of, 73–75, 84–88, 201, 203–206
  field, 87–88, 214
  garden, 84–87, 151
  obstacles to, 204, 208
  tax assessment of land, 219
  transport of, 95, 98–99
  varieties grown, 87, 88, 214
Veliz, Claudio, 233n
Viet Cong, 8, 9, 10–11, 12, 160, 161, 199, 211
  and Agricultural Affairs Committee, 70–71
  beneficial economic policy, 236–238
  benefits of land policies, 65
  comprehensive-tax origin, 217–218
  controls, economic, 225
  corvée, 224–225
  and Farmers' Association, 212
  General Uprising (1960), 60, 112, 236, 243
  growth of, 241n, 242
  and harvest wage rate, 132
  institutional changes, 18, 53, 151, 244–245
  and irrigation, 154
  and labor exchange, 130–131
  and labor market, 126, 148
  and labor policies, 129–130, 132, 211
  and land reforms, 58–65, 211, 230–236
  mass identification, 238–239
  policy of terror, 241
  rent reduction, 59, 62, 64, 211
  resistance to motor pump, 174, 223
  and rice merchants, 102–103
  and rural wages, 63, 83
  and sa mai loan, 109
  sanctions, 221–222
  subsistence directives, 225, 238
  taxes, see Taxes, Viet Cong
  trade policies, 17, 222–227
  and transport, 98
  and Viet Minh, 56
Viet Minh, 12, 18, 39, 158n, 218
  and land reform, 10, 55–57, 62, 229n
  social-institutional accomplishments (1954–1959), 53
  and Viet Cong, 56

Vietnam, 14
    Central, 231–232
    North, 20n, 218
    and the French, 21, 46–52
    see also Cochinchina; GVN
Vietnamese army, 1, 11
    and fruit cultivation, 90
    and transport, 98
Village, 20–21
    aid (GVN) in economy of, 212–215
    contested, 9
    GVN, 8
    and security, 8–9
    selection, 8
    semisecure GVN, 8–9
    semisecure Viet Cong, 9
    Viet Cong, 9
Village council, 30

Wages, 39–42, 59
    declining, 40–42

and labor shortage, 131–132, 144
    rural, 127–128
    and Viet Cong, 63, 83, 237
Warner, Denis, 53n
Water, availability of, 5
    in Mekong Delta, 19–20
    as motivation for innovation, 153
    and seasonal demand for labor, 139
    and second rice crop, 77
    and vegetable cultivation, 85
    see also Irrigation
Waterwheel (man-powered), 152, 164,
    165, 169–171
Wolf, Charles, Jr., 241–245
Work-exchange teams, Viet Cong, 130–
    131, 236

Yamada, Saburo, 215n
Yang, Lien-Shen, 114n
Yersin, Dr. H. A. E., 48
Yotopoulos, Pan A, 136

Date Due

Demco 38-297